THE WRITING OF
WRITING

Open University Press

English, Language, and Education series

General Editor: Anthony Adams

Lecturer in Education, University of Cambridge

This series is concerned with all aspects of language in education from the primary school to the tertiary sector. Its authors are experienced educators who examine both principles and practice of English subject teaching and language across the curriculum in the context of current educational and societal developments.

TITLES IN THE SERIES

Computers and Literacy
  Daniel Chandler and Stephen Marcus (eds)

Children Talk About Books: Seeing Themselves as Readers
  Donald Fry

The English Department in a Changing World
  Richard Knott

Teaching Literature for Examinations
  Robert Protherough

Developing Response to Fiction
  Robert Protherough

Microcomputers and the Language Arts
  Brent Robinson

The Quality of Writing
  Andrew Wilkinson

The Writing of Writing
  Andrew Wilkinson (ed.)

In preparation

English Teaching: Programmes and Policies
  Anthony Adams and Esmor Jones

Literary Theory and English Teaching
  Peter Griffith

THE WRITING OF WRITING

Edited by
ANDREW WILKINSON

Open University Press
Milton Keynes · *Philadelphia*

Open University Press
Open University Educational Enterprises Limited
12 Cofferidge Close
Stony Stratford
Milton Keynes MK11 1BY, England
and
242 Cherry Street
Philadelphia, PA 19106, USA

First Published 1986

British Library Cataloguing in Publication Data

The Writing of writing. — (English, language, and education)
   1. Children — Writing
   I. Wilkinson, Andrew   II. Series
   372.6'23   B1139.W7
   ISBN 0–355–15233–3

Library of Congress Cataloging in Publication Data
Main entry under title:

The Writing of writing
  (English, language, and education series)
   "Made up mainly of papers invited for the
International Writing Convention organised by the School of Education,
University of East Anglia, Norwich at Easter 1985"—Acknowledgements.
   Bibliography: p.
   1. English language—Rhetoric—Study and teaching—
Congresses.   2. English language—Composition and
exercises—Study and teaching—Congresses.
I. Wilkinson, Andrew M.   II. International Writing
Convention (1985 : University of East Anglia, Norwich)
III. University of East Anglia. School of Education.
IV. Series.
PE1404.W7276 1986   808'.042'07   86–1446
   ISBN 0–335–15233–3 (pbk.)

Text design by Clarke Williams
Typeset by Marlborough Design, Oxford
Printed by St. Edmundsbury Press, Bury St. Edmunds, Suffolk

Contents

Acknowledgements   vii
General Editor's Introduction   viii

Chapter 1   Introduction: ten propositions about writing
              Andrew Wilkinson, University of East Anglia   1

PART ONE   WRITING AND THINKING
Chapter 2   Argument and the teaching of English: a critical
              analysis
              John Dixon and Leslie Stratta, University of East Anglia   8
Chapter 3   What gets written about
              Peter Medway, University of Leeds   22

PART TWO   WRITING AND FEELING
Chapter 4   I write therefore I am
              Andrew Wilkinson, University of East Anglia   42
Chapter 5   The pleasure of writing
              Bernard Harrison, University of Strathclyde   60
Chapter 6   Writers in their place
              Bruce Bennett, University of Perth, Western Australia   75

PART THREE   FROM SPEECH TO WRITING
Chapter 7   Grammatical differentiation between speech and
              writing in children aged 8 to 12
              Katherine Perera, University of Manchester   91
Chapter 8   From speech to writing: some evidence on the
              relationship between oracy and literacy
              *Gordon Wells and Gen Ling Chang, Ontario Institute
              for Studies in Education*   109

PART FOUR   WRITING DEVELOPMENT
Chapter 9   Early writing
              Anne Bauers and John Nicholls, University of East Anglia   134
Chapter 10   Writing counts
              William Harpin, University of Nottingham   158
Chapter 11   Writing development—theory and practice
              *Eric Carlin, Western Australia College of Advanced
              Education*   177

PART FIVE   FORM AND STYLE IN WRITING
Chapter 12   Interrelations of reading and writing
             Gunther Kress, New South Wales Institute of Technology   198
Chapter 13   The development of style in children's fictional
             narrative
             Gordon Taylor, University of East Anglia   215
Chapter 14   The mapping of writing
             Diana Davis, Monash University   234

Acknowledgements

This book consists mainly of papers invited for the International Writing Convention organised by the School of Education, University of East Anglia, Norwich, at Easter 1985. All the contributors except William Harpin were able to present in person. Normally conference papers appear when all memory of the conference has faded from human consciousness. I should like to acknowledge the good will and efficiency of both contributors and Open University Press staff in ensuring that publication takes place little more than a year after the Convention.

I should like to thank the Dean of the School, Professor H.T. Sockett, and members of the academic and administrative staffs of the School for their wholehearted support. I wish to mention by name members of the Language Sector — Eric Daniels, Mike Hayhoe, Susan Maclennan, Maggie MacLure, Stephen Parker, Deirdre Pettitt, and Terry Phillips; Visiting Fellows — Ron Sinclair, Mitchell College of Advanced Education, and Jack Walton, University of New England; Lynda Williams, Administrative Assistant; and Karen Bezants, reprographics. Advanced students from the MA (Language in Education) course humanised the face of the machine. They are Betty Kulsdom, Alison Littlefair, Diane Metson, Chioma Onwere, Howard Pearson, Frances Rimmell, Eve Watkins, Erik Wilcock and Miriam Vigar. Particular thanks must go to the Convention Joint Secretary, James Bidwell, and the Convention Secretary, Eileen Chapman, who made the operation go and kept it going.

Eileen Chapman has also had a key role in the detailed preparation and editing of the papers for this volume. I am most grateful for her patience, accuracy, and unfailing good humour.

A.M. Wilkinson
November 1985

This book is essentially a companion volume to Professor Wilkinson's own *The Quality of Writing* which is published at the same time and in the same series. Wilkinson's own introduction makes clear its origins in a conference held at the University of East Anglia in the spring of 1985. It is anticipated that there will be further such conferences organised on a biennial basis (the next in 1987 on oracy) bringing together scholars in English education from across the world.

This is a much-needed enterprise. Although there are regular international conferences organised by the International Federation for the Teaching of English (IFTE) there remains a place for single-theme international conferences. This book represents a first fruit of such work and it is fitting and pleasing that it includes a high proportion of essays by writers from outside the United Kingdom.

As one who attended the conference I am well aware that a publication of this kind can hope to indicate only a part of the excitement generated by the enterprise itself. The significance of the venture was confirmed by announcement at the Convention of the setting up (by the Schools Curriculum Development Committee) of the National Writing Project and the appointment of Andrew Wilkinson as its chairman.

Anthony Adams

1 Introduction: ten propositions about writing

ANDREW WILKINSON

Conference 'proceedings' frequently compete with government reports for first prize in unreadibility. This is perhaps not surprising. At a good conference ideas are a quality of the air, and are breathed in and out by the delegates — some delegates for whom they are life itself, and others who would never have come had they realised such a thing would happen. A year after, when the experience of the conference is reduced to words on a cold page, it may at best lack conviction and at worst seem meaningless. In this selection of papers mainly invited for the International Writing Convention, 1985, it is confidently believed that this does not happen, because the quality of the ideas carries them beyond the immediate occasion of their delivery.

The Convention was held at the University of East Anglia, Norwich, between 31 March and 4 April 1985. It was the first major international conference to be held on writing in the United Kingdom, and was successful in attracting many of the world's distinguished scholars and teachers. For various reasons not all the papers submitted were eventually available for publication; some approaches were presented by workshops not susceptible of easy transference to print. So while they cannot claim to be completely representative of the best that was thought and said, nevertheless it seems to the editor that the papers selected here make a major contribution to our knowledge of the state of the art, and indicate growing points from which doubtless some thorns but also many sweet flowers may grow.

It would be impossible to derive a consensus about what the Convention actually *said*. With 400 delegates, of whom 70 were presenters, there must have been a great divergence of views. At the much smaller, much longer Dartmouth Seminar in 1966 there was a wide variety of opinion (and even a small number of shell-backs present who croaked discordantly about the world before the flood). Yet the seminar report by Dixon (1967) suffuses harmony, sweetness, and light because he drew out what he felt were the generative aspects of the discussions. That is the approach attempted here. This Introduction is not intended as an account of the Convention as a whole, but as a personal selection and interpretation of salient points from just some of the papers presented there. These may be summed up in the propositions which follow.

I write therefore I am

Also, I write therefore you are, I write therefore it (the world) is. Writing is concerned, on the one hand with the definition and redefinition, creation and re-creation of the self, others, the world, a process which we may call reflection; and on the other hand with communication with others, a process which we may call transmission. As early as 1907 Hartog formulated the latter process as 'writing for a particular audience with a particular object in view' (1907, p. 61) and the sociolinguists rapidly followed and arrived at the same point in the same words by the late 1960s. Hence the great emphasis on 'communication skills' today. These are of course necessary, but writers in this volume see dangers in a philosophy which is more concerned with means than writer and message. As Harrison (p. 66) says, 'there is a sense in which writing, or at least reflective writing, is inconceivable without the presence of a writer, discovering the world in terms of the only human experience that can be known — that is, one's own'.

I think by writing

'Writing [makes] an exact man' as Bacon (1897) says, but it makes for more than precision. Thinking is, of course, also furthered by conversation and discussion. Dixon and Stratta make explicit the logical structures of a piece of talk which apparently lacks surface connections (p. 15) and emphasize the pedagogical relationships between thinking in oral and written modes, though there are of course real differences. But Bruner (1975, p. 63) suggested that the constant use of language over and above the mere possession of it makes human beings 'profoundly different' in mental powers; 'and more particularly does it matter that one *writes* and *reads* rather than *talks* and *listens*' because this moves language towards 'context-free elaboration'. The ability to deal with complexity, extension, abstraction, is predominantly the province of the written language. This is one of the reasons why Wells *et al.* advocate 'sustained writing', and 'sustained talk': 'oral monologue ... provides an opportunity to develop some of the skills of composing, planning, selecting, marshalling and organising ideas — that are so necessary for writing' (p. 130). The need to attend to the development of cognition through writing is also a concern with Medway, who argues that 'the configuration of a writing curriculum will *tend* to foster certain kinds of thinking about the world over other kinds' (p. 30).

I feel by writing

Feeling, regarded as disturbance, is as ineducable as the weather (we often use the same terms for both — 'depression', for instance). But regarded as disturbance in response to something — the actions of someone else, for example, it is inseparably linked to an 'appraisal' or interpretation, which may be simple or complex, perceptive or superficial. Partly because it gives opportunity for reflection on one's appraisals of self and others, the act of writing enables one to understand one's own emotions and the emotions of others. Whereas the creative writing movement claimed to foster emotional development, there was little profitable discussion of what this meant. On the one hand, there were books about feeling so full of feeling that it is difficult to follow their argument: on the other, writers shied away from discussing feeling as though it were too delicate a bloom. Contributors to this volume are less inhibited. Wells *et al.* have an affective/moral group of items in their model for analysing written text. Wilkinson sees an affective model as analysing the self's stance towards self, others, environment and the human condition.

I grow by writing

My writing manifests my growth, and at the same time prompts it. But 'writing development' is often talked of, and seldom defined. Traditional 'count' measures have been available, and Harpin's study sees their significance as closely tied to the mode of writing used. Carlin sees such measures providing a useful general description over a large sample, but finds the need in individual cases for wider criteria to be used such as those of Crediton. Wells *et al.* proposed a scheme in terms of substance, form, content, and rhetorical Goals (p. 111). Bauers and Nicholls (p. 136) see beginning writing in terms of four 'levels of competence' until associative writing — initial independence — is achieved. The development of wider criteria than in the traditional 'marking scheme' is one of the features of current movements.

I have two tongues

I talk talking. I write writing. I do not talk writing, and I do not write talking, except in the preliminary stages. Historically, the written language was felt to be a model for the spoken. The euphoria produced by the invention of the sound recorder led some people to regard writing as an inadequate version of the *real* language of speech. Now they are seen as different, each with its own integrity, though related. Wells *et al.* emphasize sustained writing because of its requirement to work on and transform our experience; and the importance of the less usual sustained speaking in developing 'some of the skills of composing . . . that are so necessary for writing' (p. 130). From a linguist's point of view Perera examines the differences between spoken and written texts, noting, for example, more advanced grammatical constructions in the latter (p. 91). She speaks of writing as 'a different form of language in its own right which can lead to different ways of thinking' (p. 107).

I write reading

Because I read writing I am led to write reading. It is commonplace in schools that the best writers are the best readers, but Kress sees the relationship of a read text to a written text as a 'complex dynamic about which very little is known' (p. 214). Initially a child's reading may be diffuse, and the interrelation of reading and writing indirect. Later the child reads specific texts displaying 'an order deriving from specific genres which are oriented towards the topic or material'. The child must learn these genres. Kress places the matter in a wider social-psychological context where there are issues of the 'social place and political power attaching to any one genre, and the positioning of readers and writers (and of speakers and hearers) within them' (p. 199). As he says, that matter has fundamental implications for the content of writing curriculum.

I write genres

Traditionally, writing was considered under the four rhetorical categor-ies — narrative, description, argument, explanation. After a run of 2,000 years or so these were summarily dismissed in the 1960s when categories in terms of function and purpose became fashionable. This was a gain in that it resulted in a greater sense of reader and context. In an eagerness to further these social roles, however, people lost sight of the fact that the traditional categories were not arbitrary — they refer to four fundamental mental activities, means of organising experience: the logical (argument) and the chronological (narrative), the informational (description), and the relational (explanation). We might call them cognitive as distinct from literary genres. In this book we see a movement away from function categories. Davis finds 'function' inadequate to describe the complexities of text, and instead offers a taxonomy of essay modes based on rhetorical categories. To Kress function would just be one of aspect of genres, which he describes as 'conventionalised textual forms which derive from (larger) social/institutional structures' (p. 207). It is the genre, not the function, which requires our main attention. We need to learn the conventional, against which we may explore the unconventional. Dixon and Stratta consider the various forms of sociolinguistic behaviour represented by 'argument'.

I write places

'A sense of place' is a concept in literary criticism. Recently educationists have extended it to include the social environment, on the one hand, and all non-human phenomena on the other. To Bennett it is 'an individual's physical and social environment' (p. 75). In Wilkinson (p. 47) an awareness of the 'meaning' of environment in relation to the self is seen as one of the characteristics of a mature stance. Inglis (1969, p. 22) wrote valuably about the psychological need to 'feel at home', but a sense of alienation is also part of human experience needing interpretation. Bennett envisages a range of responses from the 'wise passiveness' of Wordsworth to angry reaction, or a seeking of a state of extra-territoriality.

I write writing

'The style is the man', said Buffon, and this is clever, but an evasion. The concept of style has always proved elusive and has recently been discussed rather in terms of styles (plural), or genres. Work on different types of oral and written narrative seems to be in advance of work in other modes. Taylor, while also taking his main theme as young children's narratives, returns to the general question of style, seeing it as a product of function, choice, a characteristic of surface structure, and related to conceptual norms (p. 217). Kress is not so much concerned with the definitions as with the process whereby the concepts of genre to be found in reading internalise themselves in the writers so that they characterise their written presentation.

I write something

The matter of content is not the least important of the current
preoccupations. The concerns of the last two decades with language
rather than literature, with functions rather than facts, with process
rather than product, with audience rather than performer, in short with
communication rather than content, these concerns have brought us to
an old truth writ large — the medium is taking over from the message.
This is being strongly resisted by contributors. Medway does find a
content, but a strange one. He examines 346 writing assignments from
12-year-olds set by 21 teachers, and finds them curious in that 'if
English as a school subject had not existed no one would have invented
it the way it was' (p. 24). He asks how empirical such a curriculum is and
finds its sources of validity outside current realities. He affirms that
'writing is potentially a very important cognitive process, too important
to be frittered away on things that do not matter'. Harrison lays much
more emphasis on the specifics of the private world and its resolution of
irresolutions. Wilkinson is concerned with the psychological content of
the writing — the quality of thought, feeling, appraisal it expresses.
Wells *et al.*, similarly include ideation and affective/moral stance in their
analytical scheme under content (p. 111). Harrison considers that the
nadir of the current retreat from content is represented by the APU's
task: 'Write a short account of anything enjoyable or exciting which has
happened to you recently' (p. 65).

The title of this volume, *The Writing of Writing*, is taken from the letter
of an eight-year-old who wrote 'at school we rite riting'. In the light of
the above propositions it can be seen that this is only one of the activities
of writing, and is as much a question as a statement.

Bibliography

Bacon, F. (1897).	*Essays*, ed. R. Whately. London, Longmans, Green & Co.
Bruner, J.S. (1975).	'Language as an Instrument of Thought' in A. Davies (ed.), *Problems of Language and Learning*. London, Heinemann.
Dixon, J. (1967).	*Growth through English*. Oxford, Oxford University Press.
Hartog, (1907).	*The Writing of English*. Oxford, Oxford University Press.
Inglis, F. (1969).	*The Englishness of English Teaching*. London, Longman.

Part One

Writing and Thinking

2 Argument and the Teaching of English: A Critical Analysis

JOHN DIXON and LESLIE STRATTA

The place of discussion and argument in everyday life

Although routines seem to take care of much of our everyday living, we do in fact have to make decisions and choices daily — or else have them made for us. Some are taken with a minimum of deliberation — off the cuff, as it were; others require time and effort to weigh up the possibilities. So we discuss or we argue; sometimes with ourselves (is it worth getting up and making an early start?), sometimes with other people (should we be trying to raise more money for the school?). For convenience, we can call this kind of 'argument' action-orientated.

But there is another kind that shades into it. This, too, can happen any day, when one's opinions, beliefs and attitudes are suddenly confirmed or called into question. Again we may sound off without further thought, but occasionally we take the time and effort to elaborate or reconsider — in other words to discuss and argue. To bring out the contrast we can call this kind of 'argument' notion- or belief -orientated.

In both kinds of 'argument' we have a broad choice of role. It is true there is a common usage of the verb 'to argue' implying that we are confronting opponents, contending with them and trying to defeat them. But as we hope to show later, the nouns 'discussion' and 'argument' in fact cover a continuum of discourse, implying social relationships that range from the antagonistic to the collaborative. Some of the most powerful institutions exclusively favour the former: set-piece debates in Parliament, or advocacy in the law courts, for instance. But in the rest of everyday life there is the possibility of something much less polarised — and less of a game with its own peculiar rules.

As teachers, then, we need to recognise that discussion and argument are more than school exercises: they are an inevitable part of daily life. Unfortunately, the most publicised everyday examples often offer the worst models. The standards of public argument are appallingly low. Thus television and radio programmes that purport to discuss serious topical issues are frequently organised as entertainment, with point-scoring, chaff and chat predominating.

However, academics working in English are certainly not blameless. Compared with the plethora of recent theoretical work on literature or narrative, there is next to nothing that analyses the nature and aims of discussion and argument. Ironically, too, the most common form of argument for advanced students of English in the United Kingdom arises from the request to 'discuss' statements about a literary text — a surprisingly esoteric exercise, as Tony Davies has noted (1982), p. 39).

Clarifying our concepts

We believe that, within the teaching of English, further progress in written argument depends on being clearer in the use of words such as narrative, argument and discussion. Narrative and argument, for example, are conventionally set in opposition to each other. In fact, the relation is more complicated. Certainly narrative — the telling of stories — is typically concerned with the actual unfolding of people's lives. But stories can be used to prove a point, and often are. This is true not only in everyday life but in literature; thus fables, parables and allegories are entirely concerned to present in story form a tacit and persuasive argument about moral or political behaviour. Not only that; since literature represents life, characters in fiction inevitably discuss and argue over their actions and beliefs. And authors, too, may interpolate their beliefs quite explicitly via the narrator or a chorus. So it would be false to say that narrative excludes discussion and argument. In fact it would be foolish for teachers to ignore the possibilites of argument within narrative, especially developmentally.

However, narrative as a *form of discourse* has its limitations. when a story uses a chain of events (like the Good Samaritan) to persuade the reader of a point of view, it typically does not make the line of argument explicit — in fact Jesus frequently had to explain the meaning of his parables. Immediately we interpret the persuasive point or significance of a story we are into a different form of discourse. One of its characteristics is that it moves from the particular to the general, and thus raises the level of abstraction. A second is that the connections between the general statements have to be logical or rational, to make sense and stand up to criticism.

The usual name for this form of discourse is argument. But, as we have already suggested in the previous section, a tradition has grown up that argument implies contention, confrontation and the desire to win. In this version adversaries are engaged in a duel. Each advocates, asserts and justifies one point of view while attempting to refute, challenge, rebut and negate the opponent's. Each seeks to confound the other, and it is not always a matter of persuasion by reasoning. The debating tradition in education has always served to reinforce this notion of argument. However, we would maintain that it is a closed form that shuts off alternative uses for argument in everyday life.

In everyday life there may well be two sides, but they may need to negotiate and reach an agreed decision. Argument will be involved, but so will something broader which we have to call discussion. And when there are no longer two sides, but a group of people working collaboratively to think through a choice of action or belief, it becomes obvious that, while arguments are not ruled out, the word discussion offers a better way of describing all that is going on. The kinds of process we are thinking of include raising questions heuristically, examining and critically scrutinising alternative positions, making tentative proposals, investigating and studying the grounds for generalised opinions, coming to conclusions or deciding that the issue cannot be completely resolved for the moment. (This is the kind of discussion and argument that is going on between us, we might add, as the line of argument for the present article is being shaped.)

In this open form of discussion and argument the emphasis may well be on exploration, not confrontation. In collaborative discussion the parties are expecting, indeed hoping, to modify their positions through joint discovery. In fact it may be misleading to imply that they actually start from initial 'positions'; in ruminating over a question they may only gradually clarify what they know or think. So against the pole of contention from prepared positions we can set that of shared rumination.

Negotiation actually implies that two positions are being taken up, however temporarily. But equally both parties will recognise that they may well need to modify their original positions by force of circumstance perhaps, or because they genuinely wish to secure agreement of the other party on a joint enterprise. This kind of discussion leads to redefinitions of positions, with qualifications or amendments that take into account the interests of other parties. Where interests are very similar, the main point of the negotiation may be to reduce apparent differences. Where interests differ, than some compromise has to be found.

All three kinds of interaction — contending, collaborating and negotiation — are familiar enough in everyday spoken dialogue. That they do exist in written form we cannot doubt. Letters, for instance, may be written to challenge a claim that has been put forward, or to support and extend it, or to argue the case for revisions that might be agreed. Similar stances can be found in review articles, editorials and many kinds of journalism. If the full range cannot be found in schools, this arises, we believe, from a fundamental misconceptionof the process of argumentation, as we hope to show.

To summarise at this point: more than one form of discourse may be used to persuade people to a point of view. Thus, narrative discourse can incorporate argument of a kind. On the other hand the significance of such 'arguments' has to be spelt out in a different, more generalised form of discourse. We have chosen to call this discussion and argument for two reasons: first, to avoid the tacit implication that argument is always adversarial, and second, positively to point to a range of collaborative ways of considering choices of action and belief. The next step is to try to clarify our conceptions of the kind(s) of discourse that embody explicit argument and discussion.

Making a start in discourse that develops a line of argument

In this section we can only be tentative. Rather than generalise, we must start with some empirical evidence, and we have chosen to start with a piece of classroom discussion. this may seem odd in an article about *written* argument. However, it is at least possible, if not highly likely, that for many young students certain forms of dialogue help them to develop a line of argument well before they are able to sustain it at the same level in written form.

Let us consider how near to — and far from — connected discourse a young discussion group may be. The following brief extract (from Barnes and Todd 1977, pp. 35–6) comes from a group of thirteen-year-olds discussing facilities for a National park:

Marianne: At the roadside there should be a lot of big car parks to accommodate all these visitors and tourists.

David: Spoil t'countryside, won't it.

Jonathan: Ah, that's what'll stop erm stop 'em from going all over the countryside, won't it.

David:	That's the big un — to stop people going all over.
Marianne:	But if there's picnic areas. If there's picnic areas then they won't need to go out into the countryside. they'd be able to see it through.
Barbara:	Yeah, but that's it . . .
David:	Yeah, but people want to go out into the countryside.
Marianne:	Not all of 'em. Just tourists that are passing by . . .

What are the features that show this is potentially a coherent discussion that is getting somewhere — a genuine line of argument? Marianne begins with a proposal. David suggests that the proposal may be flawed ('won't it'); it could have negative consequences. But when Jonathan recognises the positive effects, David agrees. Marianne, who seems to have been 'taking this in', then appears to modify or develop her initial proposal ('But if there's picnic areas'). When David suddenly sees there are people this will not suit — and actually reverses his earlier protective position towards the countryside — Marianne reminds the group that there *are* people whom the proposal would benefit ('tourists that are passing by').

Suppose now we try to make explicit a possible line of argument underlying what is being said, as a writer would have to do. What are the minimum necessary changes that will make the best of the contending, collaborating and negotiating that is going on here? Let us start from the first recommendation:

> At the roadside there should be a lot of big car parks to accommodate all these visitors and tourists. Wouldn't this spoil the countryside, *it may be objected*. *No*, this would stop people from going all over the countryside, and that's the big problem. But, if there were picnic areas, people who were just passing by would be able to see the countryside without needing to go into it. *Yet, admittedly*, there would be *other* people who would *indeed* want to go into the countryside.

We have italicised our additions, some making connections explicit, others adding contrastive emphasis (as the voice would do in spoken discussion). At first sight this may seem a very small change. But in order to be able to achieve this, Marianne or David would have to learn not only to hold the role of participant, but also to take on that of an evaluative and synthesising listener, perceiving and constructing the line of argument as the discussion itself unfolds. (Our own task, we may add, was much simpler, since we were able to make a line of argument retrospectively from a written transcript.)

Insofar as students like these can achieve this kind of constructive listening, they stand to gain an increasingly complex understanding of an issue, in which their differences of opinion can be used positively, proposals qualified, difficulties conceded, and various consequences taken into consideration. In doing so, we would maintain, they are entering into a form of discussion found particularly in education (at its best). This builds on the notion that speech is a primary means for ideas to be formulated, but moves a step further. Whereas in gossip this group might have flitted from one subject to another, in our example they have held to the subject and are developing a more complex perspective on it. It is in this kind of serious discussion, or civilized conversation, as we might call it, that we suggest the foundations of connected argument or discussion are laid.

Of course, it is one thing to lay foundations in this way, but quite another to try to construct a complex and sustained argument on your own, as a writer. Thinking of what is demanded even in the role of listener, we should not be surprised if students who are quite confident, even very advanced, as writers of narrative, find this new form of discourse difficult or even overwhelming. Likely as not, then, their first attempts to develop a complex line of argument will arise within other forms of discourse.

An example of what we have in mind appears in the course of a longer reflective account called 'The Way I Talk'. (Twomey 1984, p. 32). The writer actually begins like this: 'I live in London, near Baker Street. "Quite a posh area", you might be saying to yourself, but maybe if you heard my voice you wouldn't think so.' This could well be the opening of a short story. And there is an element of story threaded through what follows. However, towards the end the writing changes. Can we describe what is goint on?

> People are judged by their voices which, as I have experienced, is wrong. Some people are under the impression that it's a status thing. If you're poor you'll have a very Cockney, common accent and if you're rich you'll speak very genteely and politely. But does this mean that all Cockneys are rowdy, rude, ill-mannered thugs and rich people are sweetness itself?

> Everybody has a different voice and different ways of speaking. The way you speak is as natural as the way you walk or eat and nobody has the right to criticise it. I don't think I should have to change the way I talk to pass a job interview as, unless I was going to be a speech therapist, it would be irrelevant to my job. I speak English which is a language. Language is a means of talking, communicating, being understood. People do understand me so why should it matter?

> If we all spoke the same, life would be very boring. We would lose our personalities and if this happened, we would lose our individuality.

The first thing we notice is that, perhaps because this section is notion- or belief-orientated, there are recurrent generalised statements about general categories: 'People are judged . . . Everybody has a different voice . . . life would be very boring . . .' We next notice that there are few explicit connections between one statement and the next. Yet on the other hand the writer does seem at this point to be attempting to construct an argument — and we can follow it. Parts are not too carefully thought through: for instance 'does this mean that all Cockneys are rowdy, rude, ill-mannered thugs . . . ?' However, the passage does make connected sense, and if challenged we can actually reconstruct it as an imaginary dialogue in which the rational connections are made explicit. Thus:

People are judged by their voices, which, as I have experienced, is wrong.

Q1   *Why* is it wrong?

Some people are under the impression that it's a status thing.

Q2   *Can you elaborate* on this 'impression'?

If you're poor you'll have a very Cockney, common accent . . .

Q3   *What's wrong* with that belief?

(But) does this mean that all Cockneys are rowdy, rude, ill-mannered thugs . . . ?

Q4   *What's right*, then; what do you believe?

Everybody has a different voice and different ways of speaking . . . and nobody has a right to criticise it.

Q5   *Why?*

The way you speak is as natural as the way you walk or eat.

Q6   *So what follows?*

I don't think I should have to change the way I talk to pass a job interview . . . as it would be irrelevant to my job.

Q7   Any *exceptions* to that *generalisation*?

Unless I was going to be a speech therapist.

Q8   Can you positively *justify your specific way* of speaking?

I speak English which is a language. Language is a means of talking, communicating, being understood. People do understand me . . .

Q9   *Suppose* we all did speak the same?

Life would be very boring. We would lose our personalities and . . . our individuality.

What does a reconstruction like this uncover? First, even where the links between successive statements are tacit, it may be possible to construct rational relationships. In fact we have taken further this notion of tacit and explicit statements in correspondence with Professor Sally Schrofel, University of Regina, Canada. You may disagree with (the details of) some of our questions — and in one or two places, we must admit, we had to struggle — but we hope it will be agreed that, given such questions, a line of rational argument can indeed be discerned. There are elements here that are characteristic of many other arguments or discussions: when taken together these constitute what we normally call a 'line of argument':

Why you do not believe A? — the arguments you offer against (Qs 1–3)
Why you believe B? — the supporting arguments you offer (Qs 4, 5 and 8)
Consequences that follow from B (Q6)
Consequences that would follow from (an implication of) A (Q9)
Exceptions that need to be conceded (Q7)

There are three things we would add at this juncture. Our first point concerns the quality of an argument or discussion. This may depend on (at least) two things besides the line of argument: how scrupulous the writer is in any generalising that may be called for; and how precise the writer is in the choice of any general categories that may be used. Here again, our example occasionally suggests a writer who is still learning the ropes. 'Some people', for instance, in her second sentence, could have been more precise: the category she seems to want is 'all those who judge people by their voices' or something similar.

The second point is that while more mature writers might well reorganise and make more explicit the line of argument in our example, it would be a mistake to conclude that tacit connections *as such* imply immaturity in discussion and argument. Even a casual inspection of professional writers reveals how frequently they leave the connection for the reader to construe. Indeed the role of the reader, like that of the listener, is necessarily active, we would claim: one never merely 'follows' in argument or discussion.

Our third point concerns signs of progress: we would expect proposals (especially in action-orientated thinking) to be progressively more elaborated, and a wider range of consequence or conditioning factors to be considered (as was happening in the small group discussion); and we would expect general categories (especially in notion- or belief-orientated thinking) to be made progressively more precise, and generalised statements to be qualified.

Confusions that exist in practice

Standing in the way and preventing everyday discussion and argument from taking their rightful place in the English classroom are two traditions: first, the tendency in this century for English studies to focus on imaginative literature to the exclusion of many other forms of discourse, something unthinkable to earlier generations brought up on the classics; second, the longer tradition, dating back to classical rhetoricians, to place written argumentation (alongside narrative, description and exposition) as an exercise without real engagement or context (for an authoritative account see Marrou 1956, especially pp. 286–7). These two practices reinforce each other, since if the students' reading offers no inspiring models of discussion and argument, but is almost exclusively fictional, they are in no position to recognise what argument can offer. Furthermore, within the United Kingdom, any attempt to broaden the range of writing in English lessons normally ends at 16, after which the predominant, even exclusive, form of writing will be literary appreciation, or literary criticism, and this continues through most university degrees in English. Not surprisingly, teachers who are the products of this system reinforce the whole process.

What are the typical confusions and misunderstandings embodied in this approach to argumentation? Nothing shows these better than typical questions set in public examinations. Let us look closely at an example, from the Oxford Local GCE O level English language examination, Paper I, summer 1980 (see Dixon and Stratta 1982a).

> 'Just look at that damage! Vandals should be treated more severely.' 'No, that's unfair. Vandalism is the fault of our society.' What do *you* think about the causes and cures of vandalism?

A question such as this makes inordinate demands on a sixteen-year-old student. Thus:

1. The topic is a highly general category, *all* vandals and *all* vandalism 'in our society'.
2. It is assumed that the student is acquainted with *all* 'the causes and cures' — something no criminologist would claim.
3. There is the assumption, on the one hand, of sophisticated sociological knowledge (causes) and, on the other, of equally sophisticated therapeutic understanding (cures).
4. Although the 'question' apparently opens with two people arguing, it seems to propose a *statement* about the causes and cures, rather than an argument. (However, the precise force of 'What do you think *about*' seems to us very unclear.)

5.   There is no suggestion of an audience (other than the examiner) who would have any interest in what 'you' think about such matters — not surprisingly.
6.   Finally, the question is to be answered in an hour, without preparation and without reference to any sources.

Questions such as this — and they are common enough in British examinations — seem to us to encourage unsupported assertions and sloppy thinking about social behaviour. Instead of setting standards, they betray them. And because teachers are themselves so uncertain or confused about the nature of argument, such questions tend to reinforce a formulaic approach in teaching. As a result argumentative essays become a peculiarly insulated 'classroom genre' with little or no relation to everyday life. What are some of the characteristic features of this genre? They can be seen clearly in an extreme example we have already analysed elsewhere: '"Streaming in school is the best method for educating." Discuss.' (see Dixon and Stratta 1982b).

1.   The topic is an unqualified and unsupported general statement. According to the code, this is an unattributed quotation, and the teacher or examiner is in no way committed to it, despite its assertive form.
2.   The instruction is a formula such as 'Discuss'. This is pure code. There is no suggestion that the student should discuss with anyone (and certainly not with the imaginary author of the 'quotation'). The conventional pretence is that the student will be addressing an unknown general audience with his or her thoughts; the fact is that an 'essay' will be handed in to be marked.
3.   There are standard openings for the main paragraphs. For example, in the original essay they are as follows:
     ● What is streaming?
     ● The main disadvantage of streaming is . . .
     ● There is one main disadvantage . . .
     ● Alternatively you can have a mixed ability scheme . . .
     ● Personally, I think a mixture of the both (*sic*) can be very successful . . .
     The convention is that five or six paragraphs are expected and this particular conventional structure (the pros and cons ploy) fits neatly, with an opening paragraph that defines the concept and a 'conclusion' that stands back to make a seemingly personal judgement. Both the latter are part of the code.
4.   Until the final paragraph, the 'discussion' should be impersonal in style: 'There is one main disadvantage . . .' The pretence is that 'advantages' and 'disadvantages' are being magisterially reviewed

with a detachment that removes any question of personal judgements intervening.

5. It is not proper in the essay to make unsupported assertions as the 'question' does: students are expected to offer grounds within the paragraph for whatever is asserted. On the other hand, there is no expectation, conventionally, that the grounds offer will be based on evidence which has been closely scrutinised by the student; conventional opinions will be quite sufficient, so long as the clause structures are complex and grammatically correct.

In summing up the severe limitations of this classroom genre we would say three things. First, where an issue is so complex and so dependent on specialised knowledge and debate, rather than personal experience, students are doomed to failure. It would be a miracle if they learnt to develop a rational line of argument within this tradition. Second, the whole exercise seems pointless, in any case. Do students really want to argue about this topic? Who are they writing for — with what expectations of response? Such topics wrench argument and discussion from their communicative context with people in the real world. Third, we see every reason for students to explore important social concepts and issues (including vandalism or streaming), and to learn how to do this rationally. But initially we want to know what issues *they* are deeply concerned to investigate and are capable of tackling, given their current range of experience. Then we want them to weigh the evidence of their own experience and also to recognise (often enough) the need to draw on wider social experience.

A more complex model for discussion and argument

At this juncture, we want to offer an alternative — but still provisional — model to guide further work on discussion and argument in the English classroom. There have been six strands in the discussion so far which we propose to synthesise and develop.

First, we went to keep at the centre an image of argument as a *dynamic process* between people. If this is to open up the possibilities of learning to be rational, there will be the need for an open, exploratory, investigatory phase. And at times this is as far as students will feel able to go: in other words they will end up well short of fully-defined positions. There is a positive value in realising that, after careful examination, an issue is still too complex to be resolved at this moment. But if students do go further, there will be even more need systematically to check the bases for their conclusions, recommendations or decisions.

This leads to a second element in our model: the realisation that, for many broader issues, personal experience will be valid but it will not in itself offer adequate grounds for a sustained and complex argument. Learning how *to find, and evaluate further, 'public' evidence* becomes an important part of the dynamic process.

These preparatory phases will precede decisions whether to take the argument or discussion to a wider audience, and what stance(s) to take towards them. It is *the social relation with that audience* that will determine the writer's role, and this is our third element. Admittedly it is always open to writers to use the process of writing as a means of *arguing* their way *through to a conclusion* (for their own benefit). But if they want, for instance, to enlist people for a cause, resist attack, impartially set out alternative possibilities, or exchange ideas, then they have to learn how to meet the demands of these (and other) major *forms of argument and discussion* — our fourth element.

Fifthly, in all we have said so far, there hve been implicit distinctions between two major kinds of argument and discussion: those which lead to **decisions or practical recommendations** (*action-orientated*), and those which lead to *opinions and beliefs* (*notion-orientated*). Both major reasons need to be borne in mind and provided for.

Finally, writing for real audiences is in some respects the ultimate test of the efficacy of discussion and argument. So when a teacher helps students to address a wider audience, it will be valuable at the same time to find some way of communicating their response — of *eliciting audience feedback*. When this is not possible, a simulated context and audience can offer an alternative method of helping students to understand their positive achievements, as well as possible limitations.

Pointers to student development

In our view, research in argumentative writing in the teaching of English is still at a very early stage, and inevitably so, since elicited material from the classroom is so often poorly grounded in understanding. Until much more sophisticated classroom approaches have developed, the evidence for progress in students' written argument and discussion is going to be limited and skeletal. However, developing some of the ideas put forward by Wilkinson and his colleagues, we can say with some confidence that a teacher will be looking for signs that students are *moving away from* some or all of the following:

1. unsupported assertions;
2. an egocentric assumption that the reader is bound to think the same;
3. a dependence on the reader to construe ideas and relations in

ways that remove potential ambiguities and suggest coherent relations; and

4. unreflecting generalisation still without scrutiny or control.

In doing so, it seems that students will be *moving towards*:

1. attitudes, opinions and general statements supported by well grounded evidence;
2. a more flexible view of the range of consequences and implications;
3. a social ability to engage with readers with varying attitudes, opinions and values;
4. an awareness of the demands on the reader, thus a willingness to offer explicit cues as to rational coherence and overview;
5. a willingness to qualify generalisations and reformulate proposals;
6. an ability to relate personal experience to broader public knowledge which has been critically reviewed.

What these imply is that the student is learning to make a more sophisticated analysis and deal with more complex issues. At the same time, one is hoping for a growth in conscious and self-critical activity by the writer, and this will show in such characteristic things as comments on the ideological and sociocultural nature of words like 'vandal', and in a more reflective, self-critical awareness of the writer's own assumptions and perspective.

In the long term we would expect to find not a single line of development but several branching forms of discussion and argument within which development can be seen. Given the current limitations of the evidence, however, we have found the following check list (developed from Dixon and Stratta 1982b, pp. 4, 21–3) useful for focusing attention on the detailed achievements in any given piece.

- How complex and refined a rationale?
- How coherent, whether tacitly or explicitly?
- What quality of evidence, personal and/or public? What signs of objectivity, discrimination and critical review?
- What kind of stance to the topic — whether to explore an issue, advocate a line or attempt an overview . . . ?
- What kind of social relation to the audience, and with what effects on the flexible development in the line of thought?
- What control and delicacy in language and form?
- What reflexive and ideological awareness of language and thought?

Bibliography

Barnes, D. and Todd, F. (1977). *Communication and Learning in Small Groups*. London, Routledge and Kegan Paul.

Davies, T. (1982). 'Common Sense and Critical Practice' in Widdowson, P. (ed.), *Re-reading English*. London, Methuen.

Dixon, J. and Stratta, L. (1982a). 'Argument: What Does It Mean to Teach of English?', *English in Education*, vol. 16, no. 1.

Dixon, J. and Stratta, L. (1982b). *Teaching and Assessing Argument*. Southern Regional Examinations Board, Southampton.

Marrou, H.I. (1956). *A History of Education in Antiquity*, transl. G. Lamb. London, Sheed & Ward.

Twomey, A.M. (1984). 'The Way I Talk', *The English Magazine*, no. 12 (Spring). ILEA English Centre, Sutherland Street, London SW1.

Wilkinson, A.M., Barnsley, G., Hanna, P. and Swan, M. (1980). *Assessing Language Development*. Oxford, Oxford University Press.

3 What Gets Written About*

PETER MEDWAY

Initial analysis of the writing assignments

In the summer of 1983 I visited 21 classrooms in schools in the North of England where English was being taught to children to 12 years of age. I was able to interview the teachers and look at the complete collected written work done by a sample of pupils in that year, that is since the previous September. From these data I constructed a catalogue of all the writing assignments which had been set by the 21 English teachers over that period. There were 346 of them. The catalogue included information such as the title of the assignment, the terms in which it was set, the context in which it occurred, the teacher's stated intentions and my observations on the pupils' writing. I found out more about some assignments than others, so that the entries were not all equally full. By 'writing assignments' I mean tasks requiring continuous complete original pieces of writing — not language exercises, summaries, short answers or copying. The pupils' writing had in fact almost all been 'set'; hardly any had been self-assigned, although in a number of cases the pupils were able to select *either* the form *or* the topic.

A first analysis of the assignments revealed the following picture (in percentage terms):

*The research has been carried out at the University of Leeds under the supervision of Douglas Barnes with the support of a studentship from the Economic and Social Research Council. This paper presents an interim report of the research, which is not yet complete. Both the categories and the figures are still subject to modification.

Fiction	31.4	Book report	7.1
Personal account	15.0	Information	1.7
Poem	13.1	Argument	4.8
Play	3.1	Utilitarian conventional	3.4
Description	9.0	Media	2.8
Fictional document	7.6	Unclassified	0.9

These categories were not theoretically derived but were simply adaptations of common-sense terms in which I discussed the writing with the teachers. Some of them nevertheless require explanation. 'Personal accounts' are self-contained autobiographical writings, often alternatively called 'personal writing' or 'writing and experience'. 'Description', that strange form which occurs only in school (who ever heard a writer saying 'I've got a new description coming out on Thursday'?), refers to those accounts which endeavour to give a sense of something, and not simply to record features as in a surveyor's report on a house. 'Fictional documents' look like documents occurring in the real world but have been written in role by the pupils. They are often related to the novel currently being read. Pupils were asked, for instance, to write Tyke Tyler's school report, Tyke being the central character of a novel by Gene Kemp, and the letter which Tolly is reported in Leon Garfield's *Black Jack* to have written to his uncle. Diaries, manifestos, 'Wanted' posters and news clippings were similarly invented, in effect as alternative means of telling stories. 'Book reports' are the familiar reviews and character studies. Also included here are the occasional review of a TV programme and an essay on a set of letters written by a First World War soldier. The surveyor's report just mentioned would be an example of my category 'information', as in a report of research into evacuation in the Second World War and a history of the school. Facts are what is at issue in these cases. 'Argument' I use to cover any writing in which reasons and evidence are adduced for propositions, whether these assert what ought to be done or what our attitude should be on something, the pros and cons of an issue, or the truth or probability of some matter. 'Utilitarian/conventional' writing meets the requirements of everyday social and bureaucratic demands: letters of thanks, letters home from holiday, letters replying to advertisements and instructions how to get somewhere, are examples found in this work. 'Media' refers to writing which is set in order that the students may have experience of forms like the newspaper report or advertisement.

This analysis enabled me to make some observations. In the first place it was striking how fiction predominated — a third of the assignments were stories. Secondly, this was a very literary curriculum. All the categories down as far as 'fictional document' call for what Louise Rosenblatt (1978, pp. 24–5) has termed an 'aesthetic' reading, that is,

one the point of which is in the experience of the reading itself and not
in information or messages which may be abstracted for possible use
elsewhere. A Martian observer, assuming in ignorance that the forms of
writing practised in schools are ones likely to be useful in later life,
would take it that these pupils are expected to become novelists,
autobiographers, poets — and describers. Non-literary writing, by
contrast, receives little attention, although a token presence is maintained in nearly all the curricula.

This analysis left me feeling unsatisfied. For a former English teacher
the results contained few surprises. The curriculum had not been made
to look strange. Yet clearly it *was* strange: if English as a school subject
had not existed, no one would have invented it the way it was in these
schools. I needed somehow to undermine my sense of the naturalness of
this cultural form.

A further disappointment was that I had not caught what was
distinctive about this group of curricula. What that was I could not
precisely say, but the feeling confirmed my view that there were aspects
of English as it was practised which were not acknowledged in the
accounts of the practitioners. An English classroom constructed from
teachers' accounts in the 'method' texts would not be like a real one.
There appear to be *unspoken* generative principles underlying parts of
what we do as English teachers. It is not that these considerations are
suppressed — there is no conspiracy of silence; it is simply that they are
not seen.

There are, of course, far more adequate theoretically-based schemes
for classifying writing, such as those employing categories of rhetorical
function and sense of audience. But I felt that the really interesting
distinctions would escape those nets too. It appeared better to probe for
the unspoken principles in the circumstance that, while consensual
formal aims of English are generally couched in terms of *language*
(competence in writing, for example), practice necessitates that there be
non-language content for the language to be about. What *most*
contributed to the distinctive nature of the English curriculum, and of
one English curriculum as against another, might not be the forms
employed but the content which the pupils are required to read, write
and talk about. Moreover, in so far as different *writing* curricula within
English had different effects on pupils, the most significant differences
would surely derive from their having to write about different aspects of
the world. In following a writing curriculum pupils would perform
intensive processing on some aspects of their knowledge, while other
aspects would remain unarticulated and unexamined.

I therefore set out to describe and classify what the writing was about.
In the next part of the paper I show how I ended up doing this. Then I

illustrate the sort of things such as analysis enables one to say — and I say some of them.

A second analysis of what the writing was about

To try to talk about what writing is *about* is to negotiate a minefield: the 'aboutness' of writing is problematic. The very structure of the phrase 'writing about' suggests that there are two things: the writing, and some entity existing independently which is referred to by the writing. But in fact many of these 'entities referred to' — fictional characters for instance — only have an existence in so far as they are constituted by the writing. And even when entities do exist in the real world, to speak of writing as *referring* to them is difficult. There are things there and signs here, but the signs do not do anything to the things. Writing is not a spotlight which picks out aspects of the world. It is more like a dance of lights which we *see* as emblematic of patterns in the world. So when I speak of 'writing about cats', strictly speaking I am naming a sort of writing, not identifying some real connection between writing and the world.

These considerations serve to warn one against simplistic assumptions that to write about something is necessarily to engage in some way with that something. The process of writing *may* involve consulting one's real world knowledge, but it need not. One may, for instance, accomplish a piece of writing by drawing on one's knowledge of other texts.

I now proceed to the categories which I arrived at. There are three sets of these, entitled 'source of validity', 'topic' and 'mode of specification'. We will take them in order.

Source of validity
Different sorts of writing imply different sorts of validity claim. The way validity claims work is implicitly to invoke a *locus* outside the writing in which the entities represented in the writing are held to have their existence and from which the knowledge is derived which enables the writer to speak of them. As I mentioned above, this attribution to an external source may be a fiction in that the entities may only exist in so far as the writing appears to refer to them. However, fiction or not, writing generally looks and acts as if it is referring to states of affairs which exist outside itself, if not in the real world then perhaps in a place called 'the writer's imagination'. Writers are thus thought of as having *knowledge* even of those entities which they have imagined. Validity for the writing is claimed by pointing to the particular *domain* of knowledge

— such as experience or imagination — from which the entities are known. What I attempt to classify is the kind of sources which writers might invoke when challenged about the authority of their representations.

One sort of claim which writing might implicitly make is: 'This is based on knowledge of the real world.' The claim is for literal truth: 'This is how the world is; these representations correspond to actually obtaining states of affairs — to how the world is, or has been.' The 'validating source' to be adduced for one's representations might be one's own first-hand knowledge, which I here term *experience*, or it might be someone else's account of reality — book, conversation, media, or 'common knowledge' — the term I use is *report*. 'My last visit to the dentist' would have experience as its validating source, 'Evacuation from London in 1939' would have report.

Truth to 'the way it is' might, however, be claimed in a different way. A class might be asked to write about 'An autumn day'. The task could be fulfilled in two different ways. A child could write an account which reported the specific characteristics — feel, weather, scenes, occurrences — of an actual remembered day: say, 14, October 1984. The other acceptable way would be to write about a composite, idealised autumn day containing the essence of autumnness. The account would have the appearance of a report of actual occurrences, and would include statements like 'A squirrel scampers across the lawn and up the tree to check on his hoard of nuts', but this appearance would be a delusion. The day, as represented, never happened. Nevertheless the writer would not say it was an invention. Rather the claim would be that this 'ideal-type' representation is based on real knowledge and presents the truth about autumn days: not, indeed, the literal truth but another sort, the *essential* truth. This type of validating source I call *idealised knowledge*: when writing under this banner you would not wish to be held to the detail of your account but you would certainly claim to be conveying what the world is actually like.

Now, in contrast, consider writing which is avowedly invented or 'made up', in which the writer implies no claim that the report has been 'read off' the real world and has no wish for readers to suppose that any *knowledge* is being communicated to them. Immediately it is clear that further distinctions have to be made. Consider these two possible assignments, both of which would be considered as involving imagination: 'Imagine you were a child evacuated from London in 1939' and 'Imagine you are a Martian and a human *au pair* comes to live in your family'. For the writing resulting from the first of these, a mixed claim would be made: the personal story — what exactly happened in this particular case of evacuation — would be acknowledged as purely fiction: these precise events did not happen and there is no pretence that they did. On the other hand, that *type* of experience happened, and there would be an implied claim to have got it right in terms of knowledge of evacuation in general. The assertion is: 'This is what it *would have been* like, according to my best attempt to speculate on the basis of the knowledge that I have.' The source appealed to is *knowledge supplemented by imagination*, the imagination supplying the elements in which knowledge is deficient in that it is unavailable, or because we cannot know things like what it would have been like for *me* to have been there. In such writing what is constructed is a hypothesis, and truth to the nature of the world is a major consideration.

In representing Martians, on the other hand, a writer may point to pure *imagination* as the source from which the representations are derived. Such a claim would, of course, be a fiction, in that even the most apparently untrammelled fantasy is based on sort of knowledge. The point, however, is not what the actual source was, but what is claimed as the source, and in this example there is not any intention that readers should believe it to be reality. If a validity claim were to be formulated it would have to be not 'This corresponds to how things really are' but something like 'This is how I've imagined it, and what I say goes'.

I have not exhausted the possible 'sources of validity'. Two more can be distinguished. First, implicitly underwriting a large body of school writing is the writer's claimed knowledge, not of the real world, but of a fictional world created by another writer. Thus the pupils take the characters and situations of Shaw's *Pygmalion* and invent further episodes, documents and accounts, taking over and continuing the role of the original author. I label this type of source an *existing fiction*. The second source of knowledge is also other writing: not particular works, however, but general sub-genres. In these cases the originals against which the representations are to be evaluated are such types of writing as detective stories, ghost stories, SF stories, desert-island stories, naughty children stories, escape stories and hijack stories. For the most part the sources are not high literature but more popular forms of 'airport literature'. In a few cases other forms are represented: limericks, nonsense verse and myth. The point, once again, is not that these literary or sub-literary forms are the actual source of the elements in the writing (which could never have been successfully written by consulting one's knowledge of the real world) but that they would be the source which under challenge is *claimed* as authority. There is a sense in which you can get it right or wrong in horror stories. In vouching for the validity of the basic elements — you might say: 'This is how it is in horror stories.' The term I use for this sort of validating source is *discourse type*.

Finally I should mention that some writing assignments leave open as to which 'domain of knowledge' the representations are to be drawn from. A teacher who sets simply the title 'The escape' allows for response in a number of those categories. These assignments have to go in separate category: *unspecified*.

Topic

In constructing the set of categories I've called 'topic', I ask what aspect of the world are indicated as those that the writing will be about. 'Aspects of the world' is the best phrase I can find: by 'the world' I mean everything that is the case, or could conceivably be the case, including states, situations, relations, ideas and so on as well as people and things.

The distinctions I make are very simple. There is writing about *human phenomena*, writing about *non-human phenomena*, writing about phenomena which are *unspecified*, and writing about *texts* (book reports and the like). There is no profound philosophical basis for this particular carve-up of the universe: it is simply that these distinctions seem useful for what I eventually want to say about the cognitive implications of writing curricula.

I subdivide *human phenomena* but not the other categories. The distinction is mainly because of numbers: a bigger collection of assignments would make further subdivisions a sensible proposition. *Human phenomena* breaks down into *interactions* — people interacting with people or with circumstances or environments ('people in situations' would be another way of expressing it); and *persons* — people depicted in those ongoing aspects which persists across varied interactions; people as static or continuing phenomena. Persons described might of course include the self.

There is a further distinction within *interaction* which is useful because of characteristics of these particular curricula. I categorise separately those assignments in which there is a clear emphasis on the articulation of subjective experience, on what it is like to be me, the experiencing subject, in particular situations and interactions. I use the label *subjectivity* for such cases in which interactions are described as it were from the inside.

It will be clear that many topics can be dealt with in a number of ways, with appeals to a range of validating sources. As authorisation for one's description of a person one might implicitly adduce one's own experience, a report in a history, one's abstracted and idealised knowledge of a type of person, one's imaginative speculation based on a framework of knowledge of a person, an account of a person in a novel, one's knowledge of the type of person as depicted in class of popular novel or one's unconstrained imagination.

Mode of specification

In naming some aspect of the world as the subject, writing assignments may delineate the topic in various ways. The assignment may, for instance, specify a *unique* phenomenon, something which occurred or occurs at a specific identified time and place: or visit to the theatre last Thursday, Blind Pew's arrival at the Admiral Benbow Inn. Such cases I label *U*. Alternatively an assignment may designate a *type* of phenomenon. 'Family outing', for example, is a general term which covers many actual instances: each pupil will think of different examples. Similarly with 'Letter from my holiday abroad', 'The alien in my garden' and 'My secret hiding place': the terms used in the titles designate a class of phenomena and an act of selection or specification is demanded of the pupils whereby in effect they each have to decide which particular instances would count as cases of the type named. Here I use the code *T*.

At this point we realise that the terms of an assignment which names a type may at the same time indicate how the pupil is to realise the topic. There are two possibilities. 'Family outings' with its plural form invites the pupil to deal with that human phenomenon *as a class*, that is, to offer observations about family outings in general. On the other hand the form 'A family outing', which despite the singular and the indefinite article is still a name for a class and does not indicate any particular occurrence, requires the pupil to produce a representation of one unique instance of the type. Thus we have the mode of specification employed in the formulation of the assignment (T or U) and the level at which the student is expected to realise the assignment (again T or U), giving us three possible permutations:

Mode of specification	*Expected realisation*
T	T
T	U
U	U

Yet another mode of specification is found. Consider these cases: 'Write your autobiography'; 'Look out of your window and record everything which you see over the space of five minutes'; 'Write what happens after the end of the novel *A pair of Jesus boots*'. Two of these clearly earmark human phenomena as topics; what is seen out of the window, on the other hand, might be human or non-human. But none of the assignments name the type of human or non-human phenomena to be represented; *anything* could feature in an autobiography or a continuation of a novel, and who knows what might pass in front of the window; nor do they indicate specifid *unique* occurrences. What they do is indicate a *frame*: temporal (birth to present, over five minutes, afterwards), or spatial (out of your window); and then require that the pupil represent whatever phenomena occur within that frame. Such assignments I show as *FU*: the assignment specifies a frame, the pupil is to describe the unique reality inside it.

This scheme gives us in theory four possible modes of specification (TT, TU, UU and FU) against each of the topic categories. In practice it was not necessary to use them all on this data, and I omit several from the table showing how the 346 assignments were classified.

Writing curricula as cognitive programmes

As presented so far, then, this is simply a scheme for classifying writing assignments. What bearing, however, might it have on the possibilities of cognitive experience created by a writing curriculum? Something must be said about this before I present the figures. I have been at pains to emphasise that producing writing about an aspect of the world does not in itself involve a direct encounter with the world. That is a point about the *sui generis* nature of writing. A different point is that even when reality is claimed as the source, one's account actually owe more to knowledge of other accounts than to knowledge of the world. Nevertheless, there clearly is, generally speaking, *some* connection between writing about certain topics and engaging with certain aspects of the world. It would seem to make a difference to the processing one carries out on one's experience and knowledge whether one is regularly asked to write about ghosts and comic-strip characters, or people from everyday experience. If one is 'writing about experience' it is at least relevant to consult experience, and indeed this is actively promoted by some teachers. The formulation of writing assignments may at least be said to provide *opportunities* for addressing aspects of one's knowledge, and the configuration of a writing curriculum will *tend* to foster certain kinds of thinking about the world over other kinds. It is at any rate likely to be a different cognitive experience on the one hand to recall an incident from one's own life, and on the other to invent an incident in the life of an imaginary character; on the one hand to explore the motivation of a character one has invented within the conventions of detective stories, and on the other of one's own sister.

Since types of writing assignment will tend to involve types of cognitive experience, one can look at a writing curriculum and read from it a sort of cognitive programme. This is in no way to imply that any cognitive programme was intended: the intention may have been simply to provide experiences of writing. It is simply that cognitive effects follow from writing and that it is possible, at least speculatively, to characterise them.

In examining such implicit cognitive programmes consideration of the 'mode of specification' of the topics appears very relevant. Different sorts of cognitive programme seem to be implied by formulation in terms of types of phenomena, of unique instances and of frames. Behind the indication of *types* as topics there might lie some idea of *covering* a range of important or significant classes of phenomena. One knows that in some English classrooms this intention is explicit: there are teachers who consciously involve their pupils in thinking about the nature of fear, of loneliness, of love and so on. But even where no such intention has been formulated there may nevertheless be an effective programme of the kind. By contrast, the programme which could be construed as underlying the habitual framing of topics at the level of *unique instance* would be rather different. Teachers who simply designate specific aspects of reality to be dealt with are presumably less likely to be motivated by a concern for an agenda of significant issues. The object of setting 'Bonfire Night' (to be written the day after it takes place), a letter by one of the characters in *The Ghost of Thomas Kempe* describing the ghost, or 'Our visit to the airport' is probably achieved if the students produce adequate accounts: such a curriculum would tend to be just about getting the pupils to write better. The adequacy of the pupils' understanding of Bonfire Night, fictional ghosts and airports is not a major concern.

A similar case is when the teacher defines a frame and is happy to take whatever falls within it, different though the contents from individual pupils will be. Whatever lies behind the setting of such assignments it cannot be that the teacher has in mind some particular aspects of the world or of experience which it is considered important that the pupils come to grips with.

A question which it makes sense to ask of an English curriculum is 'How *empirical* is it?' My impression is that, paradoxically, for a teacher to assign a unique phenomenon as topic is rarely an indication of a determination that pupils should observe and register the recalcitrant specifics of a concrete instance. Rather what often seems to be called for is a decorous parade of appropriate conventional sentiment. This is especially the case when, as often happens, pupils are given as their writing topic some publicly marked occasion such as a Bonfire Night, Christmas or 'My birthday', experiences about which a set of ready-made attitudes are available in the culture. These attitudes and interpretations are often so strongly established that it is difficult to imagine the teacher having any intention that the pupils should express an unstereotyped vision. Such assignments are in fact best seen as part of a process of socialisation into received versions of reality.

The place where we find embodied the most powerful concern for the empirical, for the observing and registering by the pupil of reality, is in assignments of the form TU: teacher specifies type: pupil supplies unique instance. In these the teacher indicates a class of phenomena of which the pupils collectively may know or be able to imagine many instances: 'Getting stuck in a high place', 'Something my friends spoilt

for me', 'Unfairly accused'. The episode which the individual pupil
supplies will not typically come accompanied by an existing public
interpretation; it will be marked as significant only in the individual's
memory or imagination. That such experiences might be material for
public expression may indeed come to the pupil as a quite new
possibility.

Accurate recording of the concrete might constitute a base on which
more overarching ideas — categorisations, abstractions and generalisations — could then be built. One can envisage a rational cognitive
programme involving a planned Moffett-style move up the ladder of
abstraction from 'type – unique instance' (TU) to 'type – type' (TT),
from 'My dog' to 'Pets' or 'Human–animal relations'. The occurrence in
a curriculum of 'type – type' assignments might be attributable to some
such plan. But then again it might not. It might instead turn out that
those assignments in which pupils are required to say things about types
or classes of phenomena have nothing to do with those in which they are
directed towards particulars. Indeed, writing of the 'type – type' form
could conceivably have a quite different function, that of framing, not
the first tentative abstractions from empirical knowledge, but mere
decorative generalities, as indeed we tend to find when the type
specified is 'Autumn', 'Snow' or 'Fear'.

The writing assignments and the pupils' world

I hope I have said enough to indicate why I think these categories could
be relevant to a consideration of the cognitive experiences children
gain through writing, and I now turn to Table 2.1 which shows how the
346 writing assignments were classified according to the scheme I have
described. In commenting on selected features I mainly want to
illustrate the *sort* of things one can say on the basis of this analysis.

My first observation is that the number of assignments in which the
implied source of validity was to be the writers' own experience was
nearer a quarter than a third of the total. Even if all these assignments
represented genuine engagements by the pupils in reflection about their
experience, such engagement is evidently far from being the main
concern of these curricula. Writing clearly designated as about the
experience of being oneself in particular situations or types of situation
(the subjectivity category) was even less frequent.

A major activity in these curricula is representing particular human
events, incidents and situations: in the terms of this scheme, all the
entries under *subjectivity* and *interaction* in which the level specified for
the pupils' realisation of the topic is the unique instance, U. These add
up to 164 assignments, or 47.4 per cent. If we look at the sources from

Topic/Mode of specification

Row-group labels (left of table): Indicated as topic — Level/frame of specification — Level of realisation — Source of Validity

Source of Validity	Subjectivity		Human phenomena — Interaction				Person		Non-Human Phenomena		Un-Specified	Text	Other	Total	%
Level of specification	T	T	T	T	U	F	T	T	T	U					
Level of realisation	U	T	T	U	U	U	U	T	T	U					
Experience	19	4	9	12	4	6	10	14	2		1	17		98	28·3
Report	1		1	11	1	2			2	1	2			21	6·1
Idealised knowledge				1			1	3	4					9	2·6
Knowledge supplement by imagination	16	1	14	2	1	5	3	11	1		2		2	58	16·8
An existing fiction					18	12	7							37	10·7
A discourse type	2		40				1	1			24		4	72	20·8
Imagination	1		5	2		2	1	5	10		4			30	8·7
Unspecified	1		1								7			9	2·6
Other	2		1					1					8	12	3·5
Total	42	5	71	28	24	27	23	35	19	1	40	17	14	346	100
%	12·1	1·4	20·5	8·1	6·9	7·8	6·6	10·1	5·5	0·3	11·6	4·9	4·0	100	

Table 2.1 Writing assignments from 21 curricula

which these representations purport to draw, the pupils' *experience* is not the main one. Indeed, if we add to *experience* both *report* and *knowledge of the world as supplemented by imagination* we have still only accounted for 79 cases, as against fully 72 which derive from an *existing fiction* or a *discourse type* — that is, from *literary* experience. In other words, pupils spend a lot of their time depicting human life as it manifests itself in particular circumstances and settings, but the knowledge they use for this is not what they have themselves gathered in their 12 years. Instead what these curricula have them doing is recycling book knowledge, if we may use that term to cover what is acquired from works of fiction. (Bear in mind too that those 24 entries against *discourse type* which are in the *unspecified* column are also mainly stories depicting human actions and experiences and many of them should be included in the count. The reason that they are not in the main body of the chart is that the terms of the assignment don't generally specify either a type of human phenomenon or a particular phenomenon or a frame: often they simply designate a form ('Write a ghost story') or supply a title ('Night at a cottage').)

There is, of course, nothing inherently contradictory between wanting your pupils to attain insights about human behaviour and motivation, and getting them to write mostly fiction. Fiction has been very widely used as a means of generating and communicating understandings about the social world. But such an intention *would* be incompatible with heavy reliance on the sort of fiction I have here categorised as having an established *discourse type* as its source, fiction in which central elements are, in a sense, given. What is at issue in the classrooms where such writing goes on is not 'Let's get it right about what makes people tick and how they behave and how the world works' but 'Let's make it really exciting or really funny'. A good deal of attention is also paid to a 'convincing' view of the world; but such attention is in the interests not of the resulting knowledge but of the verisimilitude of the narrative. The object is not a more adequate grasp of reality but achievement of what Barthes (1968, p. 88) calls *l'effet de réel*, 'the reality effect'.

Assignments, on the other hand, which seem to have *knowledge worked on by imagination* as their source — 16.8 per cent of the total — might indeed represent a coherent cognitive programme, one for getting pupils to understand situations they have not experienced by entering into them imaginatively. However, rather than look at those more closely I propose to use my limited space to comment on the type/unique instance issue.

I suggested earlier that a line of curricular thinking might be to help pupils first to attain an unstereotyped view of particular realities and overcome preconceptions and conventional categories, and then to begin to formulate more general understandings on that sound basis.

Assignments in which the level of realisation was to be the type rather than the unique instance might be explained by such a plan. To test this we might look at those assignments in which pupils are required to give accounts of types of human phenomena based on the sources *experience* and *report*. So first let us take the twelve entries at the intersection of the column *human phenomena, interaction*, TT, and the row *experience*. The assignments are:

016/8	Should Christmas be banned?	F/G/I
110/4	Bonfire Night (in general)	F
110/9	Instructions for a blind person	P
123/9	Directions to get somewhere	P
125/7	School uniform	G/I
126/11	Christmas	F
154/8	Friends and friendship	G
159/7	Collecting militaria	P
159/13	School problems the teacher don't know about	G,I
160/9	How to use a box of matches	P
160/14	Firework code	P
161/6	Christmas in our family	F

Thus four are about annual festivals (F) and five are practical instructions or accounts of procedures (P). Only the three others and 'Should Christmas be banned?' could be vehicles for acts of classification, generalisation, analysis or evaluation (G). Three of these concern issues (I) about which a position is to be taken up.

Moving down one row, we find 11 such assignments based on *report*. These are:

013/1	Evacuation (research report)	Inf
014/6	World poverty	G,I.
053/6	Fox hunting	G,I
064/1	Blood sports	G,I
107/3	Directions (based on map)	P
107/4	Directions (based on map)	P
111/12	War — adventure or horror?	G,I
111/13	War (poem)	G,I
113/54	Pollution	G,I
154/2	Karate	Inf
160/10	Unemployment	G,I

Two are practical instructions (I have counted maps as reports), two are simply general information (Inf) and the rest (seven) are issues and involve, one would think, generalising and analysing.

So we can say two things: in relation to human phenomena, there is not very much opportunity genuinely to generalise and analyse — only ten assignments; and in only three of those ten cases is experience the avowed source. In so far as pupils deal with experience in these classes they stay at the level of the specific, moving outside it, when they do at all, mainly for purposes of writing general practical instructions (applicable to numerous particular situations) or rehearsing conventional sentiments. And, in so far as they may genuinely attempt to generalise and evaluate, it is not about experience that they do so, but rather as a rule about topics that are already packaged in the culture as 'issues'. 'Views' are what you have about public affairs which you know mainly from the media, and about the semi-public sphere of school.

Thus between the two modes of *representing*, which is what one does with experience at the level of the particular, and *generalising and analysing*, there is little connection. They operate in separate spheres on different contents, and there do not appear to be even the beginnings of a move to reach from one to the other. It is as if *simply* representing is an end in itself. The exercise is either to present an account which is acceptable in terms of tone and sentiment or to construct a vivid realisation which will enable the reader to share what it was like. The latter description seems to be true also of much of the writing in the category *knowledge worked on by imagination*: in imagining what it would be like to be blind, or evacuated, or a lion in a cage, or marooned in a space ship, or holed up in a bunker, or in creating a description of a house on fire or a Belfast street or a day in 2083, what counts is certainly the successful visualisation of detail, of the precise texture of experience.

The unspoken assumption seems to be that the sort of generalising, weighing and evaluating which one does on public issues — a process involving, at best, the posing of questions, consideration of explanations, comparison of alternative interpretations, teasing out of implications — is not appropriate for the material which one has gathered in the business of living. It is as if reality as experienced by a young adolescent of 12 is seen as unproblematic. Or, if it is problematic, then representing it in a presentational way is enough.

Compared with school curricula as a whole, English in at least some of these classrooms is undoubtedly a child-centred subject. That is to say, children are not required to pretend to be something they are not; their own honest responses and evaluations are respected and given a place. But what is acknowledged and given scope is, it seems, only one side of children's nature, their Wordsworthian capacity for freshness of vision and appreciation of the texture and variety of the world, of 'things being various'. There is surely also another side of childhood, the propensity to wonder, puzzle and speculate, to want to look beneath the surface, to ask why things are the way they are. This side, by contrast, is unregarded. English, it seems, is a good place in which to recreate or imagine experience, but a bad place to be curious.

To come at a similar point from another direction: a world is constituted by this collection of assignments, by the topics and the manner in which they are expected to be realised, and it is essentially a world of surfaces, a parade of phenomena. In it there are no causes, no structures, no underlying processes, nothing hidden or latent which needs to be revealed. *Society*, for instance, doesn't appear, nor any social forces or processes. Experiences and events just happen, and one registers them in their specificity. Phenomena just are. It is as if only that is taken to be real of which we can have unmediated knowledge through our senses or through introspection. The locus of reality is solely in inner experience and in the phenomena with which we are in immediate contact.

There is a further point to be made about this world. If a Martian archaeologist some time in the future were to come across this body of writing and, taking it to be a reflection of the world the writers lived in, attempt to derive a picture of that world, it would be a very strange picture that would result. Asking ourselves what are the most distinctive features of life in the 1980s in Britain, we might think of demographic change, population movements, economic near-crisis, unemployment, the achievement by some women of some liberation, rapid technological innovation, Boy George, video, neglected public services, glue and heroin, Greenham Common and microcomputers. These items barely appear in this collection of writing curricula. Twelve-year-olds evidently do not live in history. They may write about the history which happened in the past — in 1939 for example — but the great social processes currently occurring, the massive gear-shifting evident in our society, apparently pass them by. The young adolescent section of the population apparently has no apprehension of those processes, not even as they manifest themselves in the lives of known individuals.

It is hard to believe that this is really the case. It is more likely that the young people themselves have an awareness of the society around them, albeit an inarticulate one, and that the writing curriculum is framed in such a way that they can give no expression to that awareness. A writing curriculum provides, after all, not only an opportunity to work on selected aspects of reality, but also a model of what writing can be used on and for, of what can be written about. An inadequate model not only excludes important tracts of reality but also creates the impression that they are outside the scope of what *can* be brought under control by writing.

Writing writing/writing someting

What I have been doing in this paper is to consider the probable
cognitive effects of a writing curriculum. I have asked, if, as we know to
be the case, the process of writing can produce changes in awareness,
knowledge and understanding, then *what* changes are likely to flow from
this particular curriculum? I have suggested what they might be and have
criticised the curriculum in the light of that analysis. But in doing this I
have, in a sense, not been playing the game, since few of the teachers
intended the curriculum to have particular cognitive effects. The effects
were supposed to be on the children's ability to *write*: this is a language
curriculum, not a knowledge curriculum. To formulate serious intentions about children's knowledge and understanding of the world is to
go beyond what counts as English in the division of school responsibilities.

My point, however, is that these curricula *do* have cognitive effects
whether or not we have planned them to. English teachers sometimes
claim that anything may be written about in their lessons, the important
point being that motivated writing should occur. But what this enquiry
shows is that it is not 'anything' that gets written about, but a specific set
of things. For instance, on a big scale pupils represent human
interactions. Underneath the writing curiculum there is a highly
particular and distinctive knowledge curriculum. Presumably it is the
habit of not examining this that accounts for the lack of previous
research into what pupils write about. But since a cognitive programme
is necessarily implied in a writing programme we have no choice but to
take responsibility for it and make some decisions about what we want it
to be. The fact that, historically, content only got into the English
curiculum on the coat-tails of writing, because there had to be
something for the writing to be about, is no longer any excuse since we
now know about the relationship of language to thought and knowledge.

One writer frames the problem in this way:

> To write an essay may be an exercise of style, but it is something more; it
> is an exercise in knowledge or in thought. The pupils have not merely to
> express something in language, they have also, on certain hints supplied,
> to find the matter to be expressed . . . the lesson is a mixed exercise, partly
> of thought and partly of style . . .

The writer suggests that this is a difficulty:

> . . . you cannot carry on two subjects abreast, and make them both
> consecutive, or observe the natural course from elementary to difficult. If
> you follow the proper order for the one, you cannot be sure that the other

will bend to that order . . . you cannot frame a series of essays that will be consecutive, both as regards subject, and as regards language or expression.

On these grounds the writer was opposed to pupils writing in the composition class. They could do that in other lessons, while confining themselves in composition to the study of exemplars. The writer was Alexander Bain, Professor of Rhetoric at Aberdeen, writing in 1887 (p. 25). Nowadays we would agree that the study of exemplars is not of much use in isolation from the practice of writing, and the practice there has to be. But that leaves us with Bain's nettle, which so far I do not think we have grasped. We have avoided looking too hard at the value of the topics we set and the quality of our preparation for them.

We are now in a position to take a more positive line. We may start by affirming that writing is potentially a very important *cognitive* process, too important to be frittered away on things that do not much matter. There is no need for pupils in English to be just writing writing: let them write *something*, and let the something result in cognitive gains which might make a difference to them. Could we not begin by asking. What do pupils *need* to address themselves to? What are the bits of the world, the aspects of reality and experience which could do with receiving that intense working over which only writing can give? Starting from there, we might get both a less trivial curriculum *and* enhanced writing performance.

Bibliography

Bain, A. (1887).   *On Teaching English: with detailed examples, and an Enquiry into the Definitions of Poetry.* London, Longmans, Green & Co.

Barnes, D. and D. (1983).   'Cherishing Private souls? Writing in Fifth Year English Classes' in Arnold, R. (ed.), *Timely Voices: English Teaching in the Eighties.* Melbourne, Oxford University Press.

Barthes, R. (1968).   'L'effet de réel', *Communications*, II.

Rosenblatt, L. (1978).   *The Reader, The Text, The Poem.* Carbondale, Southern Illinois Press.

Part Two

Writing and Thinking

4 I Write Therefore I Am*

ANDREW WILKINSON

The proposition 'I communicate, therefore I am' (Wilkinson 1985) emphasises the creative nature of communication. It means, clearly, not that I exist physically, but that I exist as a personality with an identity and self-image in the social world. We can go on to say 'I communicate therefore you are' (and 'you communicate therefore I am'): and also 'I communicate therefore it is', i.e. I create the universe in which I live. The proposition in the title of this paper, 'I write therefore I am', is an aspect of the wider proposition. Let us approach it by some discussion of the wider proposition.

Three communication models

There are three basic communication models, and only three: transmission, reciprocity, and reflexion.

The simplest model, transmission, is one in which information is passed from A to B — a speaker addresses an audience, the media transmit, the actors perform, a writer writes a book. In the crudest manifestations, B cannot contribute to what A is saying. Least crude is perhaps an actor sensing the mood of an audience or a teacher grasping learning difficulties of a class.

A second model of communication is the reciprocal. In this model A communicates to B communicates to A communicates to B communicates to A, and so on. The second model of communication must of

* In abbreviated form, this paper draws on some of the arguments of Wilkinson (1986).

course comprehend the first. This is in fact the normal model in human relationships. Its basic description is 'conversation' — whether this be adult–child interaction, gossip, love talk, any situation in which there is an exchange.

A feature of this reciprocity is that the communication of A to some extent creates the communication of B, which again creates the communication of A, and thus to some extent A creates B creates A. If A for instance asks B a question he tends to determine that B will give him some sort of answer, and the meaning of the answer is prescribed in terms of the prompt or even the alternatives offered by the question.

Thus these two communication models can be designated AB and ABA. But there is a third which is reflexive: we can call this AA. A communicates with A — A communicates with self, and this is very important indeed.

Model AB — transmission

What does the first model tell us about the proposition 'I communicate therefore I am'? It tells us that we can inform, and regulate (i.e. influence, affect) other people. In other words it gives us a sense of being a source — a source of something — information, emotion, power. Even behind the various cries of a young baby, there is this sense of being a source. They mean, whatever their individual connotation, I am a force to be reckoned with. It is this model which underlies what has become known, in Goffman's terms, as 'the presentation of self' (Goffman 1969).

So AB is assertion of being on the one hand, and regulation of other things on the other. In terms of assertion it is an attempt at self-definition — I am the greatest, for example — but ultimately without social verification it is meaningless. In terms of regulation it works with objects as an absolute — lifting a weight, moving a chair. With people it has to be socially conferred. If you are king of the castle it is ultimately because in some sense you are acknowledged to be so. Of course the acknowledgement which preserves a democratic ruler is different from that which preserves a tyrant. Power is one of the things which compels acknowledgement.

As a paradigm of AB we may take the classical teacher–taught relationship — what Barnes (1976) calls transmission. The teacher transmits and the student receives. The research evidence is that teachers talk much more of the time in most lessons. Much of the information transmitted in secondary school is at low level on a cognitive scale, encouraging assimilation rather than thought. The self-statement of the teacher is inseparable from his regulatory role, in which two types of activity are present — a teaching and a control function. Often the same language does both jobs — 'Get out your books and read quietly till the end of the period', for example.

On the whole, then, the contribution of the model AB to the proposition 'I communicate therefore I am', is confined to the first clause — I communicate. There does not need to be a class response to produce validation — it could come from training, past employment, DES certification. We must turn, therefore, to an examination of the second, the ABA model.

Model ABA — reciprocity

As mentioned above, the prototype of ABA is conversation, and there are allied forms such as discussions, seminars, commercial transactions, disputations, and travesties of the interaction process such as committee meetings.

In conversation A makes a speech act to B. Whatever the speech act is it is in some sense creating B. If A asks a question B is created as an answerer, if he makes an unquestionable statement B is created as an agreer, or a commentor, and so on. But by the same token B is also creating A by the type of responses he makes. However at the affective level something else is going on. B's responses are offering his perceptions of A as a person. Approvals, agreements, favourable responses, inclusion of a good deal of phatic support are enhancing of self-image. As a result of B's feedback A is created as, say, a kinder, more intelligent person in his own eyes: but also in fact he may become so as a result of B's perceptons. In part personality is built up by the use of language to obtain reflections:

> Mirror Mirror on the wall
> Who is the fairest of us all

and by conferment by others — not only 'I communicate therefore I am' but 'I communicate therefore you are'.

Model AA — reflexion

So far we have looked at the communication models AB and ABA, i.e. without feedback, and with feedback from significant others. Let us now look at the third model, AA, the model with self as recipient of the message.

We take it that the prime example of this is thought itself — the dialogue inside the head, the interminable conversation with its questions and answers. Idiomatic expressions in our language show that this is well recognised — 'I said to myself', 'I asked myself the question', for instance. This dialogue is perpetually concerned with three basic questions: Who am I? What do I think? What do I feel? The first is concerned with self-image and body-image, the second with the assertion, examination, revision of our propositions; the third with feelings and attitudes.

In the world outside the head these processes, it would seem, are best represented in writing.

I write therefore I am

Writing is a prime means of developing our thinking and our emotions, and therefore of defining, and redefining, ourselves. This is because it gives us time and opportunity for reflection. The words are not gone as soon as spoken, but are before us on the page for consideration, and this enables us to deal with more complex ideas and the relationships between them, and to be more exact about them. These two mental activities we may call 'thinking on paper' and 'feeling on paper', though there is no absolute distinction between the two. In the rest of this chapter we shall be concerned with the latter.

The education of the affect

We sometimes use the word 'emotion' interchangeably with 'feeling'. Sometimes this makes little difference, but here a distinction is necessary.

'Emotions', such as anger, jealousy, fear, admiration, do not arise spontaneously, but have an external cause. A person is angry *about* something, jealous *of* someone, and so on. But it is not the cause itself which gives rise to the emotion, it is the judgement the person makes about it and the value he puts upon that judgement — the *appraisal* he gives it. Thus Tom's girlfriend talking sinuously to Dick occasions jealousy in Tom because he appraises the situation as threatening her preference for him, and is *disturbed* by this. Harry, seeing the same conversation, is indifferent to it and he makes no appraisal of it. In Tom's jealousy there are two elements — a cognitive element (the appraisal) and a feeling element (the disturbance). Feeling is often spoken of as 'coming over us', as something which often happens to us when we make an appraisal, something which *affects* — we speak of being 'affected by grief', or being 'seized with passion', and the implication is that we are passive in the matter. For this reason the realm of feelings (and emotions) is sometimes known as 'the affect' or 'the affective'.

An emotion may be described, therefore, as a cognitive act together with the feeling this causes. Peters (Hurst and Peters 1970, pp. 49–50) distinguishes between a cognitive act which he calls a judgement, e.g. that something is three feet high, and one which he calls an appraisal, which has a feeling side to it, e.g. that something is dangerous:

That is why the cognitive core of the emotion is referred to as an appraisal and not just as a judgement. But the feeling is inseparable from the cognition; we could not identify such feelings without reference to the understanding of the situations which evoked them.

It is important to emphasis this 'cognitive core' to the emotions as sometimes 'head' and 'heart' are spoken of as though they were completely separate. The appraisal made may be an extremely rapid one. We may take an instant dislike to someone on first meeting and on fuller acquaintance revise our opinion. In both cases the feelings of dislike or of liking would be based on an appraisal, in one case superficial. Appraisal is frequently an unconscious matter: for instance, we may dislike someone who reminds us of a past enemy, though we are not aware of the reason. This kind of reaction is sometimes called 'intuition'; nevertheless it still contains an appraisal.

There follow from regarding 'emotion' in this way two very important implications. One is that we cannot talk of emotional development as separate from cognitive development. The (emotional) response will always be related to the (cognitive) appraisal. A young child might evaluate a teacher as 'cross' or 'bossy'; an adult appraisal of the teacher might be of role as much as personality. And this brings us to the second important implication: we cannot separate emotional from social development because emotional development takes place predominantly in relation to other people. An emotion of compassion, for example, requires some being outside oneself to call it forth; so a child may try to console a companion who has fallen. As Peters (Hurst and Peters 1970, p. 50) says:

> Emotions such as jealousy, guilt, pity and envy cannot be characterised without reference to moral and social concepts such as rules, ownership, and rights. One of the main features of emotional development is the learning of the countless different ways of appraising other people and ourselves in terms of a conceptual scheme which is predominantly social in character. The education of the emotions consists largely in the development of appraisals of the sort which are appropriate in terms of moral and aesthetic criteria and which are founded on realistic beliefs about how we are placed.

It is difficult to see how 'feeling', in the sense used above, could be educated: it would be like trying to educate the weather. But when we talk about the emotions we talk about feeling plus a cognitive element, and cognition *can* be educated. As we said above, the distinction between 'feeling' and 'emotion' is not always observed. In order to avoid possible confusion many writers use the term 'affect', the 'affective', to cover both, and this is the usage we follow.

The quality of affect in writing

The quality of affect in writing cannot be described in itself but only in terms of its appraisals. In the affective model of the Crediton Project it was suggested that the major appraisals were self of self, self of others, self of environment, and self of the human condition. To simplify, we may say that these concern the degree of self-awareness writers display: their empathy with others; their sense of relationship to the non-human world; and their wisdom in the face of circumstance. In the Crediton Project and subsequent work (Wilkinson *et al.* 1980; Wilkinson 1986) we subdivided each. At the moment we shall confine ourselves to a summary.

Self
Young writers express themselves directly, without self-consciousness, but they gradually become able to understand their own motives and feelings, and their place in context — their effect on and their appearance to others, and so on. A mature poet, W.B. Yeats, contemplating his declining physical powers in 'Sailing to Byzantium', writes

> An aged man is but a paltry thing,
> A tattered coat upon a stick, unless
> Soul clap its hands and sing, an louder sing
> For every tatter in its mortal dress

Here Yeats is describing both the decayed outside image presented by old age, and at the same time his consciousness of an inner passion which needs to celebrate.

Others
Along with a growing awareness of ourselves there develops an awareness of the people, a sense of 'our neighbour as self'. Young children are necessarily egocentrical, but as they grow we expect some empathy for others to develop — some ability to realise what it is like to be in the other person's shoes. Christ's words (Matthew 22. 37–9) make the statement; Auden's paraphrase, from 'As I Walked Out One Evening',

> You shall love your crooked neighbour
> with your crooked heart

adds the word 'crooked', bringing out not only an understanding of the neighbour, but also of the self, indicating at once the difficulty of such an act, and at the same time how their very imperfections enable people to relate to each other.

Environment

Environment may be social: the atmosphere, the conventions or assumptions of social behaviour. On the other hand it may be physical — everything in the world except human beings. This latter aspect is many-faceted. It touches the ecologist's sense of the interdependence of the human and non-human, the painter's response to landscape, the carpenter's delight in the grain of wood, the poet's celebration of 'things being various' (Louis Macneice, 'Snow')

> World is crazier and more of it than we think
> Incorrigibly plural. I peel and portion
> A tangerine and spit the pips and feel
> The drunkenness of things being various.

For our purposes a response which respects the non-human world is more acceptable, or 'mature', than one which exploits it.

The human condition

The circumstances in which we find ourselves constantly change, so that we are continually having to 'come to terms with reality' and the adjustments we make will vary in their success. An immature response 'avoids' the issue, a mature one 'copes' with it. Some people deal with problems as they arise, others formulate their conduct in terms of principles. W.E. Henley, the poet, had the grim ordeal of a year in the Edinburgh Infirmary in 1873, while doctors struggled to save his right foot, the other having been amputated as a result of a tubercular disease. There he formulated the stoical views expressed in his poem 'Invictus':

> It matters not how strait the gate,
> How charged with punishment the scroll,
> I am the master of my fate,
> I am the captain of my soul.

The verse quotation we have used cannot give more than a hint of the quality of feeling they are intended to illustrate because the context is absent, and this quality is a function of the total situation rather than the particular words used. Later on, however, we shall be illustrating from longer quotations.

We shall now go on to discuss affect in the writings of children and young people in the terms just outlined — the 'affective model'.

Applications of the affective model

Self-definition

The compositions used below are taken mainly from the work of writers ages 5–18 given the title 'Myself'. In writing about 'Myself' young writers give three kinds of information. The first we might call *formal* — the sort required on an official form — name, age, even weight, address, members of family, possessions. The second is information about *actions*; many of these actions are insignificant in describing us — e.g., going to school, sleeping; others are more significant — our achievements, crimes, oddities. A third class we may call *dispositional* items — describing our temperment, character, personality. So frequently as to be almost a sub-class with younger children are lists of likes and dislikes. Thus Charlie, aged six, develops this with riotous enthusiasm:

> I like banging my heDe a gast the wall
> and I liyk Fook I liyk School liyk water
> I liyk news

An example containing all the items at a very simple level is Scott's:

> My name is Scott
> What I like best is doing sums
> I like playing football and I am six
> I am quite good and
> like this school

Here there is no organising principle apparent.

Seven- to eight-year-olds similarly have no organising principle unless they follow Charlie's method, but they are on the whole more fluent and need to write more. Their additional material takes the form of chronicle or narrative; here is a typical example by Tom (aged 6 years 11 months):

> Halow my name is Tom and I have a brouther and a sisder my brouther is called Glen my sister is called Lynne. I have a mumy and a Daddy. And now I will tell you a sory adalt saterday and Sunday

(there follows a chronicle of domestic happenings on both days). The narrative pull is so strong that with some children it obviates any attempt to write about 'themselves'.

With 10–11-year-olds in our sample a new element enters into the descriptions — some attempt at objectivity about the self, manifest in an awareness that others might have a viewpoint about the writer not corresponding to the writer's own. David (11.1) writes about himself in the third person)though not consistently) including dispositional items like 'doesn't have a very good temper' and notes a deeper self than the surface appearance indicates:

> He works quite average, but he can work quite heard when he wants to.

The objectifying device used by several children is a letter from one teacher to another about the writer. Alan (11), on the other hand, uses the expectations of others for this purpose:

> I am Alan Bader and aged 11. A bad point about me is I don't fit into the person my family would like me to be, my parents would like me to be a president or prime-minister but I would like to make living as something dangerous or adventeres like a stuntman or actor. Another bad point is I lie to get out of situations I don't like. A good point about me is I am very careful about what I say & what I do and I always chose my own disitions

The type of classificatory system and the strongly self-critical stance is one we do not encounter with younger children.

More writers at this age try to present a unified persona. Ian speaks of a tendency towards depression and attempts to arrange information around this theme; he is aware of the difference between private self and public presentaiton:

> I haven't been very well lately and was very depressed but I tried to be happy so everyone else wouldn't be depressed.

Considerations of space compel the omission of further comment on teenage writers. We may take one more piece, this time from a 17-year-old boy:

> At the age that I am at at the moment I believe there could be no harder time, I have to go out and find a job that will satisfy me for the rest of my life.

Here there is a marked contrast to the foregoing writing, partly indicated by his sense of his place in time: he is conscious that the current situation is not necessarily the only situation:

> At all the points and times in my life where I have had problems, I have always believed they would be the worst times I'll ever have.

He has a consciousness of the different forms of mental activity:

> At the moment I believe that as soon as I get a job all my big problems will be gone. Maybe that's more hope than belief . . .
>   I sometimes wonder if I would and could be a good adult. My pride likes to think so, but my reason, weighing up my pros and cons tells me I am not . . .
>   Trying to assess myself gives me a headache. It is as though you're having a fight, but its inside your head . . .

He is able to look at himself with fair objectivity:

> I believe I have my bad points like stubbornness and on some occasions a
> short temper. But I also have my good points. I have a sense of humour
> and an opinion on life which is fairly elastic, and I also believe in other
> people. Some people my age believe the world rotates round them.

The criticism of an egocentrical viewpoint is one of the things pointing
towards Ian's growing maturity.

The realisation of other people

In describing other people known to them (in response to the title 'My
Best Friend', or 'A Friend of Mine') young children again give formal
details (name, age, etc.), physical description (colour of hair, eyes, etc.)
actions, achievements, preferences and detestations. Clare (10.5) gives
height, weight, address, post code and phone number of her friend
Penny. Penny tells us that Karen's favourite food is chips; and that 'Her
worst food is Green'). We are told by Karen the Penny 'lives in a
bungalow and has no filings'; we know that Rachael takes size 3 in shoes,
that Andrea's birthday is 12 January, and that Paul's 'ears stick out a bit,
but not enough to notice'. On the other hand information about
disposition which would enable us to understand the person being
described is largely lacking, beyond descriptions like 'kind' and 'nice'.

From about 12 onwards other features begin to appear — less listing
of items, more dispositional characteristics — loyalty, understanding —
John commends the sensitivity of his friend 'for not calling when I was
doing my home work'. Reasons for friendship begin to be offered.
Stephen (13) says:

> As essential part of friendship is that we both like doing the same things. I
> think one of my best friends is myself.

Girls particularly value a 'best friend' relationship which may be
precarious ('my best friend had decided to break up. I had to stand alone
in the dinner queue'.) Michaela (14) rates as very important the
affection from her former 'best friend' as measured by presents:

> Unfortunately I was never her best friend again but we did spend more on
> each other at Christmas than on our other friends.

The intensity of friendships amongst girls occasionally approaches that
of a love affair. Boys represent themselves as having more stable
friendships. It is not without significance that a number of children of
this age designate as best friend a cat, a dog, a fishing rod, 'my snooker
table', and an imaginary companion.

At this stage friendship is described rather than accounted for, often
in terms of the things friends do together, but the influence of one friend

on another is sometimes mentioned ('I know he could be a bad influence on me, but I always keep out of trouble' says Keir (12). But occasionally we find reflexions on aspects of friendship such as the individuality of the other. Stephen says:

> No matter how a friend is close, he is always different. No matter what I think or I say a person has a mind of his own and a right to feel different. Perhaps this is a perfect friend.

In the higher age group (14–16) writers are more likely to *account* for a friendship, perhaps in terms of its history. Lorna (15.6) speaks of how Michelle first appeared as a stranger:

> When I would hear gossip about her she was often described as 'you know, the weird looking one' which, in a sentence, accurately described public opinion of her.

Growing knowledge of her, however, reveals a thoughtful individual, very perceptive about other people. The gap between appearance and reality is brought out:

> One thing I have learnt from all this is that awkward appearances are no judge of what is on the interior . . . and no one should be denied the choice of friendship because of the invility (*sic*) of what they look like, whether it is their choice or mother Nature's.

Suzanne (16) describes a friend who moved from Eire at the same time as she herself did, but whose history has been different. Rachael was unable to settle down; she did not 'come to terms with the move', idealised her early childhood, got mixed up with the wrong sort of people, and became depressed 'dull and flat' instead of 'lovely and bubbery'. There is a real attempt not just to describe Rachael's present state but to account for it in terms of her history.

With such writers individual dispositional items are observed rather than formal features mentioned by younger children. Generalisations about friendship are made, motives for friendship are perceived. Notice in the following how Andrew (16) lists loyalty, self-interest, guilt, and pity, as reasons for friendship:

> There are friends and there are friends, there is one who stands by you at all times, or another who only wants to be a friend cause you have a computer, snooker table, video, etc. Then when your dad becomes redundant you have to sell your things they then desert and shun you. Some people befriend people out of guilt or just because the feel sorry for them.

In summary we may say that young children's descriptions of others are non-selective. They consist of formal items, actions (usually non-differentiating) with a few conventional dispositional items. In the early teenage years there is an emphasis on what people do together with some dispositional comments of a rather more general nature — loyalty, understanding. But older children are more concerned to account for a relationship — it has a past as well as a present; motives are perceived; the differences between appearance and reality are commented upon. The view of friendship as an abstraction can be taken and discussed.

The world around us

Of the many aspects of environment we could have investigated the present study took the common one of 'landscape'. The title 'My Favourite Place' was offered to groups of writers ages 5–18.

Young children's writing is often lacking in a sense of place because it is uncontextualised. Repeatedly in the sample we found a brief mention of place followed by the description of an activity. Sharon (7) says:

> My favourite place is when we go to the beach at Gorlstone, and we had a picnic

The ten-year-olds however may include a certain response to the sensory aspects of the situation:

> My favourite place is sailing at Hickling.
> My brother was holding the boat and the wind blew strong and he let go. My Dad had to get his legs covered with Mud to get it. My Mother said You smell horrid.

To make the developmental point by contrast let us turn to the work Clare (15), where the environment is not only responded to in immediate terms, it is also made symbolic of inner state:

> My home isn't my home, its where I live.
> When I come along the road I come to the same gate and the same path to the same front door and prick myself on the same holly bush. But it's not the same.
> It used to be the same till my Dad left. My Dad used to have a work bench in the garage but he took that.
> He left all the furniture but when the settlement came through my Mum didn't like it and bought a new suite. I went along to choose it. It was cream with frills and deep upholstery. My Mum was very pleased with it but I thought it dominated the room, although I didn't say anything. I don't like sitting on it. The only place I feel at home is my bedroom because it had my old things there.

The idea of one's bedroom as one's favourite place occurred repeatedly with adolescents, but not with the younger children in our sample.

Finally a piece by Geoffrey (17). It has all the marks of a young writer in that it suggests the writer is a thousand years old. But actually the distancing is because it is from the first attempt at a novel:

Your room is your outward soul. When I first saw the room I was going to live in, with its dirty (not even consistently dirty) walls, and its chipped paintwork, and the indecipherable carpet, I felt it was a dreary soul for any one to have inhabited. Through the dirty windows when the sun penetrated it showed up myriads of spots of dust, like myriads of little sins, the worst of all someone else's sins.

The landlord wouldn't improve it, but he didn't mind if I did. I painted everything white, and the floor black, hid the carpet in the cupboard, and placed a single circular rush mat in the centre of the floor. The whole effect wasn't so much bare as austere. I thought it suited me well; that was my austere period. There were still spots of dust in the sunlight, even if fewer. But they were mine. My own sins were much more acceptable than other people's.

Comment is perhaps superfluous. An explanation of the deliberate symbolism is given in the first sentence, and then developed very skilfully.

A matter of choice

Underlying the analysis in the previous section are assumptions about development, the primary one being that it involves an ability to decentre. This in not the place to discuss in detail the theory of development used (see Wilkinson 1986), but it is necessary to refer an aspect of it briefly as it provides terms of analysis for the compositions in this section.

Psychoanalysts regard the individuals as maintaining themselves in 'crisis' by 'coping', on the one hand, or by 'defending', on the other. 'Coping' is coming to terms with, 'defending' is avoiding the problem, an obvious example being by retreating into fantasy, or regressing into violence (people have been known to kick their cars when they 'refuse' to start). The compositions in this section all concern the 'human condition', and we shall consider them in terms of the nature of the 'coping' or 'defending' they display (for a detailed model see Wilkinson 1986). We shall refer to writings from the collection made by Kulsdom (1985). The sample chosen describes the relationships of teenagers to older members of society, particularly parents.

Lisa depicts a situation of no understanding with a regression to rage replacing communication. 'Sallie' is accused of coming in late:

'For gods sake Sallie, you are only fifteen, how old do you think you are blody twenty one?'

'Fifteen! Yes, that is my age. I realise that so why can't you? she screamed . . . 'Dad I am not a baby any more I am growing up can't you see that? I want to go out and enjoy myself. You are only young once you know'.

The writer comments that the father 'cannot cope' with the growing independence of his daughter — there is no evidence that she is distanced from this situation. A boy, Kevin, presents a similar situation. He comes in late and finds unexpectedly his father waiting up for him.

> 'I didn't realise the time!'
> 'Don't give me that, don't you think I worry?'
> 'I can look after myself!'
> 'I'm only trying to help you!'
> 'Yer' Kevin replied while pushing past his father. 'You could have fooled me'.

However there are indications that the writer is not to be equated completely with Kevin. The title of the piece is 'Friend of Foe?' The father states his point of view, and Kevin's behaviour 'pushing past his father', is not presented uncritically. There are the beginnings of 'coping' here whereby the writer defines the problem realistically though he is far from any resolution of it.

However there were also writers who were to be more objective. Jayne calls her piece 'Carning Parnets' and describes a girl who 'fineley got chucked out of school her mem and dad couldnot controll her so she was put into a home'. The conclusion is in the form of a comment:

> Karen could not see that her Mum and Dad were just trying to help her in the first place being hard on her so she would not get hert or full into bad company that some kids do. When Karen gets older she will have kids and worrey about then the ha parents have to her

The conventional wisdom that 'time teaches' enables her to round off the incident.

Conventional solutions often occurred in the writing — undoubtedly popular wisdom has its elements of truth — experience teaches. There is forgiving and forgetting, time heals, virtue is rewarded, vice is punished, love triumphs, there are more fish in the sea. Sometimes however these solutions imply a certain passivity — wait and do nothing. Other writers describe solutions brought about by rational action rather than by waiting on events. Panu describes a girl who talked over the matter of her freedom with her parents, was given more and 'Never took advantage of it, never'. Karen's parents say to her:

> Karen we have seen how happy you are being fancy free so your mother and I have decided to let you go out with this boy on a regular basis as long as he brings you home at a reasonable time.
>   Oh Mum, dad, thank you. Karen Kissed them and went to bed. Karen's problems with her parents were solved.

On several occasions the boy friend charms the mother into submission.

It such outcomes seem perhaps slightly oversimplified the same cannot be said of some scripts like Maria's. 'Tracy' and her father abuse

one another when she comes home late, in a tension aggravated by the
fact that her mother has left home. Tracy sympathises with her mother
but a dream indicates to us that she also has feelings for her father's
plight: she dreams of her childhood in which all three played together:

> Suddenly her mother was gone from the picture and it was just her father
> as he was now. She wasn't in the park any more but in a strange house
> with her father sitting in his chair, his face in his hands. Slowly she went
> up to him touched his shoulder
> 'What's wrong' she asked slowly
> 'Vera's dead'.

It is as though the dream had been shared and he is touched by her
sympathy for in the morning he seems brighter, and she is surprised he
speaks to her nicely. He asks her to open a letter that has just arrived
from her mother.

> Tracy opened the letter and began to read it to herself at first
> 'What does it say'. Her father asked
> 'O not much, just says that she's sorry and how we're doing'.
> She folder the letter. Her father was standing over a frying pan and
> didn't say anything. Tracy felt angry but she also felt sorry for her Dad.
> 'Dad?'
> 'Eggs, Tracy?' he asked.

Tracy's complex and ambiguous feelings, the *possible* hint of a
reconciliation with the mother ('she's sorry'), her father's gesture of love
symbolised by 'Eggs, Tracy?' indicated no speedy solution but the need
to make small gains, to wait, to tolerate uncertainties.

The insights of these writers are by no means necessarily related to
their literary ability, but arise as they seek their own particular wisdoms.
Many of them are aware of the various mechanisms of defending,
particularly in others. Parents are shown as refusing to face the growing
independence of their children, both sides resorting to tantrums,
displacing their frustrations on others. One mother recognises eventually that part of her anger rises from an unconscious envy of the
blooming sexuality of her daughter. Fantasy is sometimes a solution,
particularly in romantic situations, but it is the realism rather than the
fantasy which prevails. The writers do not avoid so much as cope. The
maturity of a response does not necessarily rely on an ability to come up
with a solution, but rather on such factors as its insights, its sense of
empathy, its cognitive and imaginative grasp of the problem, as in
Maria's piece just quoted. It corresponds with what Keats called
'negative capability', that is when a writer is 'capable of being in
uncertainties, mysteries, doubts, without any irritable reaching after
facts and reason' (Keats 1960, p. 69).

Comments

Initially three possible communication relationships — AB, ABA and
AA — were mentioned. Education takes place in all three relationships.

In AB, telling people things, we have traditional method of instruction
and control by parents and teachers. It is of course fundamental but its
limitation is that it may assume A's omniscience and B's passivity. In
formal education we have too much of AB.

ABA is the basis of social life. In recent years there have been
attempts to make use of it as a learning device, in the emphasis on group
work, the activity of the learner, on interpretation rather than
transmission.

AA is what goes on inside the head — the development of the
affective and cognitive power — and this is the greatest area of neglect.
The AB model tells what to think, requires us to receive information
which far too often remains inert (a tendency encouraged by examinations). AA requires a discussion with oneself, particularly in the writing
process, to attain higher levels of thinking. AB can tell us what to feel of
course. But that is not adequate. The perceptions of ABA need to be
explored, understood, made use of in the self-education of the emotions
which is one of the features of AA. Of the various ways in which the AA
dialogue can be developed one of the main ones is the process of writing.
The grey soul reflects before the white page and in that mirror begins to
learn understanding.

Bibliography

Barnes, D. (1976). *From Communication to Curriculum.* Harmondsworth, Penguin.

Barnsley, G. and Wilkinson, A. (1981). 'The Development of Moral Judgments in Children's Writing', *Educational Review* vol. 33, no. 1.

Bruner, J.S. (1967). *Towards a Theory of Instruction.* Cambridge, Mass. Harvard University Press.

Carlin, E. (1978). 'Theories and Measures of Writing Development'. M.Ed. dissertation, University of Exeter.

DES (1979). *Aspects of Secondary Education in English: A Survey by H.M. Inspectors of Schools.* London, HMSO.

Gleason, J.B. (1977).
'Talking to Children: Some notes on Feedback, in C.E. Snow and C.A. Ferguson, *Talking to Children: Language Input and Acquisition*. London, Cambridge University Press.

Goffman, E. (1969).
The Presentation of Self in Everyday Life. London, Allen Lane.

Haaf, R.A. and Bell, R.Q. (1967).
'A facial Dimension in Visual Discrimination by Human Infants', *Child Development*, vol. 38, p. 893–9.

Hurst, P.H. and Peters, R.S. (1970).
The Logic of Education. London, Kegan Paul.

Keats, J. (1960).
Letters, *ed.* Buxton Forman, 4th edn. Oxford, Oxford University Press.

Kulsdom, B. (1985).
'Moral Development in the Writing of Adolescents'. Study in part-fulfilment of requirements for MA in Education, University of East Anglia, Norwich.

Newson, J. and Newson, E. (1975).
'Intersubjectivity and the transmission of culture', *Bulletin of British Psychological Society*, vol. 28.

Porch, B.E. (1974).
'Communication' in G.G. Hirchbergm, L. Lewis and P. Vaghan (eds), *Rehibilitation: a Manual for the Case of the Disabled and Elderly*. Philadelphia, Lippincott.

Secord, P.R. and Backman, C.W. (1974).
Social Psychology. London, McGraw-Hill/Kogaskusha Ltd.

Sternglass, M. (1981).
'Assessing Reading, Writing and Reasoning', *College English*, March.

Sternglass, M. (1982).
'Applications of the Wilkinson Model of Writing Maturity to College Writing', *College Composition and Communication*, vol. 33, no. 2, May.

Sternglass, M. (forthcoming).
Fostering Cognitive Growth in Writing.

Stratta, L., Dixon, J. and Wilkinson, A. (1974).
Patterns of Language. London, Heinemann.

Wilkinson, A. (1985).
'I communicate, therefore I am', *Educational Review*, vol. 37, no. 1.

Wilkinson, A. (1986).
The Quality of Writing. Milton Keynes, Open University Press.

Wilkinson, A., Barnsley, G.
Assessing Language Development. Oxford,

Hanna, P. and Swan, M. (1980).

Oxford University Press.

Wilkinson, A. with Davies, A. and Atkinson, D. (1965).

Spoken English. Educational Review Occasional Publications no. 2, University of Birmingham.

Wilkinson, A. and Hanna, P. (1980).

'The Development of Style in Children's Writing', *Educational Review*, vol. 32, no. 2.

Wilkinson, A. and Worsley, G. (unpublished paper).

'The Language of Feeling in the Writing of Late Adolescents'.

Wills, D.M. (1977).

'The Ordinary Devoted Mother and her Blind Baby', *The Psychoanalytic Study of the Child*, vol. 34.

Wittstein, S.S. (1983).

'Four Case Studies: An Analysis and Assessmentof Inner-City High School Student Writing Using Three Measures of the Wilkinson Model of Writing Maturity'. Unpublished thesis for the Degree of Doctor of Education in the University of Cincinati.

Worsley, G. (1983).

'The Quality of Feeling in the Writing of Older Adolescents'. Unpublished MA dissertation, University of East Anglia School of Education.

5 The Pleasure of Writing

BERNARD D. HARRISON

What and where the pleasure

> When I went for a walk with my daughter earlier today I saw two cricket
> sidescreens as a couple reading newspapers; that's the way it struck
> me . . . I find that my thinking is fluid, and I'm often out of phase with it.
> I'll start to write something and then discover what I'd been thinking
> about.

Craig Raine's reflection on a morning walk in Haffenden (1981, p. 184)
— relaxed in tone, not rigidly tidy in context — lies somewhere between
talking and writing. Its easy, conversational style conveys a sense that
writing, like talking, can be an unforced, quite natural activity. This view
of writing provides grain for a plump question concerning the
experience of writing, and issues of writing development. Educationists
share a well-grounded belief that good performance in reading is
achieved through discovering the pleasure of reading; can they argue
with as much conviction for a comparable pleasure through writing?
    Faced with this question, members of my M.Ed. classes tend to react
with some scepticism, if not dismay. They dwell on the motor difficulties
that young (and some older) children may have in learning to write, let
alone writing to learn; on problems of spelling, punctuation and syntax;
on the requirements of public examinations, and so on. Furthermore,
they have argued, it is all very well to claim that writing is a natural
activity which ought to contain the pleasure to be found in any real
engagement with learning; but if this is so, why do they find the prospect
of writing, say, a course essay to be so alarming, compared to the more

or less pleasant experience of small-group discussion, or reading one of
the better texts recommended on the course book-list? It has to be
conceded, to their objections, that writing does undoubtedly involve
particular difficulties, and that the difficulties are not just to do with
motor skills or problems of formal accuracy, but with the organisation of
ideas. While writing involves, in part, a compressing, distilling and
reshaping of talk, it also provides scope for a particular kind of
ideas-making that does not happen so readily in spoken discourse; it
prompts a kind of echo-sounding in the mind, seeking (in Raine's
phrase) to 'discover what I'd been thinking about'. Some of the
discomfort of writing may be explained by this, in that we sit before a
blank white, sheet of paper, rather like a radar operator waiting for blips
on a screen — blips which may or may not prove to be of significance.
The writer's necessary dependence on inner resources brings a sense of
ordeal to the task, of stage-fright in the face of the blank paper, of
self-doubt, of helplessness when few ideas form, followed by uncomfortable excitement when they eddy round without control. This quest
of writing, to deliver ideas and experiences previously unwritten on to
paper, is an oddly private, sometimes discomfortingly lonely task; all who
have attempted it will feel a degree of sympathy with the would-be writer
Grand, depicted by Camus in *The Plague*, who doomed himself to
polishing and perfecting the opening sentence of his never-to-be-
finished novel each day of his life, never progressing beyond that
sentence.

Writing, then, demands a good deal, especially of the inexperienced
learner-writer. I am thinking here of any writing which involves
reflection, rather than of that writing which simply involves the modes of
processing and reprocessing information that microtechnology now
provides. For while there may be many varieties of writing that involve
reflection, it is only through reflection that the writer is involved as a
learner. Notes taken from a board or from dictation, vocabulary lists,
copying or mechanical summarising from a text book may (or may not)
aid, or at least decorate learning; but these activities in themselves are no
more to be confused with learning as such than is a piece of chalk, or a
cap and gown.

There are, of course, vastly different levels as well as varieties of
reflective writing, just as there are different levels of reading which
involves understanding — that is, reading which is more than 'barking at
print'. In reading, the kind of attention that is required, say, for a bus
ticket or for *The Sun* is of a different order from that required for a book
by, say Charles Darwin or Virginia Woolf. A structuralist or post-
structuralist viewpoint might be that there is as much meat for thought
in the homely propaganda of a *Sun* editorial or a bus ticket as there is in
the subjectivity of *To the Lighthouse* or the drama of *The Voyage of the*

Beagle, on the grounds that there is a whole social history to be 'decoded' from *The Sun* or from a bus ticket. That argument has some plausibility, but in highlighting so exclusively the 'creativity' of the reader, rather than the inherent 'quality' of the text, there lies a danger of neglecting the actual kind of experience which is available 'out there' in the text. Similarly, in writing, there exists a tension between the event 'out there' in the world (a text, a townscape, an issue), and the writer's experience of that event. As with reading, writing depends on a personal presence in the world. But terms like 'personal' and 'impersonal' writing do not, perhaps, suggest the subtle and variable interaction of an individual in relation to the world as well as they ought. There are, from time to time, fashionable chages of emphasis in education — from respect for the learner to respect for what ought to be learned, from the importance of the text to the importance of the reader, and (almost conversely) from 'personal' to 'impersonal' modes of writing. It is worth noting that while such shifts of opinion can help to redress an imbalance, they may fall into the familiar either/or trap that never allows more than half of a case to be admitted at any one time. Without contraries there is no progression; but educational theory needs to take full, steady account of both the learner and the world, if it is not to be shifted like dust in the wind of public opinion. As far as learning through writing is concerned, this implies a concern for both the writer and the topic, for 'process' as a way to achieving 'product', for the contextual conditions (of the person who is learning through writing) that may generate a regard for formal aspects of writing.

Constraints on freedom

This chapter opened by querying whether pleasure can be found in writing; the question is of central importance to teachers, since motivation in learning ought to involve at least some degree of pleasure in one form or another, unless education is to be based on repression and punishment. There is ample testimony available — from poets, novelists, journalists, diarists, autobiographers and letter-writers and also from generations of schoolchildren and their teachers (see, for example, Tolstoy (1967) — to confirm that writing can bring pleasure. Educationists such as Hourd (1949), Pym (1956), Holbrook (1961), Britton *et al.* (1975), Wilkinson *et al.* (1980) and Protherough (1983) have, while placing varying emphases on the role of writing in learning, made common claims for an essential pleasure principle in writing, which ought to be encouraged at all levels of learning in schools. After all, the very nature of writing — at least, of reflective writing — implies an emphasis on personal activity in learning, requiring conditions where the teacher *has* to stand back from the learner, to allow it to happen.

Thus to provide the conditions for reflective writing is to go with the grain of sound learning theory.

Reflecting on his work as a poet, Raine has claimed that 'writing is a perfectly natural activity . . . [and] is the slave of sense experience — unpaid, but eager to serve'. (Haffenden 1981, p. 182); but he also admits to being 'really worried' about publication. His sense of a discrepancy between the experience of writing as a natural, pleasantly absorbing activity on the one hand, and the discomfort of enduring critical scrutiny on the other, is the problem that educationists have termed as 'audience-sense'; it is acknowledged by Britton *et al.* (1975) and many others to be such an extensive problem for learner-writers that the pleasure-principle in writing becomes endangered in schools.

Apart from the masses of mechanical writing that school learners still endure each week, their scope for freedom, even when engaged in reflective writing, is limited by many constraints, some more justifiable than others. The onus is on them (as with professional writers) to ensure that what they write is readable, reasonably well ordered and reasonably accurate in formal terms. Beyond that, they may be subject to any number of random whims of individual teachers, from a request to draw large margins to a requirement to be interesting and 'sincere' (to mention some of the arbitrary demands I myself have made on school learner-writers).

One escape route from such arbitrary requirements is to impose some kind of standard on all teachers and pupils from the centre; this has been attempted in recent years by the Assessment of Performance Unit (APU), which was set up in the United Kingdom by the Department of Education and Science in the 1990s to investigate various aspects of pupils' language performance in schools. In APU (1978) it outlined the most ambitious attempt in modern times at a national standardisation of language performance in schools. Couched in mild terms as a 'discussion' document, its preamble recognised the desirability of varieties of writing and varieties of audience in school writing. But when it moved on to proposals for evaluation, the respect for 'variety' was sunk under a weight of requirements that would seem to be no less arbitrary than, say, were mine in my own classroom:

We propose to evaluate writing in two ways:

i.   overall impression
ii. spelling and punctuation

. . . One would expect the impression makers to take into account the internal coherence of the writing, the selection and organisation of the content, and the style, including its appropriateness to the audience and the use of grammatical forms acceptable in different kinds of written English . . .

As well as being arbitrary, these versions of 'style' and 'content' were inept; on this point; on this point Wilkinson *et al.* (1980, p. 27) commented that 'style is fundamental — it is by style not language that we communicate. Content is fundamental — it is in some measure what the people are who make writings for our reading.' This is to introduce complex aesthetic issues which may not seem, of themselves, to relate to my present topic. But since my thrust of argument is towards recognition of a *comprehensive* writing norm (embracing an individual, within a social norm) for the writer, the notion that 'style' is simply adjustable to 'appropriateness to the audience' has to be discarded as a naive error. The unique, unmanufacturable source of writing style is explored in a key section of Proust's *Remembrance of Things Past* (1981, p. 593) when the author reflects of the essential style of '*Bergottisme*':

> An author of memoirs of our time, wishing to write without too obviously seeming to be writing like Saint-Simon, might at a pinch give us the first line of his portrait of Villars: 'He was a rather tall man, dark — with an alert, expressive physiognomy,' but what law of determination could bring him to the discovery of Saint-Simon's next line, which begins with 'and, to tell the truth, a trifle mad'?

The APU was out of its depth in attempting to cope with anything that constitutes 'individuality' in writing; for what is true of Proust and Saint-Simon is no less true of ten-year-old Claire in Rotherham or of 15-year-old Robert in Daventry. Its attempt to define criteria for judging the quality of writing came from a pressure to standardise writing performance, and its failure to do so deserves no sympathy. It faces the problem that confronts any researchers who are not practising teachers, in that its ghostly team of programmers and impression-markers is removed from the living presence and intentionality of the learner. Its work carries the danger that, far from engaging the learner's reflective activity, it might encourage more refined versions of unreality in writing, which could damage essential threads in the learning process, as teachers and learners conspire to identify government 'standards' of reflective subjectivity.

Private and public worlds

Perhaps the wrongness in the conception of the APU lay not so much in envisaging standards to assess organisaton, spelling, punctuation and so on (such standards are needed, even if they are arbitrary and ought therefore to change from time to time), but in the assumption that the Unit had something direct to contribute to an individual's well-being in learning. There are sound educational reasons why there should be some essential separation between an actual class of school pupils engaged on reflective writing, and the statistical graveyard of a government department. The ill effects of direct intervention were reported, for instance, by the head of a Welsh primary school, who revealed: 'As for the writing test, I am left almost speechless. Whose was the inspired brain that hatched such a stimulating writing task as 'Write a short account of anything enjoyable or exciting which has happened to you recently'?' The head was convinced that the tests showed the compliers were 'totally out of touch with children, their concerns and the right ways of stimulating them into producing their best written work'. Replying to the head's criticism, Dr Tom Gorman, Director of the APU's language programme, explained that the task had been left deliberately unspecific 'to obtain examples of autobiographical narrative'. He also defended a set of lifeless, stylised drawings on the grounds that they were deliberately stylised 'because their function was to get pupils to observe, not to stimulate them' (reported in the *Times Educational Supplement*, 6 June 1980).

The innocence of this reply reveals the innocence of any world-be evaluator of schools and school achievement, who has no direct involvement in the teaching of children, and (in this case) what they write. It has to be said, too, that there is nothing in APU (1984) to reassure the dismayed headteacher. While evaluation is a desirable, indeed an unavoidable aspect of teaching and learning through writing, it needs to depend on a good deal more than raw scraps of writing 'observed' out of context. Evaluation involves both learner and teacher, as well as other important parties, such as parents. It is an infinitely more sensitive, interwoven activity than grades or mark sheets or outside observers can discover. Criteria for evaluation ought also to allow as much space as possible for self-evaluation, since the learner-writer is in a unique position to give an illuminating account of the difficulties, the failures and the successes of trying to 'get it right' through writing. Writing development, like any craft, requires both a flow of activity and also a continuous appraisal of work in progress. The pleasure-principle is best safeguarded by encouraging a flow first, and by ensuring that appraisal is an anxiety-free as possible. For this to be achieved, the learner-writer should not only understand the criteria for appraisal, but ought to be able to contribute to these. Teachers and parents in the West *know* it is wrong, that toddlers in élite Japanese kindergartens should be assessed and streamed for social 'maturity' (the high rate of child suicides in the Japanese middle class is but further confirmation of the wrongness). The purpose of play is, essentially, play, and children simply need provision for safe, interesting play — sometimes with adults, but on terms that please the child as well as the adult. As with play, the 'game' of writing can be self-justifying; through absorption in the writing task the learner discovers the world; this world is discovered in personal terms, but through the writing 'game' it is communicated to others and shared with them. In this way writing is a private, but not solipsistic activity; like all language acts, it involves both expression and communication, neither of which can be divorced from the other. The impulse to express implies a desire to communicate, which in turn depends on having something to tell.

In dwelling on a personal and even pleasure dimension in writing, I wish now to look further at problems that fact the learner (and therefore the teacher) when writing as an individual in a world shared by others. As was suggested earlier, terms like 'personal' and 'impersonal' can lead only too quickly to an either/or trap and to sterile debate. This happens, for instance, whenever 'personal', 'expressive', 'free' or 'creative' writing is unilaterally advocated or (as is now more likely) condemned. To complain about egotistical outpourings in writing need not require a campaign against expressive writing; as for 'personal' writing, there is a sense in which writing, or at least reflective writing, is inconceivable without the presence of a writer, discovering the world in terms of the only human experience that can be known — that is, one's own. Similarly, the 'impersonal' concerns of the world cannot be met without regard for the statistically irreducible requirements of those many individual lives that compose a society and its structures. Where writing is concerned it is worth reminding ourselves that while varieties of writing are a desirable outcome of varieties of experience in the world, these varieties could suffer from being too rigidly compartmentalised — into, say, writing that is private and writing that is for the world, or (to introduce now fashionable terms) writing that is 'affective' and writing that is 'cognitive', or writing to 'express' and writing to 'argue'.

Has this happened? There was evidence, for example in Allen (1980) of a movement in the 1970s away from recognition of the comprehensive quality of poetic and literary forms of language, towards utilitarian version of language as a 'tool' for learning and communications systems. This trend was reflected, furthermore, in the kinds of 'English, language and communication' projects approved by the Schools Council over about two decades, where only one (which investigated the reading interests among children of secondary school age) sustained an aesthetic or literary emphasis on its investigations.

Ironically, the Schools Council 'Arts and the Adolescent' Project, which provided valuable commentaries on English and Drama in the context of the arts curriculum, was not among the English or language projects. One book in particular that emerged from this project, Witkin (1974), provided an influential counterbalance to the 'language as a tool' movement.Witkin recognised that, in the struggle to win a place in the world, the private world of the individual learner should not be neglected. This timely plea for a proper regard of subjectivity in learning needs now to be modified, perhaps, in order to move beyond yet another either/or divisive half-truth, where writing is concerned (writing that is 'either' private, intimate, poetic, and 'affective', or public, impersonal, transactional and 'cognitive'). I have argued elsewhere against the harm done to writing development (and to language development in general) when a myth is followed that affection and cognition somehow conduct themselves as separate activities of the mind (Harrison 1983; Harrison and Gordon 1983). We are, after all, the language we are talking about, flesh and bone together. And since the social structure that determine our lives in the world are subject to the influence of all the individuals who compose that world, it is connections rather than differences between public and private aspects of living that the learner needs to make; in this, the life-game of learning to write is the life-game of negotiating a place in the world on one's own as well as the world's terms. To write personally need not imply a withdrawing from the world but, rather, an active (not resigned, or self-obliterating) coming to terms with it.

Composing personal sense

Yet in order to develop beyond itself, personal writing does need, sometimes, to be allowed to 'regress' into a more private, confessional mode; this can help, for instance, in the case of shy children, who educational opportunities are now recognised to be at risk. Justifiably, the needs of these children tend to be seen in terms of increasing confidence in talk, rather than in listening, reading or writing, where they may already be performing well enough. But writing provides a unique opportunity for admitting feeling and asserting points of view, without running an immediate risk of confrontation — with peers or with teachers. An example of the benefit to be gained is available from the letters of a teenage girl, written to me as a kind of continuous journal over a period of some eighteen months. Her progress at school (including her English studies, for which I was responsible) and her personal happiness had been affected by a familiar enough set of problems — family difficulties, loss of belief in the 'point' of her studies, a first love affair, and so on; and she was, at the point when she began to write the letters, painfully shy. Within the space of some thirty or so letters she submitted herself (and her chosen reader) to a sustained, self-probing account of her state of feelings during that time, moving gradually towards a more confident, self-assertive pattern in both her writing and her living. In her final, 'signing-off' letter she revealed a readiness to move beyond being unduly private — though she acknowledged, too, that she has some inner qualities which are worth respect from both herself and the world (Harrison, forthcoming).

> I feel stronger now than I have ever felt in the last six years. Perhaps I appear a weak person to a lot of people, but I know that I am not so weak. I admit I am rather soft and easily hurt but other people cannot sway me when I really believe something. I think I have become stronger because I feel more confident in myself and I think David and Richard have helped me a lot. People have often avoided laughing at me openly, for fear of hurting me, and although at the time I was grateful, I now realise it hindered me because I always took myself and other people seriously. I could never laugh at myself because, I felt so self-conscious and inhibited that I could not bear any form of criticism, even if it was only a joke . . . David and Richard have helped me to learn how to laugh at myself because of their warmth and perseverance. When Richard first made jokes about me I felt ever so hurt and confused because I had never been really made fun of before. I used to walk into the classroom and he would call me 'Muscles', making me want to shrivel up to nothing. At the beginning I lost quite a lot of self-confidence and became more inhibited because I felt he must despise me. I really began to feel I must be weird for him to say such mad things. I do not recall feeling so hurt because of David and I think I probably felt at ease with David from the beginning. It is only very recently that I have felt able to talk to Richard, because somehow people who appear very confident in themselves, make feel uncertain of myself. I used to think I would never feel at ease with Richard but now I can talk to him and feel grateful to him because I made no effort whatsoever to offer any friendship or warmth. It was not because I did not want to, I just could not but Richard and David really broke through my shell and I am glad they did . . .

Having reasserted her place in the world and with her friends, she went on to explain why she needed to write; it was, she found, her chance of discovering — from within herself — what had seemed to be vanished patterns of confidence and well-being in her younger self:

> I think I must have written all this because I want to know what I have lost in myself which caused me to feel so discounted and restless. Why, when I was younger could I be content deep inside me, even though there were rules, restrictions and fears? I suppose I accepted everything, whereas now I feel more resentful if anything is forced on me. I cannot feel at peace very often and in a way I am more tense and aggressive. When I say I am more aggressive I do not mean I want to physically fight people, but when people keep bumping into me in the corridor and trivial things like that, I feel more irritated than I should. Sometimes, when I am feeling disgruntled I think, perhaps it is because I find it difficult to accept the fact that I am growing up. If I can tell myself, 'I am never going to be a child again, so I must remember how precious it was, and now I am going to move on', perhaps I will accept it easier. It is strange that I should find such an inevitable thing hard to accept, but I think I am probably

frightened. When I was a child, I could depend on other people whereas now I am more aware of being an individual with my own thoughts. I just want to live my life true to myself and it is not easy.

Moving from a sense that she 'must have written all this because I want to know what I have lost in myself', she concluded that she has decided to take full responsibility from now on, for living a life 'true to myself'. Throughout the months of her writing these letters, it was she who had done the thinking and self-searching, gradually helping herself to clearer thoughts.

Sarah's letters dwell — a shade self-pityingly perhaps — on the difficulties of inheriting the world. Yet to suggest that the world should adjust to the individual writer, as much as the individual to the world, is not just to wish to make life easier for the young; it is to plead for some essential space to be granted in learning through writing. This may involve a willingness by the teacher to play no more than the modest role of an attentive reader, who is not so much concerned with evaluating 'product' as in ascertaining the personal intention of the writer — that is, what the writing points towards, as a focus of the writer's sincere interest. An essential art of teaching consists in learning *not* to intervene; the teacher's role as trusting audience may be all that is needed, rather than any scientific apparatus of 'objective' criteria for evaluation. Any teaching which places external conformity (in curriculum, in rules, in learning patterns) before respect for individual humanness is likely to have ill effects, whatever its declared 'ideals' or 'standards', since it conspires to consign any weakness of selfhood (for example, through a wooden-headed denouncing of a confessional piece of writing as 'egotisitcal' or 'onanistic') to the imprisonment of solipsism, through not being allowed.

A zest for meaning

Guntrip's account of this problem (1968) helps to clarify a key aspect of the learner–teacher, or writer–reader relationship: that mutuality of recognition involves admitting 'weaknesses' in our undeveloped or undistorted selves. Through the writer's trust in the reader a stronger form of self-trust is gained. In frailty, by paradox, lies the way to strength; in Guntrip's words, 'A natural human being would be more likely to start from "I feel, therefore I am"' (Guntrip 1968, p. 65). Winnicott, whose work is more widely recognised among educationists, intended to place greater emphasis on the robustness of the individual who has been given what he termed a 'good-enough' start in life. Basic to Winnicott's thought is the provision of a 'play-area' or 'potentially creative space' for the learner in the world, a space which is then filled with the products of the learner's creative imagination (Winnicott 1971). Making things available for their play-space is not to be confounded with imposing things on them (a belief in only the parent-figure's version of God, or rigid rules of writing practice) nor with a wholesale refusal to choose on behalf of the child, like the father who

> refused to allow his daughter to meet any fairy story, or any idea such as that of a witch or a fairy or a prince, because he wanted his child to have only a personal personality; the poor child was being asked to start again with the building up of the ideas and artistic achievement of the centuries. The scheme did not work . . . (Winnicott 1965, p. 101).

The learner-writer depends on interesting provision, in order to write well; without stories, allegories, homilies, histories, as well as their own experience they have no correlative for their own intuitions, dark of light, about the world. The emphasis here is made on personal engagement, rather than implant; on the teacher as a providing, reassuring presence, rather than restricting director and manipulator; on individual growth rather than unreal success based on a compliance with outside demands at the expense of inner needs. The worst immorality is to oblige the learner to comply at the expense of the inner life; since writing is such a personal, private activity, the writer–reader relationship is a particularly delicate one in this respect, since to write is not necessarily to wish to be published (with its risk of being 'damned'). The quality of what we teach, of what we choose to make available in the learner's play-area is crucial to the quality of the learner's writing; this, perhaps, is where sharp scrutiny and evaluation are of the essence. As far as schools are concerned, there is still much to be achieved, in aiming towards more free, confident, friendly and simple relationships between those who teach and those who are taught. Teaching and learning — even when the age gap is wide, as is usually the case in schools — is at best a collaborative venture; evaluation, like respect, is at best a two-way business.

The links between personal or private, and impersonal public modes of writing are far more important than their differences. A healthy community depends on the vigorous, non-compliant participation of its individual members. As far as writing is concerned, the zestful involvement of a non-specialist public in the world's affairs remains essential — a zest which is also critical, prepared to dissent, wary of undue dependance on the 'expert', alert to the dangers of expertise and knowledge becoming used (by lawyers, teachers, doctors, defence experts, government officials, and so on) against, rather than on behalf, of people.

Through learning to talk, listen, read and write we do not merely learn how to use a tool for living; we *become* the language and, according to our individualities, we have the power to influence language. Plain speech is to be commended, and jargon deplored, because it enables all those who share a language to share all aspects of social and cultural life that are embraced by the language, while jargon resists that sharing. This may seem too obvious a point to need labouring, yet even as highly experienced and respected a teacher of English as Meek has offered to concede that 'to be literate at the present time is to assume that reading and writing will become even more specialised according to the area of their functionaries. Doctors can't read lawyer's briefs, and solicitors are not necessarily competent with computers' (Meek 1980, p. 32).

This judgement, given in the context of a discussion on children's literature as part of an attack on 'high culture' notions of children's books, prompts immediate common-sense objections — that we *ought* to know what doctors are saying and writing about patients; that legal language ought to be accessible to all whom the law concerns; that we should examine, on our own terms, the enthusiasms of architects, educationists, hospital administrators, lawyers, and all who have power in social planning. It is in fact part of Meek's own argument that teachers should remember how 'studies of response cannot now disregard what the reader brings *to* the book'; yet while she applies this to fiction texts, she has an altogether more passive view of the so-called 'transactional' literacy (a term taken from Moffett via Britton's Writing Research Unit) with its separate status from that of fiction. She attacks aspects of modern 'functional literacy' but she recommends a too limited version of 'pleasure' in declaring that our 'chief investment in literacy will be as a support for our social role, and, thereafter, for our pleasure'. This seems, again, to imply a separation of what is personal and private from the world of utility and transactions, to be followed by a turning of the alienated self to the less serious but harmless world of fiction for pleasure (as compensation for the 'sacrifice' of self to the world?). The too reduced, split-off version of pleasure implied here involves a dilemma for writing, as for reading and for all language. If a mechanistic view of humanity as so many servile components in the social machine is to be resisted, how can the public world be made more pleasurable and even bearable, with room for individual subjectivity *within* that world? As teachers of language we believe in the power of language to do this, since acts of language require both expression and communication. Language enables recognition for the individual; yet we acknowledge that language can be operated against, as well as on behalf of individuals, even to the extent of imposing alien forms of language on them, through contempt or ignorance of the claims of their subjectivity. Jargon and propaganda and but different aspects of such abuse of language and of people.

The opening section of this paper introduced some reservations about hand-me-down post-structuralist attitudes that would seem to deny original creativity in the writer (and by implication, any composer or user of language). The 'structuralism versus creativity' conflict has tended, like the 'atheism versus belief' debate of earlier times, to attract inflexible commitment on one side or another, as well as having many confused doubters in the middle. Since I have dwelled, in what might seem anti-structuralist spirit, on the importance of individual validity and pleasure in both personal and public modes of writing, I should like to conclude my case by invoking the views of a distinguished structuralist, Roland Barthes, on these issues. Barthes is best known for his scheme of semiological analysis; his earlier development of Saussurean linguistics was concerned with system and structure in language rather than with its creative possibilities. Yet works such as *The Pleasure of the Text* (1975) and *A Lover's Discourse* (1978) revealed a fascination with the creative ambiguity of language. He recognised that language, creatively used, has two aspects that operate simultaneoulsy — an aspect which conforms to, and an aspect which subverts normal usage — and that pleasure lies in experienceing these aspects simultaneously. Through this 'cohabitation' of two aspects of language, individuals develop in language, and develop through a language. In his preface to *A Lover's Discourse*, Barthes explains that the need to write this book grew from a sense that intimate modes of language (*'le discours amoureux'*) tend more and more to be employed in extreme privacy. The forms of intimate discourse are unknown or disparaged in the public discourse of the arts and sciences; yet they need, not only for their own sake, but for the sake of the public forms which have displayed them, to be granted affirmation. On behalf of writers, and of the communities in which they write, I could not agree more.

Bibliography

Allen, D. (1980).	*English since 1965: How Much Growth:* London, Heinemann.
APU (Assessment of Performance Unit) (1978).	*Language Performance*. London, Department of Education and Science, HMSO.
APU (1984).	*Language Performance in Schools. 1982 Secondary Report*. London, Department of Education and Science, HMSO.
Barthes, R. (1975).	*The Pleasure of the Text* (trans. R. Miller). New York, Hill and Wang.
Barthes, R. (1978).	*A Lover's Discourse* (trans. R. Howard). New York, Hill and Wang.

Bennett, N. and Desforges, C. (1985). *Recent Advances in Classroom Research.* Edinburgh, Scottish Academic Press.

Britton, J.N., Burgess, T., Martin, N., McLeod, A. and Rosen, H. (1975). *The Development of Writing Abilities (11–18).* London, Macmillan Educational.

Camus, A. (1984). *The Plague* (trans. S. Gilbert). Harmondsworth, Penguin.

Guntrip, H. (1968). *Schizoid Phenomena: Object Relations and the Self.* London, Tavistock Press.

Gusdorf, G. (1965). *Speaking.* Evanston, Il, North Western University Press.

Haffenden, J. (1981). *Viewpoints: Poets in Conversation.* London, Faber.

Harrison, B.T. (1983). *Learning through Writing.* London, NFER/Nelson.

Harrison, B.T. (forthcoming). *A Case of Shyness: Sarah's Letters.* Bedford Way Paper, University of London Institute of Education.

Harrison, B.T. and Gordon, H. (1983). 'Metaphor is Thought: Does Northtown need Poetry?', *Educational Review*, vol. 35, no. 3.

Holbrook, D. (1961). *English for Maturity.* Cambridge, Cambridge University Press.

Hourd, M. (1949). *The Education of the Poetic Spirit.* London, Heinemann.

Meek, M. (1980). 'Prolegomena for a Study of Children's Literature' in Benton, M. (ed.) *Approaches to Research in Children's Literature.* Southampton, University of Southampton.

Protherough, R. (1983). *Encouraging Writing.* London, Methuen.

Proust, M. (1981). *Remembrance of Things Past* (trans. C.K. Scott Moncrieff, and T. Kilmartin). London, Chatto.

Pym, D. (1956). *Free Writing.* London, University of London Press.

Tolstoy, L. (1967). 'The School at Yasnaya Polyana' in *Tolstoy on Education* (trans. Weiner). Original publication 1882. Chicago, University of Chicago Press.

Wilkinson, A. (1985). 'Writing' in Bennett and Desforges (1985).

Wilkinson, A., Barnsley, G. *Assessing Language Development.* Oxford,

Hanna, P. and Swan, M.   Oxford University Press.
(1980).
Winnicott, D. (1965).   *Maturational Processes and the Facilitating Environment*. London, Tavistock Press.
Winnicott, D. (1971).   *Playing and Reality*. Harmondsworth, Penguin.
Witkin, R. (1974).   *The Intelligence of Feeling*. London, Heinemann.

6 Writers in Their Place

BRUCE BENNETT

The central role of place

A general neglect of place in literary criticism has its counterpart in educational research on writing. In both spheres universalist assumptions have erected barriers to place and culture-specific modes of investigation and analysis. My argument here is twofold: that, as teachers, we should be more aware of the function of place in the formation of the self and hence in our own and our students' writing; and that as researchers who write about writing, we should resist the temptation to gloss over differences between places in our description and interpretation or writing processes and products. 'Place' will be here defined as an individual's physical and social environment. Thus defined, place has a central role in the drama of writing.

For many professional writers of fiction the *construction* of place in their work is a matter of the greatest interest and concern. Welty (1956) has given some reasons for this:

> It is by the nature of itself that fiction is all bound up in the local. The internal reason for that is surely that *feelings* are bound up in place. The human mind is a mass of associations — associations more poetic even than actual. I say 'the Yorkshire moors' and you will say 'Wuthering Heights', and I have only to murmur 'If Father were only alive' for you to come back with 'We could go to Moscow', which is certainly not so. The truth is, fiction depends for its life on place. Location is the crossroads of circumstance, the proving ground of What happened? Who's here? Who's coming? — that is the heart's field.

A regrowth of regional fiction, poetry and drama in recent years seems to spring from this kind of recognition. Hardy, Faulkner and Welty herself, as 'regional' writers, were forerunners of recent works such as Graham Swift's novel *Waterland* (1983) and Caryl Churchill's play *Fen*, which powerfully record the impact of East Anglia upon the human imagination. Randolph Stow's novel *The Girl Green as Elderflower* (1980) grows from the landscape, idiom and legends of Suffolk. In John Fowles's psychological saga *Daniel Martin* (1978) the protagonist's attempt to find himself involves a not uncommon process in the fiction of our times: he returns to his native county, Devon, where, in sensuous contact with landscape, vegetation and the remnants of a rural community, he re-establishes a sense of direction which may guide him through the latter part of his life.

The process of recovery, through writing, of a sense of belonging may tell us much about the writer *and* the place. D.H. Lawrence's assertion of the reality of an active spirit of place is dependent upon the existence of sensitive individuals who may respond to that spirit. In responding, the writer may locate those details and associations which comprise, in Eudora Welty's words, 'the heart's field'. Rushdie (1982, p. 18) has described how this process occurred during the composing of *Midnight's Children*, and stresses the significance of the writer's 'position' in relation to the environment which he or she constructs:

> Writers in my position, exiles or emigrants or expatriates, are haunted by an urge to look back, even at the risk of being mutated into pillars of salt. But if we do look back, we must also do so in the knowledge — which gives rise to profound uncertainties — that our physical alienation [from India] almost inevitably means that we will not be capable of reclaiming precisely the thing that was lost: that we will, in short, create fictions, not actual cities or villages, but invisible ones, imaginary homelands, Indias of the mind. Writing my book in North London, looking out through my window on to a city scene totally unlike the ones I was imagining on to paper, I was constantly plagued by this problem, until I felt obliged to face it in the text, to make clear that (in spite of my original and, I suppose, somewhat Proustian ambition to unlock the gates of lost time so that the past reappeared as it actually had been, unaffected by the distortions of memory) what I was actually writing was a novel of memory and about memory, so that my India was just that: 'my' India, a version and no more than one version of all the hundreds of millions of possible versions. I tried to make it as imaginatively true as I could, but imaginative truth is simultaneously honourable and suspect, and I knew that my India may only have been one to which I (who am no longer what I was, and who by quitting Bombay never became what perhaps I was meant to be) was willing to admit I belonged.

In spite of the disclaimers here, Rushdie's creation of an imaginary homeland in his novel has enabled millions of other readers to inhabit vicariously the country of his mind; and often, if the reviews are to be believed, with a sense that they have been put more closely in touch with an actual India. Such is the power of imaginative truth-telling about place. Yet readers' responses will differ: the response to Rushdie's novel was generally more negative in India than in Britain, for instance, indicating the gaps which may exist between readers according to their own location and circumstances.

Only a few writing researchers have attempted to take on board the complex and difficult implications of such insights from literature. One who has, Andrew Wilkinson, has argued in a paper included in the present volume that the self's growing awareness of, and interaction with its environment should be considered as a major process in the writer's development towards an organic sensibility. Such development may occur around points of crisis or dislocation in an individual's life, as appears to be the case in 15-year-old Clare's response to the topic 'My Favourite Place' (see p. 53):

My home isn't my home, its where I live.
When I come along the road I come to the same gate and the same path to the same front door and prick myself on the same holly bush. But it's not the same.
  It used to be the same till my Dad left. My Dad used to have a work bench in the garage but he took that.
  He left all the furniture but when the settlement came through my Mum didn't like it and bought a new suite. I went along to choose it. It was cream with frills and deep upholstery. My Mum was very pleased with it but I thought it dominated the room, although I didn't say anything. I don't like sitting on it. The only place I feel at home is my bedroom because it had my old things there.

Here the writer reflects upon details and aspects of her home, which has become transformed for her since the day of her father's departure. Mother and daughter buy new furniture after the settlement. But the only room in which the daughter feels 'at home' is her bedroom, in which her old things are kept. In this fine piece of writing details of place are used symbolically and repetition of significant words builds an appropriate tone. The research design for this project did not include case studies. If it had, it might have tested the hypothesis that a development in writing abilities and in identity formation occurred in this episode of writing.

The encouragement of writers to formulate and convey a sense of place is also evident in Fred Inglis's aptly titled *The Englishness of English Teaching* (1969) in which, as in Wilkinson, a 'humanising' function for English teaching is assumed. For Inglis, English teaching should contribute to fostering, creating and 'making real' the following:

1. a sense of the past
2. a sense of place
3. a language of tenderness
4. a sense of coherence
5. powers of discrimination

Inglis stresses the importance of a sense of place by arguing that to 'feel at home' is 'exactly what *is* needed in an English lesson, or in a life-time'. English teaching (including writing) should include 'key images of place and home (of belonging, of roots and continuity)'. But this should not preclude the development of a critical and perhaps outraged awareness: 'Whether one opts on the side of an uncritical and sincere neighbourliness, or whether a sense of the outrage done to the landscape drives one in anguish to forfeit human contact, it is relevant to know what the children feel' (Inglis 1969, pp. 22–3).

One of the most enterprising pieces of research dealing with the relationship of writers to place is Paquette (1981) which analyses the journals of eight London East End adolescent students before, during and after a trip which they made together to Canada. Paquette's study recognises that it is possible to go stale in the place where you live, to fail to notice things, so that they become clichés. This piece of common sense is transformed into a revealing account, through case studies of his writers and their writing, of the ways in which writing can change in response to new stimuli in a different environment. The thesis contains some suggestive findings about the importance of audience. For, as Paquette has argued (1984, p. 78):

> Writers do not write in solitude any more than speakers speak in solitude. The private act of writing on paper should not be construed as a vision of solitary man, for the act of writing is the act of sharing shaped meaning with real and construed others who influence the shaping by their incorporation within the self of the writer.

If we restrict the number of listening partners (or indeed the quality of engagement of those construed listening partners whom we carry about in our heads) we will restrict the range and quality of our writing. The sharp sense of difference which Paquette's English students noticed in the west Canadian environment, including the sense of space and of social relations, together with a new sense of their English families and friends as an audience for whom they had to contextualise their experience, led in certain cases to an improvement in the quality of their writing. Further studies would be necessary to understand the reason for blockages to change in the writing of those few who did not respond to the change of environment. The notion that changing one's environment and one's audience will improve the quality of one's written or other responses to place may moreover deny the value of those 'tribal' responses to place which we find in relatively closed communities around the world. These are problems which research seems not to have fully addressed as yet.

Another kind of analysis is that which stays closer to the evidence of written products rather than analysing the writer in his or her environment. Alan Purves's continuing study (1983) of compositions by pre-university students in several countries on the topic 'My Native Town' is an example of this kind of research. Purves and his colleagues have derived a number of 'dimensions of difference' from these composition: single or multiple focus, abstract, personal or impersonal, metaphorical or literal (or elaborate or plain) and logically or analogically organised. These dimensions were found to distinguish compositions between and within language groups. The interpretation of this kind of research is fraught with difficulties, but important hypotheses may emerge from it about the relationship between writing and place. We might thereby learn to question more intelligently the extent to which a sense of place varies according to a writer's nation, region, vocation, ethnic group and other factors. Hypothetical statements about the ways in which communities are supposed to 'produce' communities of writers (and readers) could also be examined more closely. For these reasons, among others, the proposal for an International Educational Assessment (IEA) Written Composition Study across a number of countries deserves the full support of the international community of writing researchers (Kadar-Fulop and de Glopper 1985).

Whether the relationship between writing and place is investigated on a broad or narrow scale will depend upon the aims, resources and interests of the investigator. The Western Australian Writing Research Project (Bennett *et al.* 1980; Bennett 1983a), for instance, adopted a deliberately narrow frame in order to probe at some depth into the backgrounds and circumstances of a number of 'case study' writers. The rationale for such case studies has been justified enthusiastically by Nancy Martin (1984, p. 49):

> Anthropologists, clinical psychologists and social workers, for instance, have always been concerned with case studies. Their validity in these fields is unquestioned, yet educational research has for too long been straitjacketed by procedures (and philosophies) derived from technological models, and the weight of the educational establishment is still behind them. The mould, though, is beginning to crack . . .

Martin's own ethnographic approach to the study of English involved case studies of several Western Australian high schools (Martin 1980). Shirley Brice Heath's case study (1983) of three communities and their language (including written language) is another example of this approach, in which the different patterns of socialisation of her three communities are shown to contribute to an explanation of the nature and quality of their 'literacy'.

The research project

Members of the Western Australian Writing Research Project team with whom I worked accepted the view that an in-depth study of writing should not ignore the writer's social and geographic context, situation and intentions. Among the eleven published case studies of 15–17-year-olds which were an outcome of this project, along with a number of unpublished studies, various kinds of 'pairing' now seem feasible in order to compare and contrast characteristics of individual writers. Such an approach enables us to include 'marginal' figures who would not be foregrounded in a study dominated by norms and averages, but who, by virtue of their marginality, can reveal much about the context of situation. Two such 'characters' are Michael, an Aboriginal student at a country high school, and Marion, a Eurasian student at a metropolitan high school. They were each visited and interviewed by the present writer over a period of three years (Bennett 1979; 1980). The composition of case-study accounts of these two writers and their writing involved an attempt to 'place' the individuals as objectively as possible within their homes, schools, communities and geographical terrains as well as to record their individual perceptions of place, school and community and their roles in relation to them. In each case their writing behaviour was a key factor in defining a sense of the role and significance of place in their lives.

As the author of these case studies, I was concerned to allow the subjects to influence my point of view and style. My attempted objectivity was thus strictly relative. The model I had in mind was that of the good novelist or short-story writer, who is flexible enough to vary his technique according to what the subject seems to demand. (One of the reasons for this was that I wanted teachers, who would be the main readers of the case-study booklets, to become interested in the subjects.) In the event, I used more naturalistic techniques in the case study of Michael. As a consequence, this study exhibits a greater 'distance' between its author and its subject than the study of Marion, which is more impressionistic, involved and free-flowing; the degrees of distance also reflect the different degrees of rapport which I achieved with these individuals. Such inter-subjective variations are inevitable, it would seem, in participant–observer research of this kind; they certainly make interpretation complex. But when such complexities have been taken into account, the resultant understanding may be more revealing and more durable than statistical averages or an enforced objectivity in which an inflexible form is imposed on quite various subjects.

Michael

In the case of Michael, an Aboriginal student at a high school in wheat-farming country 120 km from Perth, the capital city of Western Australia, it seemed important to establish some 'social facts'. An Australian Government Committee of Inquiry into Education and Training (the Williams Report of 1979) showed that the circumstances of Aboriginal people varied greatly in Australia. In a depleted population of 106,000 in a total Australian population of 13 million (now nearly 15 million), 46 per cent of Aborigines were less than 15 years old; 26 per cent had not attended school, 53 per cent had received some primary education and only 20 per cent had schooling of secondary or higher standard, including no more than 1900 who had gone as far as grade 10 (Michael's year) or beyond. In 1976, 79 were enrolled at universities and 151 at colleges of advanced education. In remaining at school for grade 10, and deciding to repeat the year, Michael was in a small minority of Aboriginal students who had proceeded to secondary schooling and a much smaller minority who had remained there until the age of 16. The Williams Report quotes an Australian Council for Educational Research survey, which found that among Aboriginal children at school the general level of literacy and numeracy was 15–20 per cent below that of the whole school population.

The generalised view of Michael which many European Australians would assimilate through the media is summed up in a newspaper report about conditions in Michael's home town:

> Aborigines in M —
> The Chairman of the National Aboriginal Conference Rev. Cedric Jacobs has claimed that urgent action was needed to overcome appalling social problems ... including distressing alcohol and unemployment problems.
> 'The situation is serious and could lead to violence. There is no work available and many people are on the dole. They are spending their dole money on alcohol. They are starting this at a very young age.'

Michael lived in a house on the outskirts of town with his grandmother and an extended family of varying size. This family, and the Aboriginal community of the town, appeared to be the major determinants of his attitude of schooling generally, and to writing. The flat landscape, ploughed, seeded and harvested once each year, the railway line and the wheat silo were his chief geographical landmarks, though he was also very observant by comparison with many of his white schoolmates about details of local fauna and flora. In his community, and his town and its hinterland, Michael had accumulated a reservoir of experience which

the school scarcely ever tapped, and to which one or two teachers were
actively hostile. (Traditional Aboriginal attitudes to land ownership and
use from the beginnings of Australia's British and European history
have been a perennial source of conflict; and it was this clash of values
which seemed to underlie the hostility of these teachers, who identified
with the land-owning farmers of the districts.)

The extraordinary difficuty which Michael had in writing, and his lack
of interest in it seemed to relate directly to place, family and community;
his physical and emotional conditions for writing were negative and
general expectations of his achievement were low. The rare occasions on
which a sympathetic English teacher stimulated Michael to write at
some length, and with apparent interest, emphasised the usual antipathy
between his own experience and that which the school promulgated —
an antipathy which grows from wthat Douglas Barnes *et al.* (1969, pp.
11–16) have described more generally as a discrepancy between school
knowledge and action knowledge. Yet any application of a universalist
deprivation theory to Michael would be a poor substitute for the
culture-specific base out of which his experience grows and how it
interacts with the wider Australian community.

Michael's relations with family, land, school and peer group indicate a
necessarily complex basis for analysis of his writing behaviour. One of
the chief lessons for this researcher was that the extended family of a
largely alienated minority group in an Australian country town provided
a compensating co-operative support system, in which one of Michael's
sisters, who was a strong reader and writer, did the necessary writing of
personal letters, bills and accounts for other members of the group,
while they helped her out in other ways.

Michael's history after he left school was typical of many of his people.
After working for a time as relief odd-job man for the shire council in
his country town he went to the city, where he was unable to find work.
After a year he returned to his country town, where he now works as a
garbage collector, gardener and odd-job man for the council. Marginalised by conditions and pressures in his home town, he would remain a
marginal figure in the power structures of the community at large; his
attempts at writing in school may be interpreted as symbolising this
wider powerlessness.

Marion

Another, quite different set of responses to place and community is
indicated in the case of Marion, a Eurasian immigrant to Australia from
Singapore. The Singapore ethos from which Marion emigrated was
competitive rather than co-operative, though she was protected from

this to a large extent by her convent upbringing. Sensitive, intelligent and remarkably self-aware at 16 and 17, she oscillated between the desire to achieve highly in Australian society — to become a doctor — and the wish to retreat to easier, less threatening circumstances. Like the Aboriginal boy living on the fringes of his country town, the Asian girl, an only daughter from a relatively affluent suburban family in a metropolitan beach-side suburb, was subject to racial intolerance and ignorance, but it was less concentrated, more diffused for her by a greater number of people and a more mobile lifestyle.

Marion used private writing in a way unknown to Michael to explore her feelings and attitudes. Whereas Michael saw no point or purpose in writing for himself and could only occasionally be induced to put pen to paper, Marion saw at least two distinct purposes: the utilitarian one of expressing knowledge of her school subjects which would enable her to pass examinations and hence achieve her academic and vocational ambitions; and the personal need to explore her thoughts and feelings in imaginatively created situations. Although she would sometimes express the latter purpose as 'escape' it was clearly an important element in her development as a thinking and feeling person, enabling her to play roles, to entertain different hypotheses about herself, her environment and the community she inhabited, but of which she felt 'on the edge'. Here is an example of Marion's writing on a topic set for her by the class teacher, which reveals some original responses to her physical and social environment:

> Nude bathing is disgusting
> and should be prohibited

Nude bathing, now that the long not months of summer are approaching, will become a very sensitive topic; the sensitivity not being entirely due to sunburn. All the staunch workers for righteousness and stalwarts of the Church will be going around broadcasting the decadence and immorality of 'Swannie' Beach with the vigour and energy usually attributed to the flies during a heatwave. Old faithful reasons such as exposing one's personals is detrimental to the pesonality as well as to society will be heard with as much frequency as Coca Cola advertisements. It is then refreshing, I feel, to hear a slightly different view of the undesirable commodities of nude bathing; in brief, my own intelligent and well thought out opinion.

It is apparent to any self-critical and observant citizen of our fair land that Australians in general are not conscious and therefore not very concerned about their body beautiful, besides the fact that they find it necessary a summer-time accessory to attain a 'beaut' tan if they are able to do so. On the whole, both females and males believe in letting themselves go both virtually and literally, consuming every edible item in sight from fat drenched steak and chips to cream buns and fairy floss, with a minimum of hard physical exercise between the frequent meals. This results in the all too familiar beer-belly, double chin, flabby arms, un-contoured ankles, and the dreaded wobbles around the thighs, hips and posterior. What more detrimental sight could one observe in the nude? What more callous injustice could be done to a human body? Of course I would find nude bathing disgusting if the bathers should take it upon themselves to deface what could be a beautiful work of art; the human body made in God's image and ruined by man's selfish, piggish, uncouth appetite. It would be a great blow to human pride to expose these monstrosities in the bare, ruthless light of day.

Apart from this ruination of figures displaying themselves on our white sandy shores, I have nothing against nude bathing, except for the fact that if would cost rather a lot in sunburn cream.

In this, as in many other pieces of writing, Marion exhibits a witty and intelligent control over her material. Her 'place' is not fixed and immutable, but a series of refractive glasses on her experiences.

By increasing her powers of self-analysis and her ability to project herself into other people's situations in her writing Marion was, according to our usual way of thinking, gaining in maturity and extending her humanity. While Marion was more capable than most to write about school as a 'prison' (which she did on more than one occasion) her writing always exuded a sense that she was intelligently in control of her environment. What gave her writing its particular 'edge' was a sense of friction with her surroundings which she, to a much greater extent than Michael, felt she could manipulate to her way of thinking.

Discussion: self and environment

Beyond Michael and Marion lie quite different ethnic communities and traditional ways of living in Australia. Their attitudes to writing are shaped by family and communal pressures as much as by the school they attend or the friends they make there. In addition, Michael's country town, with its special climate (encouraging outdoor activities) and social and economic organisations, differs considerably from Marion's relatively affluent suburban situation — that of an only child without extended family commitments and with the leisure, family encourage-ment and financial resources to take up music as a hobby. Both individuals are nevertheless marginalised (though one is rendered much more powerless) by a traditionally British-Australian ethos, whose exclusiveness varies in strength in different places in Australia but is a necessary element in any social analysis of the impact of place upon these writers and their writing.

What happens when place is held relatively constant? Can the environment then be seen to determine a certain set of responses? On the contrary, it seems that individuals still perceive differently and consturct different versions of place, though this may vary according to the 'tribal' nature of different communities. The paring of case studies may again provide insights into the reasons for similarities and differences in students' construction of place in their writings as well as the influence of their environment upon them (though it would be foolish to expect conclusive proof from this approach). Two friends through their senior years at a Western Australian country high school, Wendy and Caroline (Bennett 1983b), demonstrate how place may be responded to, and reconstructed in imagination, in quite contrary ways. Caroline, the 'converger', was more conformist and more successful at school and in the community; in her written constructions of place she was generally literal-minded and less 'literary' than her schoolfriend Wendy. Wendy, the 'diverger', was a dreamer, who invested her perceived world with the intertextuality and metaphorical equivalences which derive, in part at least, from wide reading and a variety of writing tasks and audiences (she was an inveterate letter writer). Whereas Wendy, the 'high metaphoriser' tended to transform what she saw and was considered 'a bit mad' by her schoolmates, Caroline was a practical, career-orientated girl who seemed most likely to 'get on' in the part of the world which she inhabited. If either girl could be considered to speak and write 'tribally' — with the middle-class outlook of school and town most embedded in her own attitudes and values — it would be Caroline; yet Wendy carried the seeds of a 'prophetic' voice. Conceivably, in another place and society the two girls' roles might be reversed. yet both would be seen to have a complicated and provisional 'hold' on their place of habitation.

Clearly, the role of place in children's and adolescents' writing, as in the work of professional writers, requires further investigation. Writing researchers might learn much in the course of their investigations from the introspections and self-analysis of experienced writers for whom place has been a significant factor in their work. A sample of kinds of response might be collected and analysed, ranging from those which exhibit what Wordsworth called a wise passiveness before their natural environment to those which express an angry rejection of place. Another group might be those fantasists who choose a state of extra-territoriality, ignoring the physical and social environment in favour of a world of fables and dreams. Such studies, among professional writers and among students, could illuminate the needs of individual psyche in relation to place — both the natural and built elements of the environment. The currently unfashionable topological psychology of Kurt Lewin (1935), which takes into account the fields of force in an individual's 'life space' and their relation to the individual's geographical environment could be helpful. Taine's attempts to explain human creativity by a combination of climatic, biological and social factors (Kahn, 1935), might also be re-examined; and recent sociological accounts (Laurenson and Swingewood 1972; Berger and Luckman 1973) of literary activity and associated modes of constructing reality could contribute to a fuller sense of the 'socialisation' of the writer.

A complete explanation of how writers possess, and are possessed by the places they inhabit may never be achieved. But somewhere between pure determinism and pure existentialism lies a territory of partial explanations which may best satisfy our need to understand how the self responds to, and is in turn influenced by its environment. It is a field of valid and important activity for the teacher and writing researcher.

Bibliography

Barnes, D., Britton, J. and Rosen, H. (1969). *Language, the Learner and the School.* Harmondsworth, Peguin Education.

Bennett, B. (1979). *Michael: A Case Study.* Writing Research Project, University of Western Australia.

Bennett, B. (1980). *Marion: A Case Study.* Writing Research Project, University of Western Australia.

Bennett, B. (1983*a*). 'Writers and their Writing 15–17' in Freedman, *et al.* (1983), pp. 190–206.

Bennett, B. (1983*b*). 'The Necessity of Metaphor' in R. Arnold (ed.), *Timely Voices: English Teaching in the Eighties.* Melbourne, Oxford University Press.

Bennett, B., Bowes, D., Jeffery, C., McPhail, S., Sooby, A. and Walker, A. (1980). 'An Investigation of the Process of Writing and Development of Writing Abilities 15 to 17'. Report to ERDC, Canberra.

Berger, P. and Luckman, T. (1973). *The Social Construction of Reality.* Harmondsworth, Penguin.

Freedman, A., Pringle, I. and Yalden, J. (1983). *Learning to Write: First Language Second Language.* London, Longmans.

Heath, S.B. (1983). *Ways with Words: Language, Life and Work in Communities and Classrooms.* Cambridge, Cambridge University Press.

Inglis, F. (1969).   *The Englishness of English Teaching.* London, Longmans.

Kadar-Fulop, J. and de Glopper, K. (1985).   'Proposal for an International Student-Composition Corpus'. typescript, National Institute for Education, Budapest, April.

Kahn, S.T. (1985).   *Science and Aesthetic Judgment: A Study in Taine's Critical Method.* London, Routledge and Kegan Paul.

Laurenson, D. and Swingewood A. (1972).   *The Sociology of Literature.* London, Paladin.

Lewin, K. (1935).   *A Dynamic Theory of Personality: Selected Papers by Kurt Lewin* (trans. D.K. Adams and K.E. Zener New York, McGraw-Hill.

Martin, N. (1980).   'What Goes on in English Lessons: Case Studies from Government High Schools in Western Australia'. Education Department, Western Australia, 1980.

Martin, N. (1984).   'Researchers and Learners' in M. Meek and J. Miller (eds.), *Changing English: Essays for Harold Rosen.* London, Heinemann Educational.

Paquette, J. (1981).   'The Influence of the Sense of Audience on the Writing Processes of Eight Adolescent Boys'. Unpublished doctoral thesis. Unversity of London Institute of Education.

Paquette, J. (1984).   'On Writing Something to Somebody' in J. Britton (ed.), *English Teaching: an International Exchange.* London, Heinemann.

Purves, A. (1983).   'Language Processing: Reading and Writing', *College English*, vol. 45, no. 2, February, pp. 129–40.

Rushdie, S. (1982).   'Imaginary Homelands', *London Review of Books*, 7–20 October.

Welty, Eudora (1956).   'Places in Fiction', *The South Atlantic Quarterly, vol. 55, no. 1 (January); reprinted in S.K. Kumar and K. McKean (eds.), Critical Approaches to Fiction.* New York, McGraw-Hill, 1968, p. 251.

Wilkinson, A.M. (1986).   'I write – therefore I am', paper included in this volume.

Part Three

From Speech to Writing

7 Grammatical Differentiation Between Speech and Writing in Children Aged 8 to 12

KATHARINE PERERA

Primary school teachers often complain that their pupils 'write as they speak'. In an earlier study (Perera, forthcoming), I attempted to show that, in fact, young children's writing shows more evidence of differentiation from their speech than that lament would suggest. The study took published corpora of data and compared the speech of 53 twelve-year-olds with the writing of 28 twelve-year-olds and 48 nine-year-olds. This comparison yielded some useful information but, because of the way the data were presented, it had the limitation that it was not possible to compare the same children as both speakers and writers. This paper, therefore, presents a smaller follow-up study, comparing the speech and writing of 48 monolingual English-speaking children in Wales. The data come from a language development project at the Polytechnic of Wales: the speech samples are published (Fawcett and Perkins 1980); the writing samples by the same children are, as yet, unpublished, and I am grateful to Robin Fawcett for providing access to transcripts and writing. The 48 Children come from three groups, aged eight, ten and 12, with 16 in each group; each contains eight boys and eight girls, from four different 'classes of family background'. When recorded, the children were within three months of eight, ten or 12. So a reference to 'eight-year-olds' encompasses children between 7.9 and 8.3.

For the collection of the spoken data, the children were tape-recorded as, in groups of three, they made a construction out of Lego bricks. They were then interviewed individually by Perkins, who asked them to describe what they had made and to talk about other games they played. For the writing task, the children had to write about the Lego construction they had built.

The data for this study come from a grammatical analysis of the first three pages of the transcript of the adult–child interview for all 48 children and from an analysis of the 48 pieces of writing they produced. So the corpus consists of language samples from the same children talking and writing about the same topic. It is a small amount of data, on a limited topic, so the findings can only be tentative, but, because they are generally in accord with the results of the earlier, larger study, I believe they may have some general applicability.

Constructions typical of spoken language

Differentiation between speech and writing by children works in two ways. On the one hand, as they get older they use in their writing grammatical constructions that are more advanced than those they use in their speech (O'Donnell *et al.* 1967); on the other hand, they use in their speech an increasing proportion of specifically oral constructions. This section will examine the oral constructions that the children in the study used in their speech, because such an examination throws some light on what they are doing in their writing.

Excluded from the analysis are all those constructions that are heavily dependent on the situation in which the speech occurs: deictic items like 'this', 'that', 'here' and 'there', that the children use when they point to things in the room; expressions like 'you know', 'isn't it' and all other question forms, since they seem to require the presence of a listener; and the false starts, redundant repetitions and ungrammatical sequences that are a result of the pressures of producing spontaneous speech. Even after excluding all of these, there are still in the spoken data eight different constructions that we think of as characteristically oral. In the examples that follow, the name and age of the speaker are given, together with the volume and page reference in Fawcett and Perkins (1980). Although the oral constructions are illustrated from the speech of children, it is important to emphasise that all these expressions occur frequently in the spontaneous speech of adults — there is nothing immature about them.

The first is the clause initiator 'well'. This is so familiar that it needs only one example:

(1)   'well I de'cided to put the gàrage on/

(Andrew (8); II, 24)

This is by far the most common oral expression in the data. Between them, the 48 children use 137 instances of 'well'.

The next most frequent type of oral construction is the use of 'this' and 'these' for specific indefinite reference; that is, when the speaker has a specific person or object in mind which has not yet been introduced to the listener. (This use is different from deictic 'this', because it is not referring to something physically present in the situation.) For example:

(2)   well there's 'this bùmpety thing/

(Sarah (8); II, 57)

(3)   they 'had to run 'under this 'dark tùnnel/

(Rachael (10); III, 59)

(4)   it's 'got 'these 'things that 'catch the márbles/

(Peter (12); IV, 20)'

In more formal contexts, including writing, 'this' and 'these' would be replaced by 'a' and 'some', e.g. 'They had to run under a dark tunnel', 'It's got some things that catch the marbles'.

The third type of oral construction is the group of 'vague completers'. They include expressions like 'or something':

(5)   it 'might be a 'children's hòme or something/

(Andrew (8); II, 24)

and 'an all that', as in:

(6)   we was 'looking for pièces an all that/

(Neil (10); III, 182(

They have been described in studies by Dines (1979, pp. 13–31) and Scott (1983) under the general heading of 'and stuff'. The most famous adult use of one of these vague completers was probably in the film where Groucho Marx said to his leading lady, 'let's get married or something' and she replied, 'Let's get married or nothing'. Sadly, the example of 'or nothing' in (7) is not a witty riposte but simply a non-standard version of 'or anything':

(7)   they 'wouldn't let him óut or nothing/

(Sarah (12); IV, 306)

These completers seem to be used when the speaker feels that more could be said but that perhaps it is unnecessary to be more explicit.

There is quite a range used by the children, from the highly colloquial *'and that'* to the more formal 'and things like that'.

The fourth category is the recapitulatory pronoun. In this construction, the speaker uses a noun phrase at the beginnning of the sentence and then abandons it syntactically, filling its grammatical slot with a pronoun, for example:

(8)   well my 'nan 'she got some bóoks/ from the lïbrary/
(Sharon (8); II, 266)

(9)   wèll/ Nèil/ you knów/ he 'started 'building a well he 'put the 'bottom of the 'house by thére/
(Jason (10); III, 193)

(10)   'this mán/ he . . . was 'selling ícecreams/
(Jane (12); IV, 220)

In more formal styles, the initial noun phrase would serve as the subject of the sentence and the pronoun would not appear at all, for example: 'My nan got some books from the library'.

The fifth set of examples features the word 'like'. There are uses of 'like' which are perfectly normal in non-colloquial contexts, such as: 'She looks like her mother'. The only instances included here are those like (11) and (12) which are clearly not part of the formal language:

(11)   we were 'going to make 'like a 'big 'house with a pòrch/
(Martyn (10); III, 87)

(12)   'like there's 'these two 'rubber bànds/
(Peter (12); IV, 20)

Similarly, 'sort of' and 'kind of' have both a neutral and a markedly colloquial use. The neutral use is where the meaning is 'a type of', as in 'Stilton is a sort or cheese'. In this use, the expressions occur between a determiner and a noun. It is not always possible with the construction, 'It's a sort of *x*', to tell whether it is being used literally or colloquially. Therefore, conservatively, all such constructions are excluded from the analysis, leaving only those like (13) and (14) that are clearly colloquial:

(13)   we 'kind of 'lean on a trèe/
(Richard (8); II, 237)

(14)   we 'sort of ran óut of these/
(Rachael (10); III, 57)

The sixth type of oral construction is the tag statement, which speakers seem to use for emphasis:

(15)   it's the 'one we 'do in jàzz band/ it ís/
(Nicola (8); II, 171)

(16)   it's hàrd it is/

(Neil (10); III, 182)

(17)   'that was 'going to 'be like a dànger spot/thát was/

(Martyn (12); IV, 185)

The last of these oral constructions is the amplificatory noun-phrase tag. In this construction, the speaker uses a pronoun first and then, as if aware that the reference of the pronoun may not be clear to the listener, adds an explanatory noun phrase at the end:

(18)   we 'sort of ran óut of these/ 'these the 'red brícks sort of thing/

(Rachael (10); III, 57(

(19)   the 'girl who cálled her 'sister out of it/ the'fire

(Andrea (12); IV, 250)

Table 7.1 gives the occurrence of these oral constructions in the corpus of children's speech. In order to take account of the different number of words used by each age group (given at the top of the Table) all the figures are presented as occurrences per hundred words; the actual number of instances is given in brackets. The figures for the totals reveal the most striking aspect of this analysis: that there is a dramatic increase in the use of these colloquial constructions between the ages of eight and ten, from 1.86 per 100 words to 3.46, an increase of 86 per cent. All of the constructions, apart from the recapitulatory pronoun, show an increase from age eight to ten. Those that reveal the greatest gain are: the tag statement; vague completers; 'well'; and 'this and 'these'.

The figures in Table 7.1 provide evidence that, far from dying out of children's speech, oral constructions are becoming much more prominent.

The fact that they hardly occur in writing is, therefore, that much more remarkable. Because that is the case. In the 48 pieces of writing produced by these same children, there are only two examples — both in the same sentence:

(20)   We used these sort of tiles for the roof.

(Bryan, 12)

This can be contrasted with the 283 instances in speech, produced by 45 of the 48 children. The virtual absence of oral constructions in the children's writing is not a freak result: in 90 unpublished pieces of writing by nine-year-olds in the Bristol Language Development Project there are only these three examples (I am grateful to Gordon Wells and Barry Kroll for access to this material):

(21)   Well have a guess

(Mary, 9)

(22)   But then he saw this elephant.

(Philip, 9)

(23)   These men were cannibals.

(Philip, 9)

Construction	8 yrs (no of words = 3010)	10 yrs (no of words = 3926)	12 yrs (no of words = 3768)
well	0.86 (26)	1.71 (67)	1.17 (44)
this/these	0.40 (12)	0.76 (30)	0.53 (20)
vague completer	0.23 (7)	0.46 (18)	0.27 (10)
recapitulatory pronoun	0.17 (5)	0.13 (5)	0.11 (4)
like	0.07 (2)	0.13 (5)	0.19 (7)
sort of/kind of	0.10 (3)	0.13 (5)	0.08 (3)
tag statement	0.03 (1)	0.13 (5)	0.03 (1)
amplificatory NP tag		0.03 (1)	0.05 (2)
Total	1.86 (56)	3.46 (136)	2.42 (91)

Table 7·1   Oral constructions in the speech of children aged 8–12
(occurence per hundred words, with number of instances in brackets)

It is tempting to think that there is something in the constructions themselves that inhibits their use in writing. But a search through many hundreds of pieces of children's writing does produce occasional examples — and indeed adults sometimes use them in personal letters in order to establish a warm, friendly tone of voice. Here, from a variety of sources, are examples of some colloquial constructions occurring exceptionally, in writing:

(24)   When we arrived at dover we saw the white cliffs and everything.
                    (12 yrs, Handscombe (1967, p. 42))

(25)   The boy's father he has a job and family to take care.
                    (adult, Shaughnessy (1977, p. 67))

(26)   We arrived on top of a flat hill kind of.
                    (12 yrs, Handscombe (1967, p. 56))

(27)   In the morning they both went out, the two eldest.
                    (11 yrs, Burgess *et al.*, (1973, p. 124))

(28)   The skin has got like pimples on.
                    (11 yrs, Rosen and Rosen (1973, p. 134))

So there is nothing inherent in these constructions which prohibits their use in writing; rather, children have learnt, highly successfully, that they are not a normal part of the written language. they can only have learnt this from the reading they do, and from the stories that they have had read to them. This means that, as young as eight (almost as soon as they can write independently), children are differentiating the written from the spoken language and are not simply writing down what they would say.

There are a number of reasons why we may not always be aware, perhaps, of the amount of learning that is involved in children's avoidance of these constructions in their writing. first, it is a negative virtue to leave something erroneous out — we are more conscious of errors that are present than of signs of learning marked only by absence. Secondly, as adults we are so used to written language that we think it is somehow 'natural' that these constructions do not occur; whereas, in fact, such knowledge can be acquired only through considerable exposure to written language. And thirdly, we are probably not aware of how frequent these constructions are in speech: they rarely feature in grammatical descriptions and when they do get mentioned it may be in disparaging terms, as if they are errors of some kind.

Constructions typical of written language

We can now consider the written texts in the corpus, because the other side of the differentiation coin is children's use in their writing of constructions that occur rarely or never in their speech. There are two main reasons why writers use structures that are uncommon in speech: first, they are able to use psycholinguistically complex constructions because, unlike speakers, they have plenty of planning time; speakers who spend too long planning their utterances tend to be interrupted and to lose their speaking turn altogether. Also, writers can pause in the middle of a construction without losing their way because the first part is already safely trapped on the page and can be re-read as often as necessary. (However, re-reading while writing is a skill that has to be learned. Research by Graves (1979, pp. 312–19) shows that beginning writers do not take advantage of the physical presence of their chosen words but rather compose additively, one word or phrase at a time, often with disjointed results. So it is not surprising that some of the more demanding constructions, which will probably require the young writer to re-read while composing, do not appear with any frequency in children's writing until the age of ten or 12.)

The second reason for the occurrence of specifically literary constructions in writing is that writers have a need for grammatical varitey. This necessity arises from one of the most fundamental differences between speech and writing — the fact that writing cannot convey the expressive features of the spoken voice. Speakers can very their rate, volume, pitch height, rhythm and intonation patterns, partly to relieve their speech of monotony but also to place emphasis appropriately on the important parts of the message. Because writers have none of this variety available, repetitive grammatical patterns are more noticeable and more boring in writing than they are in speech. So, to achieve a pleasing style, writers have to vary their grammatical constructions. Writers also need to manipulate grammatical structure in order to get the emphasis in the right place. It is possible to indicate emphasis in writing by underlining or capitalisation but such devices are not approved of in formal styles and, interestingly, none of the children used them.

Another difference between speech and writing is that writing is, on the whole, more formal than speech. We have already seen that children reveal an early awareness of this by their avoidance of informal constructions in writing. In addition, a few of the older children in the sample use in their writing some notably formal constructions that do not occur at all in their speech at this age, e.g.

(29) When one person had finished he sent for the next one, *and so on*.
(Huw, 10)

(30) We used blocks to make a fridge, beds *etc.*
(Stuart, 12)

These examples seem to be formal equivalents of the vague completers used in speech. In his spoken account, Stuart uses a vague completer for a similar purpose:

(31)   we . . . 'put in 'pieces of 'légo/ for 'different óbjects/ 'like a frídge or something/

$\qquad$ (Stuart (12); IV, 26)

His selection of 'etc.' in writing, rather than 'or something', shows a sensitivity to the different requirements of the two modes. In (32), Peter, aged 12, attempts an appositive noun phrase:

(32)   We had the test in the Library and we (Alan and Stewart) made a house.

In speech, such an idea may well be expressed by an amplificatory noun phrase, tagged on at the end of the sentence: 'we made a house — Alan and Stewart and me'. It is apparent that Peter does not get the formal construction quite right; in his brackets he should have written 'Alan and Stewart and I' but, of course, mistakes are especially likely to occur in a construction that is new to the user and still in process of being acquired. Such errors can be seen as a sign of growth.

One aspect of the formality of writing is the tendency to make the links between ideas more explicit than would be necessary in speech. Sharon demonstrates this with her use of 'for instance':

(33)   We kept adding different ideas, for instance, kitchen windows, gates, trees, doors.

$\qquad$ (Sharon, 10)

In speech, such specification is often simply added, without any overt indicator of the relationship. Sharon's friend, Janet, provides an example of the typically implicit spoken form as they play with the Lego together:

(34)   well 'you got some 'funny idéas gátes/shútters/

$\qquad$ (Janet (10); III, 242)

Another type of linguistic formality is illustrated by ten-year-old Richard in a letter about his Lego construction:

(35)   If you meet an architect interested in our farm we would willingly give him or her the plans.

He shows here that he can use the singular pronoun after a non-specific singular noun. That this is a rather formal construction is apparent from the fact that, colloquially, many adults would use the plural 'them' instead: 'we would willingly give them the plans'. In addition, Richard seems surprisingly mature in being aware that if he had used generic 'he' and written 'we would willingly give him the plans', he could have been accused of sexism.

As well as being more formal than speech, writing also tends to be less redundant. One of the grammatical ways in which redundancy is decreased is by the use of non-finite rather than finite subordinate clauses. There are some types of clause that are normally non-finite, even in speech — for example, adverbial clauses of purpose (such as 'he went home to rest'). But most non-finite adverbial clauses are more typical of written than spoken language, e.g.

(36)   After constructing the kitchen I started on the car.

(Janet, 10)

(37)   Janet had the most amusing idea of building a multi-coloured wall, first of all using red, then blue, then yellow.

(Sharon, 10)

The finite version of the adverbial in (36) would be:

(38)   After I had constructed the kitchen I started on the car.

Similarly, non-finite relative clauses are generally more common in writing than in speech. Examples (39) to (41) show how some of the children use them in writing:

(39)   I was one of the children chosen to take part in the project.

(Siân, 10)

(40)   We made the windmill out of ten Lego bricks piled on top of each other.

(Ann-Marie, 12)

(41)   Amanda's house had one little person walking up to the front door.

(Heidi, 12)

The more redundant, more speech-like version of (39), for example, would be:

(42)   I was one of the children who were chosen to take part in the project.

In the corpus studied there were approximately twice as many of these two non-finite constructions in the children's writing as in their speech. The figures are given in Table 7.2. The difference between the two modes is much more marked in the 12-year-olds than in the two younger age-groups, suggesting that the children are becoming increasingly aware that lower redundancy is preferable in written style and are acquiring the grammatical means that enable them to achieve it.

We know that writing lacks the intonation features of speech. An important function of intonation is to signal the focus of information in a clause. The unmarked position for the focus is the end of the clause, where we most often put those parts of the message that are either new or important, or both. However, any part of the clause can be made prominent by the speaker; but the writer, in contrast, generally had to make sure that the focus of information coincides with the end of the clause. If the normal clause order of subject, verb and complementation will not achieve end-focus, then there are grammatical devices the writer can use. One is to move a normally final-place adverbial to the front of the sentence, as in (43) and (44):

(43)   On top there was a chimney.

(Gary, 8)

(44)   Outside the garden I put a little bus-stop sign.

(Kathryn, 10)

For Kathryn, in (44), 'the little bus-stop sign' is the most important part of the sentence. If, more prosaically, she had written, 'I put a little bus-stop sign outside the garden', it would have been hidden in the middle of the sentence and would have lost its prominence. In example (45), there are two kinds of word-order alteration:

(45)   By the side of it we put a bus-stop where stood two children.

(Siân, 12)

Speech		Writing	
8 yrs. (no. of words = 3010)	0.10 (3)	8 yrs (No. of words = 1414)	0.14 (2)
10 yrs. (No. of words = 3926)	0.31 (12)	10 yrs (No. of words = 2677)	0.45 (12)
12 yrs. (No. of words = 3768)	0.24 (9)	12 yrs. (No. of words = 3348)	0.60 (20)

Table 7.2 Redundancy-reducing constructions in children's speech and writing (occurrence per hundred words, with number of instances in brackets)

In the first clause there is another instance of adverbial fronting, which allows the focus to fall on the new information, 'a bus-stop'; and in the second clause the verb is fronted, causing the subject, 'two children', to occur, unusually, at the end of the sentence. The result is rather awkward but it does show that Siân is striving to achieve effects which she knows can be obtained.

For writers, then, the last position in the clause is the most salient. The next most important position is the beginning. The first element in the clause, the point of departure for the utterance, is called by many grammarians, including Quirk *et al.* (1972, p. 945), the 'theme'. The skilful handling of successive themes is essential in writing because a major way in which written and spoken language differ is that the writer, unlike the speaker, has to produce a sustained, coherent discourse, without help or intervention from a conversational partner. This means that sentences have to have a structure which is not only internally consistent but which also links smoothly with the preceding text. The theme generally expresses given information — information that has already been introduced. If new material keeps appearing at the beginning of the clauses, the result is a very jerky disjointed passage which is uncomfortable to read. So, being able to maintain thematic continuity is a necessary skill for a writer. Examples (46) and (47) show these young writes using unusual grammatical constructions in order to maintain continuity. Kathryn links the second sentence in (46) to the first by taking up the theme of the garden:

(46)   While Louise and Rachael built the bungalow, I made a start on the garden. In the garden were two trees and around the garden I placed a fence.

(Kathryn, 10)

If she had written 'two trees were in the garden', she would have had new material at the beginning of the clause, and given material at the end — the reverse of the pattern she needs. By using adverbial fronting, she is able to achieve thematic continuity and appropriate end-focus at the same time. In example (47) Stuart clearly wants 'we' to be the theme of his second sentence (taking up the idea of 'two other boys and myself' from the first):

(47)   Last Monday the 3rd two other boys and myself did a test for the Polytechnic of Wales, building with lego bricks. We were given a choice, we could either build a small individual thing ourselves or build one big thing all together.

(Stuart, 12)

To achieve his chosen theme, he uses a passive verb phrase: 'we were given the choice'. If he had used the active verb phrase which would be more likely in speech, he would have had to write something like 'A man called Mr Perkins gave us a choice', which would have introduced a new and unwanted theme.

On the whole, most of the children in the sample are very good at maintaining thematic continuity in their writing; but to show what can go wrong, here is the opening of one of the very few pieces that are less successful in this regard (each theme is italicised):

> (48) *The house* was big and *I* lived in it. but *the bridge* was big.
> *The gate and a door* was red and *the cars* were blue.
> *The dog and the pig* were pink.
>
> (Sharon, 89)

In six clauses each theme is new, with not one taking up an idea already mentioned. The stilted language this produces seems strangely reminiscent of some reading schemes.

A much more common problem occurs when thematic continuity is maintained by repeating the same theme over and over again. This gives thematic continuity without thematic variety, for example:

> (49) *I* made a garden with flowers in it. *I* did a fence.
> *I* was going to do a bus stop. *I* did a table outside and a chair. *I* put a cake on the table. *I* put an egg on the table.
>
> (Jennifer, 8)

Such repetition of a pronominal theme is common and unremarkable in speech:

> (50) wéll/ we de'cided 'first of áll/ to 'do the hòuse/ 'so we 'started to 'build the hóuse/ and we 'thought we'd 'make a 'little gárden/to go wíth it/ and we 'thought we'd 'have some péople/
>
> (Sheryl (10); III, 289)

However, to be succesful, a writer has to create thematic variety while maintaining thematic continuity and getting the focus in the right place. At (51) and (52) there are examples which suggest that their writers might be aware of the need for thematic variety.

> (51) We used blocks to make a fridge, beds etc. We then built the roof which was flat. We then put a fence round and put a tree and flowers and made a garden. *A bus stop* was put outside.
>
> (Stuart, 12)

> (52) We built the house because it was very simple and we had a lot of bricks to build it with. *Around the house* we put a fence and three gates in it. We built a bus stop outside the house with three people waiting for a bus. *Inside the fence* we put two trees.
>
> (Sarah, 12)

Stuart has used 'we' three times and then starts the fourth sentence with 'a bus stop'. This is not entirely successful since it sounds rather clumsy; and, being new information, 'a bus stop' really needs to go later in the clause. But if Stuart had not used the passive and had written instead 'we put a bus stop outside', he would have repeated 'we' for the fourth time. His choice of an unusual construction indicates perhaps that he is becoming sensitive to some aspects of the overall structure of a piece of writing. Sarah, in (52), manages rather better by using fronted place adverbials. 'Around the house' and 'inside the fence' both take up ideas already mentioned so thematic continuity is maintained. If she had used normal sentence order, all five main clauses in this extract would have begun with *we*. Some of the older writers in the sample show that they are able to sustain both thematic continuity and thematic variety over several sentences, for example:

(53) In the Lego boxes there were hundreds of different pieces. Some had only one hole. Others went up to twelve. They had arch shapes, straight lines and some had a circle shape. Nearly everything was used to make our mansion.

(Ann-Marie, 12)

From examples (43) to (53), it is apparent that end focus, thematic continuity and thematic variety are interrelated. So when an unusual construction, such as adverbial fronting, is used, it is rarely possible to associate it definitively with just one of the three stylistic factors. Adult writers use a number of grammatical constructions to achieve focus, continuity and variety. (A description is given in Perera 1984, Chapters 4 and 5.) In this corpus of data, there are three that seem to be being used by the children for these stylistic purposes, though it is important to stress that there is no suggestion that the children are consciously aware either of the effects or of the means they use to achieve them. The three discourse-structuring constructions they use are passive verb phrases, fronted place adverbials and reordered clause constituents. Although these constructions do occur in their speech, they are much less common than in their writing; the figures are given in Table 7.3.

Speech		Writing	
8 yrs.	0.17	8 yrs.	0.28
(No. of words	(5)	(No. of words	(4)
= 3010)		= 1414)	
10 yrs.	0.23	10 yrs.	0.49
(No. of words	(9)	(No. of words	(13)
= 3926)		= 2677)	
12 yrs.	0.21	12 yrs.	1.11
(No. of words	(8)	(No. of words	(37)
= 3768)		= 3348)	

Table 7.3 Discourse-structuring constructions in children's speech and writing (occurrence per hundred words, with number of instances in brackets)

The figures for speech do not alter very much between the ages of eight and 12, whereas for writing they increase considerably from eight to ten and more than double between ten and 12. This suggests that by the age of 12, at least some children are becoming aware of the grammatical resources they can exploit in their writing. Some of the children make errors in using the literary constructions; this underlines the fact that these new forms are still in the process of being acquired. For example, the repetition of the adverbials in (54) and (55) indicates a certain lack of faith in the fronted versions:

(54) And in the garden I put little seeds in it.

              (Nicola, 8)

(55) In the front of it we put a tree there.

              (Siân, 12)

The figures in Tables 7.2 and 7.3 give the occurence of typically written constructions across whole age-groups. Like this, it is not possible to see how far they reflect typical usage for the group and how far they derive from just a few exceptional subjects. Therefore, Table 7.4 shows how many children out of the 16 in each age group are using in their writing the three main types of literary construction that have been described.

	8-year-olds	10-years-olds	12-year-olds
'Formal' constructions	0	3	3
Redundancy-reducing constructions	2	7	7
Discourse-structuring constructions	4	8	11

Table 7.4 Number of children in each age-group using literary constructions in writing

The figures show there is an increase, with age, in the number of children using the constructions, not just in the number of constructions being used.

It is necessary to emphasise that there is no intrinsic merit in the constructions that have been illustrated: they are valuable only in so far as they enable writers to express their intentions more clearly, concisely and elegantly than they could have done without them. Further, I do not believe there is any value in teachers setting exercises for children to make finite clauses non-finite, to move place adverbials to the fronts of sentences, or to turn active sentences into passives. The use of these constructions will be learned most naturally by reading, and by drafting and redrafting sustained pieces of writing.

We know that for a written text to be successful it is necessary for there to be links between sentences. But such links alone are not sufficient. It is possible to make up pseudo-discourses where each sentence is linked impeccably to the preceding one and yet there is a lack of global coherence. Writers have to impose an overall pattern of organisation on their work as well as taking care of local connections between sentences. (There is some evidence (Atwell 1981) that global coherence is harder to achieve.) The global structure may be chronological, spatial, logical or a combination of these. It is well known that the chronological pattern is by far the easiest and is the one that young writers use most often. Many of the children in the sample organise their account of making a Lego construction in a chronological way. Table 7.5 lists the time adverbials that they use as one means of achieving this overall structural coherence. The most striking thing is the much greater variety of adverbials in the written accounts. In speech they often sequence their actions simply with 'and' or 'then', e.g.

	Speech			Writing		
	8 yrs	10 yrs	12 yrs	8 yrs	10 yrs	12 yrs
then	+	+	+	+	+	+
when + finite clause	+	+		+	+	+
first		+	+	+	+	+
first of all		+	+	+	+	+
at/in the end			+		+	+
after + finite clause				+	+	+
after that				+	+	+
after + NP					+	
soon				+		
at the start				+		
last of all				+		
secondly					+	
next					+	
sometimes					+	
in time					+	
at the time					+	
straight away					+	
to begin with					+	
while + finite clause					+	
after + non-finite clause					+	
in the beginning						+
afterwards						+
eventually						+
finally						+
at last						+
on the third go						+
before + finite clause						+
once + finite clause						+

Table 7.5 Time adverbials in children's speech and writing

(56)   well we 'started to make the hóuse/ then we 'thought that it would
'be a bit big/ . . . 'then we 'started just to 'build thàt bit/ the 'little hóuse/
and 'then we all thought 'well we 'might as well 'put a gàrage there/ on
the sìde/ and 'then we 'found all the féncing/ so we de'cided to have the
fénce/ and the trées/ and 'then we had the dóor/

(Suzanne (12); IV, 207)

There are written accounts rather like that from some of the
eight-year-olds but generally the ten- and 12-year-olds use a wider
range of structuring devices. Again, there seems to be a realisation
among the older children that special effort is needed to establish a
coherent written text.

I have already suggested that we may not notice that children are
editing oral constructions out of their writing. Similarly, we may not be
aware that they are using in their writing constructions that they rarely
use orally. The reason for this is chiefly that they are such simple
constructions that educated adults probably use many of them in
spontaneous speech. But it seems fair to hypothesise the it is the
pressure writing imposes to produce an extended, coherent piece of
language that forces children to start experimenting with these
constructions. As the new forms of language become more familiar, and
as a widening range of speech situations present themselves, then young
people may extend their oral repertoire by 'borrowing' some of their
newly-acquired literary constructions when the need for them arises.

This small-scale study has shown that even though the language of
children's writing at the age of 12 may still seem simple and speech-like
to adults, the fact is that it is not really like children's speech at all.

Conclusion

Finally we can consider the implications of this reseach for the teaching
of writing. Being aware that children are doing something different in
writing from speech may alert teachers to signs of development:
instances of constructions that show a sensitivity to discourse structure,
for example, may gleam through a piece that is badly written, poorly
punctuated and atrociously spelt — and provide encouraging evidence
that something is being learnt. Such awareness will allow teachers to
make a differential response to errors — treating differently those that
arise from haste or carelessness and that those suggest the writer is
trying out a new construction but has not got it right yet.

The fact that some of the grammatical developments in writing seem
to arise from the need to structure a discourse coherently points to the
importance of encouraging children to write continuous passages from
an early age. Writing one-sentence responses to questions will not

provide the stimulus necessary to develop these constructions. As children generally do not use many of the more typically written constructions in their speech, it follows that they need to learn them by reading extensively. It also highlights the value of the teacher reading aloud to the class, throughout the junior years and beyond, because, in this way, children are able to absorb structures of sentence and discourse organisation from written material that would be too difficult for them to read themselves. This is particularly important for weaker readers. If their only experience of written language comes from the rather stilted prose of remedial reading schemes, then it is no wonder that their own writing is flat and dull.

We know that different types of writing have different patterns of organisation: that narratives are structurally different from descriptions, and so on. Therefore, it follows that children need to read and hear read not only stories but also as wide a range as possible of non-fiction, so that they have developed a feel for the necessary linguistic constructions before they are required to use them in their own writing.

Finally, at an International Writing Convention, I know it is not necessary to make a case for writing — but elsewhere there are people who argue that with the advent of telephones and tape-recorders the need for writing has greatly diminished. Quite apart from the practical disadvantages of dependence of such machines, I believe that the argument is seriously flawed. Writing is not merely a way of recording speech, a kind of inefficient tape-recorder, but a different form of language in its own right which can lead to different ways of thinking. Because written language provides different opportunities from speech and imposes different requirements, it forces the writer to use language in different ways. These different experiences of language are then available to be fed back into speech. So, for some children at any rate, writing is not just a reflection or a record of their oral competence but is also an important agent in their language development. This suggests that it is dangerous to adopt a narrowly functional approach to the teaching of writing. Even if, as adults, we are to do no more writing than signing our Christmas cards, learning to write fluently and extensively would still be important because of its influence on both language and thinking.

Bibliography

Atwell, M.A. (1981).   'The Evolution of Text: the Interrelationship of Reading and Writing in the Composing Process'. Ed. D. thesis, Indiana University.

Burgess, C. *et al.* (1973). *Understanging Children Writing.* Harmondsworth, Penguin.

Dines, E. (1979). 'Variation in Discourse — and stuff like that', *Language in Society*, vol. 8.

Fawcett, R. and Perkins, M. (1980). *Child Language Transcripts 6–12*, vols. II–IV. Pontypridd, Polytechnic of Wales.

Graves, D.H. (1979). 'What Children Show Us about Revision', *Language Arts*, vol. 56.

Handscombe, R.J. (1967). 'The Written Language of Eleven- and Twelve-year-old Children'. Nuffield foreign languages teaching materials project, reports and occasional papers, no. 25. The Nuffield Foundation.

O'Donnell, R.C., Griffin, W.J. and Norris, R.C. (1967). *Syntax of Kindergarten and Elementary School Children: A Transformational Analysis.* Champaign, IL National Council of Teachers of English.

Perera, K. (1984). *Children's Writing and Reading.* Oxford, Blackwell.

Perera, K. (forthcoming). 'Language Acquisition and Writing' in Fletcher, P. and Garman, M. *Language Acquisition* (2nd edn). Cambridge, Cambridge University Press.

Quirk, R., Greenbaum, S., Leech, G.N. and Svartvik, J. (1972). *A Grammar of Contemporary English.* London, Longman.

Rosen, C. and Rosen, H. (1973). *The Language of Primary School Children.* Harmondsworth, Penguin.

Scott, C.M. (1983). 'You know and all that stuff: acquisition in school children'. Paper presented at ASHA Convention, Cincinnati.

Shaughnessy, M.P. (1977). *Errors and Expectations: A Guide for the Teacher of Basic Writing.* New York, Oxford University Press.

8

From Speech to Writing: Some Evidence on the Relationship Between Oracy and Literacy

GORDON WELLS and GEN LING CHANG

The focus of the present study was not originally on writing or on the relationship between written and spoken language. It grew instead out of a more general longitudinal investigation of language development and of the relationship between language and educational achievement, in which a representative sample of 32 children was followed from the age of 15 months until the last year of their primary schooling (see Wells (1981; forthcoming) for details). However, during the course of the study, a variety of samples of speech and writing were collected and in the most recent phase of the research we have begun to look at some of these in more detail.

At the last assessment, which was made when the children were aged 10 years 3 months, we asked each of them to carry out a number of tasks in speech and writing. Amongst the writing tasks there were two in a narrative genre: to write a personal narrative with the title 'The Happiest Day in my Life', and to make up a story to fit a cartoon showning a hunter with his dog, brought to bay at the edge of a cliff by a motley collection of animals. Amongst the spoken tasks there was one that was roughly comparable to the first of the written tasks: in the course of an interview, each child was asked to describe a typical school day. It is the samples of speech and writing that were produced in response to these narrative tasks that will form the subject-matter of this paper.

At the stage when we had been investigating the factors that were most influential in accounting for educational attainment at the end of the primary stage of education (Wells, *et al.* 1984), we had made a holistic assessment of the spoken and written texts, task by task. Five people had independently ranked all the texts (from which the writers' names had been removed) for each task and then a final rank order had been arrived at by consensus decision. While we were engaged in this task, we had become aware of a number of other questions that were raised by our procedure and by the material that we were assessing. In the present study, therefore, we decided to reexamine the narrative texts in order to find out:

What are the characteristics that were most influential in accounting for the order in which the texts were ranked?

What is the relationship between the spoken and written texts produced by individual children and how do the processes of production in the two modes differ?

Are the qualitative differences between texts that had allowed us to rank the children from most to least successful as speakers and as writers merely the result of individual differences, or do they represent different stages in common sequences of development in the two modes?

The strategy that we actually followed was to look first at the written texts in order to attempt to answer the first and the third questions with respect to writing. The spoken texts were then considered in a similar manner. Finally, the two sets were compared in order to attempt an answer to the second question. The same sequence will be followed in this paper.

Analysing the written texts

Considering of our writing samples led us to adopt a model with four dimensions, each subsuming a number of further categories as shown in Figure 8.1.

Substance
Handwriting, spelling, punctuation

Form
Vocabulary, grammar

Producer   Surface text

Content
Ideation. Affective/moral stance

Rhetorical Goals
Awareness of reader. Overall purpose

Figure 8.1   Model for the analysis of children's written texts

Before moving to a consideration of some of the actual texts, a few comments about the model as a whole are required. First, although designed for the analysis of finished products, it is clear that, as one moves through the model from 'substance' to 'rhetorical goals', the categories become progressively more process-orientated. However, we feel justified in claiming that it is not only think-aloud protocols but also the resulting written texts that can provide evidence concerning the processes involved in written production.

Secondly, we must express some hesitation about the allocation of the categories to the four main dimensions. Selections from the resources of vocabulary and grammar, for example, operate together at the level of form to express the content that the writer chooses to communicate. About the appropriate location for punctuation, however, we must acknowledge some uncertainty. Like intonation, to which it partially corresponds, it is not clear whether it should not more properly be put under 'form' than under 'substance'. The justification for including it under the latter, together with spelling and handwriting is that, in its realisation as a set of conventional symbols, it is specific to the graphic medium in very much the same way as spelling.

A further point that we wish to emphasise is that we do not conceive of these dimensions as prescribing a temporal sequence (from bottom to top) through which writing should proceed. Still less do we believe that writers actually follow such a sequence. How a writer starts is likely to vary from one writer to another and from one occasion to another and so is the distribution of the writer's attention as the task proceeds. Problems can arise at every level, as is suggested by the points at which writers pause with concentrated attention and by the revisions that they sometimes make before proceeding. More of the young writer's attention must undoubtedly be given to the dimensions of substance and form than is the case with expert writers, but we should assume that, like the expert, he or she moves between all the dimensions as the demands of the developing text require.   However, what distinguishes the young writer from the expert is the constraints that problems on one dimension may place upon successful operation at the others. Uncertainty about the correct spelling of a particular word, for example, can lead to the selection of an 'easier' alternative and the trains of thought called up by the word chosen can have repercussions on every other dimension. To some extent, of course, such constraints may be instructionally induced: if correct spelling is not made an issue, for example, the need to restrict oneself to words that one can spell disappears.

Finally, a point about ideation. For the texts that we are about to consider, ideation can be thought of as being concerned chiefly with narrative structure and the generation of appropriate content to fit the overall plan for the story — to the extent that such a plan is being developed. Included here also are characterisation and other devices that enrich the story beyond the bare skeleton. With othe genres of writing, other structures would be required, but these will not concern us here. It is worth noting, however, that for young writers there is a major difference between the narrative genre and almost all others in that, for most children, the basic narrative structure is already familiar from their experience of having stories told or read to them and from their own reading and is therefore fairly readily available when they come to write. In most other genres, by contrast, the appropriate structure has to be created as part of the act of writing. It is probably for this reason that most children write more easily and at greater length when composing a narrative than they do when working in any other genre.

The evidence from the narrative samples

Let us start with Rosie, to see what is achieved by the lowest ranked of our 32 writers. (Ranks on the spoken and written tasks are based on holistic assessments from the previous phase of the research, p. 110 above).

> once upon a time there is a giraffe
> in the jungle and there is a snax
> in the jungle but there is a elephant
> in the jungle The Ebb

The intention to write a story is signalled by the opening phrase, 'once upon a time' and, although brief, her story has a conventional closing in 'the end'. Beyond that, however, there is little that could be called a narrative, as she does not get beyond the introduction of some of the protagonists, using the simple active affirmative declarative form to state their location. There is some attempt at variation in the linking, '*but there is a elephant*', but the significance of this, if any, never becomes apparent.

In this sample Rosie's spelling is conventional, but this can be attributed to the fact that most of the words were spelled on the picture provided. Her account of 'The Happiest Day' is less successful from this point of view, showing that, without support, she has not yet reached the stage of phonetic spelling, ('Boon' for 'book', 'fat' for 'for'), nor is she fully consistent, as she spells 'Christmas' without an 'r' on the second occasion. Neither piece has any punctuation and the handwriting is very immature, with some letters poorly formed and the spacing irregular.

> at christmas my mum bought
> me a bice at chistmas my mum
> bought me a wireless
> and a colouring Boon

There are achievements, but it would appear that the labour involved in the very act of writing (her letter formation suggests that she has great

difficulty in the creation of recognisably conventional graphic substance), means that she can give very little attention to the selection and
shaping of material in order to meet a higher level goal.

Let us now turn to Jason.

One day a hunter was hunting
for lioms and he whet into
The jungle. He was being chased
buy a rhino and a lion and monkeys
snakes, elephant, bird and tortoises
The hunter shouted help. The
hunter fired a pule but it was
sud with blags. The hunter game
to a died end so the hunter
jumpd off the cliff. We
dont no woaat hapend to the
hunter

Jason's story contains a number of events, all relating to the principal
character, the hunter. There is also a brief introduction and a form of
resolution: 'We don't know what happened to the hunter'. This does not
add up to a very satisfactory story but, compared with Rosie's attempt,
this is considerably more mature, with some variety in the sentence
structure (for example, 'He was being chased') and a linking with 'and
so'. In his 'Happiest Day' we find the same characteristics and, in
addition, an explicit attempt to explain why he was happy: 'because I can
do jumps on it (the bike)'.

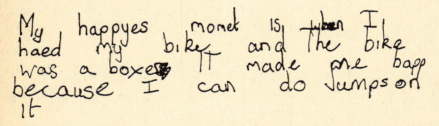

My happyes monet is, when I
haed my bike and the bike
was a boxe It made me bapp
because I can do Jumps on
it

However, the overriding impression is still of the difficulty that he
experiences with the written substance, indicated in his case by the
awkwardness of the handwriting and the number of crossings out. The
spelling, too, although more recognisably phonetic than Rosie's,
suggests that he has some difficulty in matching letters to sounds: 'The

hunter fired a pulet (bullet) but it was fuld with blags (blanks)'. The punctuation, on the other hand, shows that he is able to identify the major meaning boundaries and, in the Hunter story, all the sentences begin with a capital letter and most end with a full stop.

The following story, by Nancy, was ranked only one higher than Jasons, yet it is in many ways very much superior.

> One hot afternow Professor forget-Me-Not set of on a long long long larny frow the jungle. He tack his rifall got on his elephant an set of frow the Afreky Jungle. Afte one nite and one day he came two a spout where he cond make camp as he was camping on top of the clift a grop of anemals came along and fietad Professor forget-Me-Nots dog bones at thiss he ran up two the clift pratale nocking the Professor of the clift. The anemals became fens with the Professor and his dog bones the name the animals Jombow the elephant and wochout the Draft and hisn the snake and Toby Lefbehid. Shell and hard-shell the tortoises and beeky and mij the Baird and Gody the lion, and warm rine the rhinocero.
>
> The elephant Jombow taken the professor and his dog aroad the Jugell he take spesamins of places and fings like hat after a muthe with them he had two go back two england two his famle but he did not want two go bake without them. So he said will you come back two england So they agreed two go with him.

Apart from the digression in which the animals are named — and even this adds a humorous flavour — there is a clear story line with the events in the later part clearly motivated by those that precede. There is also a satisfying resolution. Sentence structure is varied and anaphoric pronouns are used appropriately.

Nancy's 'Happiest Day' (not quoted in full) shows some of the same achievements. It starts well: 'On Saturday 22th May 19.82 Was the day two rember in my Famly for it was my sister's weding two be marid two Richard.' In what follows, there is a tendency for the 'and then' strategy to take over, but there is considerable detail, as in the following sentences: 'When we got home we had a samwig two eat then we had a wosh and cleed are teeth then we got chage When we got down stern's the driver of the car was wateing for us so we went strate in two the car and two the chaner (church)'.

Both pieces, in fact, make quite interesting reading. So why was Nancy ranked so low? there can be no certainty about the answer but a probable explanation is to be found in the spelling. Both pieces are relatively long and quite neatly and legibly printed. They are only difficult to read if one is put off by the unconventionality of the spelling. This is certainly a constraint as far as the reader is concerned although, judging by the length and fluency of both pieces, the writer did not find this a problem. However, in the context of an assessment of educational attainment it is perhaps not surprising that such unconventional spelling was judged to be a serious flaw.

The next piece was one of the longest we received and it illustrates why teachers so often equate length with quality, particularly in the early stages.

The Angry Animals

Once there was an old scientist he was walking through Jungle When he thought about how he was going to get back he could not remember the way he came. Neither could the dog. 'I thought a dog was a mans best friend' said the old scientist. So they were lost. Soon it got very dark So they spent the night uner a tree. The next morning he and dog were very hungry and they saw the monkeys eating bananas the lions eating meat would be very nice cooked. The elephants drinking cool clean freash water from the river. everywhere they looked they saw animals eating things It made him feel very hungry indeed so he frightened all the elephants away from the river with his shot gun firing It into the air the dog chased them away as well. He pinched the meat from the lion that Made him very Angry so he chased him the old scientist ran and ran as fast as his legs could carry him he ran so fast that he lost the lion running through the long grass. He pinched the bananas from the monkeys that made them so mad they started running up and down the trees jumping and swinging on the branches and also screaming there heads off it was so loud and it made a terrible racket. He had pinched all the food and drink that he had seen. The dog and the scientist lit a fire And made a cosy bed of long grass and had a magnificent feast. All of the animals were so mad they crowded around the scientist and the dog and chased them to a cliff they got nearer and near 'Cant you do something dog' said the scientist 'you are usless' then the dog started barking the loudest he could and all the animals fled every where they wer safe. They found there way back and the scientist was very pleased 'Well maybe your not so useless after all' he said with a smile.

Greater length gives scope for a more interesting development of the topic. But what is impressive about this story is the clear evidence of planning. The animals' attack on the scientist andhis dog is a response to having their food stolen and the stealing of the food was prompted by the protagonists seeing the animals eating when they were themselves hungry which, in turn, was a consequence of their getting lost in the jungle. Samantha achieves a sustained narrative structure, with several well-developed episodes, all of which must have been planned, at least in outline, before she began to write. This is underlined by the second thread that runs through the story: the dog's initial failure to live up to its reputation as man's best friend and then its final vindication.

In addition to the overall effect, there are other achievements on all dimensions in the proposed descriptive model. The hunter is characterised as 'an old scientist' and it is his explicit response to his initial predicament which movitates the train of events that leads to the climax. The temporal sequence of events is clearly marked with such phrases as 'it got dark', 'the next morning'; causal links are similarly made explicit. Sentence structure is varied, and dependent and relative clauses are used to add detail and to convey the protagonist's thoughts, e.g. 'the lions eating meat *which would be very nice cooked*'. The choice of vocabulary goes beyond the obvious ('cool clean fresh water', 'cosy bed', 'magnificent feast') and there are a number of colloquial phrases, such as 'they were so mad that . . .', 'screaming their heads off' and 'a terrible racket', that add considerably to the evocation of the animals' angry response to the theft of their food.

Her 'Happiest Day' showed many of the same qualities.

> The happiest moment in my life is when I went to Majorca last year. We stayed in a little village called portals Nouse it was a quite village with a lovely beach on sunny days we used to walk along the road to the beach there was a restaurant & a Super market. We used to sit on the beach & every day a man used to come to the beach & throw Grapes at you he sold fruit & one day I had half of a pineapple. We went snorkelling & the water was so clear you could see the rocks & fish there were some pedilos and We Went out for a ride every day. The sun was shineing all the time and the food in the hotel was beautiful it was wondeful in Majorca.

Overall, the account is well structured. The moment is clearly situated — a holiday in a Majorcan village. A number of enjoyable activities are described with interesting details, such as the throwing of grapes, and the water being so clear that the rocks and fishes could be seen. The piece concludes with two more general statements and a summary that reiterates the main theme of a happy experience.

There are limitations in both pieces of writing, of course: an erratic use of punctuation and occasional unconventional spelling. But these are infelicities that might have been corrected on a re-reading, if there had been an opportunity. Certainly, these stories vindicate those who argue with Smith (1982) that, where 'composition' and 'transcription' are competing for attention, it is more important to concentrate first on solving problems of composition. Samantha's two pieces of writing were both ranked number five.

The final child to be considered is, in the opinion of most of the judges, already a competent writer. Consider, first, Jonathan's account of his happiest day.

The Happiest Moment of my Life

> The happiest moment of my life was as I bit into a rich, meaty cornish pasty after a day's weary travelling (at least that was what it seemed like) and a week's holiday of golden sands, ice creams and sun stretched out before me. We were camping on a quiet grassy hill, hill especially. I felt tha nothing could be better. I was right.

Jonathan was not unique amongst the children in the sample in showing an awareness of the reader through the use of 'asides' ('at least that was what is seemed like') but he was certainly unique in his ability to marshal his resources in a sustained manner to achieve a deliberate and concentrated effect. The achievements are too numerous to catalogue, but particularly worthy of attention is the construction of the first sentence, in which the moment of biting into the pasty is seen as a hilltop, from which the writer looks back down one side to the past, to the weary travelling, and forward down the other side to the pleasures stretched out before him. It is also notable that, as the title suggests, he does select a particular moment — that of the first bite into the pasty. Equally effective is the contrast between this long first sentence and the two short final ones.

His story of the hunter was equally short — too short in the opinion of at least one of the judges. But it too stands out as being distinctly and almost self-consciously literary in its conception.

> 'Where's the Ark?'
>   Noah twisted his fingers awkwardly behind his back as the animals stared at him.
>   'But how *can* you forget to build an ark?' asked the giraffe. 'I left a lovely field of juicy worms to come here' chirped a bird indignantly. 'I demand compensation!'
>   Meanwhile Noah was slowly walking backward, and eventually fell off the cliff. Luckily he fell on a wooden raft. 'Good old Noah!' yelled the animals, and dived on with him.

The story is indeed somewhat short and the author more than a little whimsical in his anachronistic interpretation of the cartoon. But neither of those signs of irreverence detracts from the achievements of the writing. Once again, it is sufficient to consider just the first two sentences. The sense of a predicament is achieved immediately through the phrase 'twisted his hands awkwardly behind his back' and, with 'the animals stared at him', a feeling of suspense is created, which is resolved in the unexpected question by the giraffe. In this same question, there is a different sort of sophistication in the use of italic script to represent the spoken emphasis on 'can'.

But the most interesting feature of the whole story is its inter-textuality — the assumption that the reader will recall the biblical story of Noah and understand the giraffe's incredulity that Noah should have forgotten to build an ark. For a ten-year-old to manage the literary allusion with such assurance is, in our opinion, an indication not only of his outstanding ability as a writer but also of the richness of his personal literary experience.

Some tentative generalizations about the development of narrative writing

Although the number of samples in the previous section is small, those that were considered are sufficient to demonstrate the very great range of ability that one finds amongst a representative group of ten-year-olds. What is more, even from these five children one gets a sense of a developmental progression, which is reinforced by examining the two types of narrative produced by all the 32 children. At the same time, however, one also gets a sense of diversity in the areas in which children demonstrate strengths and weaknesses. The tentative conclusion we would draw from this analysis, therefore, is that there is no simple linear sequence of development that is followed by all children. However, even if there is little support for a single linear sequence, it is still possible that within some or all of the categories that are associated with each of the dimensions, there is a developmental progression. On the basis of our analysis of these samples of writing we set out in Figure 8.2, for each of the categories identified in Figure 8.1, our best estimate as to what that progression is. Being based only on a relatively small cross-section of children writing in response to topics that they had not themselves proposed, the suggestion is extremely tentative. However, it will form the basis for a new longitudinal investigation that we are about to embark on, one of the aims of which is to put it to the test and either reject or modify and develop it.

The first of our initial questions we can answer with more confidence. What, we wanted to know, were the factors most influential in accounting for the order in which the samples of writing were ranked? The first approach we took to answering this question was quantitative in nature and focused on the level of form. However the results can be briefly stated. None of the measures of syntactic structure — length or complexity — was significantly correlated with the judges' rank order. Frequency of use of clauses of reported speech, on the other hand, was related to rank order on the accounts of both the 'Happiest Day' (written) and the 'School Day' (oral). An evaluation of vocabulary, in terms of the proportion of words selected that are relatively infrequently used, also showed a positive relationship between a greater use of less common words and the rank assigned to the text (Wells *et al.* 1984). Both positive results were tentatively interpreted as indicating that what the judges were responding to was not complexity or correctness of linguistic form *per se* but the selection from these resources to fulfil effectively the demands of the tasks.

RHETORICAL GOALS		CONTENT	
Overall Purpose	*Awareness of Reader*	*Affective/ Moral Structure*	*Ideation (Narrative Structure)*
Clear plan	Shows awareness of reader's state of knowledge	Implicit affective response	Two or more events in chronological sequence
Summarises		Explicit affective response	Beginning/ending
Evidence of intended effect	Explains		Causal links made explicit
	Asides to reader	Affective response motivates action	
Evaluates			Setting provided
		Empathy	Clear motivation of action
		Simple moral	
			Climax/ resolution
		Self-awareness	
			Characterisation
		Expresses ambivalence	
			Nested episodes
			Character drives plot

FORM			SUBSTANCE	
Grammar	*Vocabulary*	*Punctuation*	*Spelling*	*Handwriting*
Simple active declarative sentences	Basic vocabulary only	Marks major meaning boundaries	Salient sounds only	Idiosyncratic letter shapes
Varied sentences	Uses common modifiers	Periods and capitals at sentence boundaries	All sounds	Conventional letter shapes
Dependent clauses	Selects some less common verbs		Consonants correct	Spaces between words
Relative clauses	Uses adverbs	Question marks	Phonetically consistent	Upper and lower case used appropriately
Pronominal cohesion	Selects verbs with manner component	Exclamation marks	Mainly conventional	Prints legibly
Clausal cohesion	Varied and effective selection of vocabulary	Quotation marks	Accurate except for occasional errors	Cursive writing
Concord of tenses		Commas		
Controls choice of sentence type for effect		Paragraphing		

Figure 8.2　Observed progression in the development of children's narrative writing
Note: The progression is to be read as occurring from top to bottom within categories.

This interpretation was confirmed by the qualitative examination of the narrative texts described above, from which it was clear that it was the effectiveness with which the children had written a narrative that best predicted the rankings assigned by the judges. Control of linguistic form contributed to this judgement — appropriate use of tenses and temporal adverbials to relate the events within the narrative, the use of cohesion to achieve coherence without simple repetition and the selection of vocabularly items that particularised events, characters and their motives and feelings. But it was the extent to which the children managed the dimensions of ideation and rhetorical goals to which the greatest weight was given.

Few of the children showed evidence of deliberately attempting to achieve a rhetorical goal other than that of writing a narrative of the kind specified by the task. Jonathan was an obvious exception and there were one or two others who introduced humour, often through asides to the reader. There was also relatively little evidence of an affective or moral stance to the content of the narratives, although most of the children were able to convey their response to the events that made up their happiest day, either explicitly or implicitly through what they chose to write about. In the story of the hunter, too, quite a high proportion described their protagonist's response to his predicament and, in some of the more effective stories, this response motivated much of the subsequent action.

However, the description of the protagonist's response to his situation brings us to a consideration of narrative structure, of which, according to Mandler and Johnson (1977, p.119), it is an essential component.

> The essential structure of a single episode story is that a protagonist is introduced in the setting, there follows an episode in which something happens, causing the protagonist to respond to it, which in turn brings about some event or state of affairs that ends the episode. The simplest story must have at least four propositions, representing a setting, beginning, development, and ending, if it is to be considered a story.

Kroll, who was the originator of the narrative tasks used in this study, applied a story-grammar analysis to the samples of writing produced by a group of nine-year-old children from the Bristol study and reported that this approach failed to discriminate adequately between the stories he examined (Kroll and Anson 1983). In the present investigation, however, with a less complicated version of the model, we found a good fit between management of the narrative structure and the judges' rankings. This was particularly true in the case of the Hunter story, less so in the account of the 'Happiest Day'. In the former, the minimum four-part narrative structure was used by 24 of the 32 children and 21 of these were assigned ranks between 1 and 23. Quite a number of children went beyond the minimum of one episode and either recounted a sequence of related episodes leading to a climax and resolution (Samantha) or, in a few cases, nested one episode inside another. These children were, in general, judged to have written more successful stories.

Other features of narrative structure that were noted in the stories of those children judged to be more successful were:

- an extended description of the setting, using clearly visualized detail, e.g. 'It was a plesant day in North Africa. Filthy Menasty was making another trap to capture wild animals. He was doing this to make the biggest zoo in the whole world' (Tony).

- the use of reported speech and, in some cases, sustained dialogue (Jonathan).

- characterisation, either through a description of the externally apparent features of the protagonist (Nancy) or through revealing the protagonist's inner state (Samantha, Jonathan).

- making one or other of the forms characterisation motivate the events of the story (Samantha, Jonathan).

Significantly, six of the eight most higly ranked Hunter stories displayed this last feature, together with one or more of the others. In sum, at least as far as the five judges were concerned, it was the ability to plan and compose an interesting and well-constructed story, as evidence by the final product, that was the most important criterion for success in narrative writing.

The relationship between speech and writing

The issue we wish to explore in this section was clearly posed more than a decade ago by Connie and Harold Rosen. As they put it: 'to understand what kinds of problems young children face when they write we have to work out in what ways speaking (which they do very well) and writing (which is new to them) differ' (1973, p. 267). What is clear is that, in moving between spoken and written language, the nature of the message itself changes, in response to the different purposes that the two linguistic modes usually serve and to the inter- and intera-personal contexts in which they are typically used. Writing is not simply speech written down.

Part of the problem that writers experience, as Olson (1977) and Bereiter and Scardamalia (1982a) have, from their different perspectives, made clear, is to be found in the different strategies for text production that are necessary when the support of a conversational partner is withdrawn. Under these conditions, the major responsibility for sustaining the flow and connectedness of the text is placed firmly on the producer. However, since sustained text production can occur in both speech and writing, the important comparison for our purposes is not that between writing and conversation but that between what we shall call written and oral 'monologue'. We should therefore look more closely at similarities and differences between texts produced in these two conditions. As a first step in this direction, we shall compare the spoken and written personal narratives produced by just four of the children we have already met.

First, the tasks. The written task has already been described: to write an account of 'My Happiest Day'. The oral task was embedded in an interview between the individual child and a member of the research team and was tape-recorded with the child's knowledge. The purpose of the interview was twofold: to obtain information about the child's home environment, as he or she perceived it, and about his impressions of school, and simultaneously to obtain a sample of the child's spontaneous speech. In all parts of the interview, the researcher encouraged the child to give extended answers and, once a question had been asked, support was reduced to a minimum level of attentive gaze and the occasional acknowledgement. In planning the interview, it was decided in advance to use the response to the request to describe a typical school day to provide the speech sample on which to base various measures of oral langauge ability.

However, the decision to use this sample of speech for the specific purpose of a direct comparison between oral and written narratives was not taken until after all the interviews had been carried out, by which time it was too late to attempt to match the tasks more closely. A different request, such as to describe the most frightening experience the child has ever had, for example, would have posed demands more similar to those of the written task. Nevertheless, despite the less than perfect match, there are sufficient similarities between the two tasks in their requirement that the child produce a sustained narrative mono-logue to justify making a comparison between the resulting oral and written texts.

Rosie's 'Happiest Day', it will be recalled, was extremely short, consisting of only two sentences with almost identical structure:

at christmas my mum bought me a bag
at christmas my mum bought me a wireless and a colouring book

There is no narrative structure and the relevance of the content to the title is left entirely implicit.

Her School Day, on the other hand, while shorter than most of the other children's, still contains considerably more information than her written text.

1   When I goes to school . . I either gets told off. or gets
2   smacked (laughs) . . . or sometimes I gets. picked on by all
3   the rest of them. or sometimes it's either me who's getting
4   – it's either – or it's either . . Sandy. the one who sits
5   next to me . . sometime Sandy. gets it . . . . .
6   I don't have dinners no more . . .
7   I used to get picked on. in this class . . . and when I used
8   to go up – when I used to go up – go somewhere for Miss.
9   I used to go – I used to go 'silly cow' . . 'cos I don't like
10   our teacher. I never like that teacher . .
11   Three – three time – three years I've been in that school . .
12   And then at home time we got to put our chairs up . .
13   And then when we gets at home we got to have – we either has
14   chips. what our ma cooks. or either. we goes up the shops
15   and then – we goes up the shops to get it.
16   And then we we g – we goes to – and when – and we goes to
17   bed. me and Donna used to play cards until our ma comes up . . .
18   Don't know what else to say.

(the lines are numbered for ease of reference. Periods mark pauses, with the number of periods corresponding to the number of seconds of noticeable silence. ' – ' indicates a false start.) As with her handwriting, Rosie's speech in this situation lacks fluency but, once the listener has overcome that problem, it is relatively easy to pick out the main episodes. From 12 onwards, these follow the chronological sequence of the day. The principle on which these episodes are selected for mention (with the possible exception of 12) seems to be their significance for the narrator, although this is, quite reasonably, not made explicit. They are clearly based on specific occasions but offered as instances of the sort of things that happen on a typical school day.

It is noticeable that none of the events mentioned is connected with the official purpose of schooling. Instead, in that part of the account where some mention of lessons might be expected, she gives her emotional response to her experience at school, with a quite explicit statement of her feelings about the teacher.

Viewed in terms of the model proposed for the description of writing, we might say that Rosie's achievements in this text include features at the level of ideation — explicit expression of affective response, action motivated by the response (9) and, at the level of rhetorical goals, an aside, motivated by awareness of the listener's needs (4–5). The constraints are a lack of fluency, an intermittent and only partial control of narrative structure and, most conspicuously, an apparent absence of

any overall plan. Nevertheless, compare with her written narrative, this
is a much more successful attempt.

Jason's written account of his 'Happiest Day' (p. 114) was also short
but, in its capturing of a particular moment, it demonstrates a number of
achievements. In three sentences, he locates the moment — when he got
his bike — specifies what sort of bike and then gives the reason for his
happiness. If one ignores the limitations of form and substance, there is
coherence in this brief account, although little elaboration.

His oral account contains much more information.

1   Oh – I wake up in the morning and . . and I used to get – I get up
2   Huh I goes – I – I used to go downstairs. get dressed
3   This was inour other – old house
4   So I used to. get up get dressed go – go downstairs and have my
5   breakfast near the fire.
6   Then I used to go to school . . . . . .
7   I – I used to go to school . . . probably have a f – 'nother fight. and
8   *Interviewer: Probably have what?*
9   Another fight *Interviewer: All right Carry on* . . .
10 And in – in the dinner hour I prob – probably got sent to the
11 headmistress again. and then do – do some. p – um pick –
12 some. work got to – got to go back tothe headmistress get a –
13 a sort of star . .
14 And then . . . I used. to come home play on my bike for a bit.
15 down the park. I used to – I used to sneak down – I used to sneak
16 down the bottom bit of the park.
17 And then. then um. I used to come in h – have a bath and then
18 go to bed

The narrative follows chronological sequence throughout and goes from
getting up to going to bed. As with Rosie, there is no mention of school
work and most of the account is taken up with what happens outside the
school. What is particularly interesting in this piece is, after the first
utterance, the consistent use of the past tense and frequent use of the
marker of habitual aspect 'used to'. In line 3, this is explained: his
account to a period in the past, when he lived at 'the old house'. The
inclusion of this aside shows awareness of his listener's needs. However,
several other events are not explained, such as why he had a fight and
what was so interesting about the bottom bit of the park. Some
interesting details are introduced, such as 'breakfast near the fire',
receiving 'a sort of star' and 'sneaking down to the bottom bit of the
park'. What is clear from these brief comments is that, despite the rather
frequent disfluencies, there are achievements at all levels, even though,
in the selection of information for inclusion, there is little evidence of an
overall plan.

For children like Rosie and Jason, then, the request for a narrative monologue in the oral mode enables them to display achievements that are apparently out of their reach in the written mode. At the same time it must be recognised that, even in the oral mode, their skills of composition are severely limited.

When we come to consider the more successful communicators, Samantha and Jonathan, the situation is somewhat different. Given the more discursive nature of oral monologue, both succeed in giving a well-organised account of a typical school day and both provide specific details to give interest to their accounts. (For reasons of space, it is impossible to quote these texts in full.) Samantha walks to school: 'We have to take a slow walk up and there's this sweet shop and I go in usually and get some chewing gums or bubble gums.' Jonathan, first thing: 'I usually managed to find some excuse or other for staying in for five minutes. For example Sovereign's there on top of me. That's our dog (laughing)'. In describing what goes on in school, both give examples of lessons and, interestingly, both offer comments on the examples they give. Samantha: 'Then we get our maths books 'cos we always have maths after sums on the board in the morning'; Joanathan: 'On the other days Miss reads us a story sometimes if she's got a story. You know a long one. Reads it in bits. The last one we had was The Lion, the Witch and the Wardrobe which I've read about ten times and know nearly off by heart'.

Like all the other children, both generated more text in the oral mode than in the written and, as in their written narratives, both showed an ability to select appropriate content and to shape it to achieve an overall effect. However, the sense of a deliberately constructed overall plan is weaker in the oral texts, as the chronological sequence of the school day already provides the main framework. In both oral texts, too, we find a less varied pattern of linking and of organising the information structure of the clause: 'I' or 'we' is the subject in the majority of main clauses and 'and' or 'and then' is the most frequent link between them. In certain respects, therefore, their oral texts are less satisfactory, as narratives, than those they wrote.

But that, of course, is to apply standards that are based on writing — standards, moreover, that most of the children would probably not even have recognised as applying to speech. However, even by these standards, several of the children's accounts of the school day were quite effective. And it is probable that, if the topic had been less constraining it its strong demands for a chronological, 'and then', sequence, many of them would have been more successful. This is an issue which we intend to address in future research.

From speech to writing

Considering both types of task together, now, we can see that there is a complex relationship between speech and writing, both in the course of development and at any particular point in that development. In either mode, the production of a narrative monologue involves an interaction between children's control of the medium of expression — the form and substance—and their compositional abilities. Factors that will affect this interaction, in either mode, include their interest in the task, the availability of relevant content and appropriate discourse schemata, the specificity of their awareness of the knowledge of the prospective receiver and, of course, the pedagogical context.

What becomes progressively more important in distinguishing the two modes is the differing facilitations and constraints afforded by the actual processes of production and by the adjustments that the composer must make to take account of the different modes of reception. For both production and reception, the most important dimension on which the two modes differ is probably that of time. As Chafe (1982) has argued, the differing characteristic patterns in which information is organised in speech and writing can largely be accounted for in terms of the differing degrees of matching in the speed at which chunks of information can be processed via language by sender and receiver in the two modes. The relatively unlimited time available to the writer enormously facilitates the planning and revising aspects of composition, as compared with the constraint of having to keep going when composing in speech.

The second dimension of difference to which Chafe draws attention is that of 'involvement'. In the oral mode, even in monologue, the speaker can usually see his or her audience and receives continuous feedback, which subtly affects the ongoing planning at all levels. On the other hand, where the audience is absent and in additional often unknown, as in writing, there is little sense of inter-personal involvement. This difference in the sender–receiver relationship, when combined with the difference between the two modes in the availability of the prosodic and paralinguistic accompaniments to speech, affects not only the organisation of the content in the two modes, but also the principles on which the content is selected. Although any general comparisons will need to be qualified for more specific sub-categories, it is usually the case that, in writing, there is a relatively greater emphasis on logical structure, explicit marking of relationships, choice of more precise vocabulary, and so on. By comparison, in the oral mode there is a relatively greater concern to maintain solidarity with the listener, by remaining within the realm of the shared and familiar meanings and expression of conversation.

This differentiation of the modes of speaking and writing takes time to develop, of course, and it is only in the narratives of the most mature children, such as Jonathan, that it is clearly apparent. But, as it develops, we can recognise a parallel differentiation in the way in which the medium of expression interacts with the processes of composition. At this stage in our research, and aware of the very severe limitations of the data on which we have been working, we should very tentatively like to propose the following developmental sequence, emphasising that it is based only on a study of children's spoken and written narratives. Whether it applies also to other forms of monologue still remains to be seen.

In the early stages (that is, typically, at the beginning of schooling), the relatively well-developed control of speech allows the child to give his or her attention, in the production of oral monologue, to the task of composing, unhindered by the additional constraints of having to solve problems of expression. At this stage, therefore, we find some children producing quite complex oral narratives (Fox 1983). However, the patterns of organisation that underlie such monologues are not ideally suited to the development of the more complex compositional skills that are characteristic of writing. This requires a medium in which one can take stock of where one has got to and plan where one is going and which gives time to allow alternatives to be considered and revisions to be made. Furthermore, some degree of fluency and control of the substance and form of writing has to be achieved before the written medium can fulfil these requirements. Once this is the case, however, as for example with Samantha, we find that control of composition is more effectively manifested in the written than in the oral mode. At the still later stage of development illustrated by Jonathan, compositional skills eveloped through writing are drawn upon in the oral mode, allowing the speaker to generate a distinctive form, that of the spoken monologue.

Crucial to the later stages of this developmental progression, of course, is extensive experience of the written mode as a receiver, first in listening to stories read aloud and then as a reader oneself. Where such experiences are lacking, children may gain control over the substance of written mode, but have little facility in handling the other dimensions. Certainly, differences in the extent of such experiences, we have found, go a long way towards explaining why some children became much more successful writers than others (Wells, forthcoming).

Some implications of this investigation

In keeping with the theme of this conference, this paper has focused mainly on writing. At the present time, there is a renewed interest in writing, both amongst researchers and in schools and colleges. In our view, this is entirely to be welcomed; first, because of the opportunities for active, 'intentional' learning that are provided by the requirement to work on and transform one's knowledge and experience that any piece of sustained writing demands (Bereiter and Scardamalia 1982*b*); secondly, because of the individualised response from the reader/ teacher that the resulting text is likely to elicit. For both these reasons, there is much to recommend a more prominent place being given to sustained writing in all subjects of the curriculum, particularly when the writing assignment grows naturally out of the other activities in which the pupils are engaged.

However, in concluding, we should like to make a plea for an equally important place being given to speech, particularly *sustained* speech, by pupils. The arguments against allowing pupils to speak at any length are obvious — at least to some teachers: there is insufficient time, if the content of the curriculum is to be covered; what pupils have to say is often irrelevant, if not inaccurate; and, most dangerous of all, pupil talk is a threat to the teacher's control. Such arguments rest, of course, on a particular view of the relationship between learning and teaching which assumes that only teachers know and that their task is to transmit their knowledge to well-disciplined pupils with as little interference from the pupils' extra-curricular interests and experience as possible. The arguments against such a conception of education are also well-known and have been clearly and cogently stated in a number of places, notably by Barnes (1976). These arguments are, in our view, correct.

Influenced by the spirit of the times, an by such development projects as Tough (1977), few teachers now demand total silence in their classrooms, at least not in the primary years. However, this does not mean that pupil talk is seriously valued, as our longitudinal observations showed all too plainly (Wells, forthcoming). Pupils are allowed to talk among themselves when engaged in most activities and they are actively encouraged to respond to teachers' questions and to contribute to teacher-led discussions. But there are, according to our data, few classrooms in which pupils are given the opportunity to engage in sustained, task-orientated discussion with their peers or to speak at length on a topic on which, either inside or outside the school, they have acquired expertise.

There are several reasons for believing such opportunities for sustained oral production to be important. First, there is the impetus actively to work on and transform knowledge gained from their experience and research in order to make it meaningful to others. Second, there is the development of confidence in themselves as knowers and communicators that occurs when children are successfully able to present their knowledge to others. All of us who have to make conference presentations, such as the present one (when spoken), know how valuable the experience is in helping us to clarify and evaluate our ideas. We believe that the experiences, observations and responses of young children, too, can become more meaningful to them by being reflected on and reorganised for, and in the act of, telling. Equally important is the opportunity for peer response, both the discussion which aims at clarification and amplification and that which, through question and comment, provokes the speaker to think more deeply and carefully about what he or she has said.

In the present context, however, the advantage of oral monologue that we particularly wish to emphasise is that it provides an opportunity to develop some of the skills of composing — planning, selecting, marshalling and organising ideas — that are so necessary for writing, and that it does so in a medium in which pupils feel more at ease and in which they are more likely to be successful.

Bibliography

Barnes, D. (1976). *From Communication to Curriculum.* Harmondsworth, Penguin

Bereiter, C. and Scardamalia, M. (1982a). 'From Conversation to composition: the Role of Instruction in a Developmental Process' in R. Glaser (ed.), *Advances in Instructional Psychology*. Hillsdale, NJ, Lawrence Erlbaum.

Bereiter, C. and Scaradamalia, M. (1982b). 'Schooling and the growth of Intentional Cognition: Helping Children Take Charge of their own Minds' in Z. Lamm (ed), *New Trends in Education*. Tel Aviv, Yachdev.

Bereiter, C. and Scardamalia, M. (1985). 'Children's difficulties in Learning to Compose' in G. Wells and J. Nicholls (eds), *Language and Learning: an Interactional Perspective*. Lewes, E. Sussex. Falmer Press.

Chafe, W. (1982).   'Integration and Involvement in Speaking, Writing and Oral Literature' in D. Tannen (ed), *Spoken and Written Language: Exploring Orality and Literacy.* Norwood, NJ. Ablex.

Fox, G. (1983).   'Talking like a Book: Young Children's Early Narratives' in M. Meek (ed.), *Opening Moves.* Bedford Papers, 17. London, London University Institute for Education.

Kroll, B. and Anson, C. (1983).   'Analysing Structure in Children's Fictional Narrative' in H. Cowie, (ed.) *The Development of Children's Imaginative Writing.* New York, St. Marin's Press.

Mandler, J.M. and Johnson, N.C. (1977).   'Remembrance of Things Parsed: Story Structure and Recall'. *Cognitive Psychology*, vol. 9. pp. 111–51.

Olson, D.R. (1977).   'From Utterance to Text: the Bias of Language in Speech and Writing'. *Harvard Educational Review*, vol. 47. pp. 257 257–81.

Rosen, C. and Rosen, H. (1973).   *The Language of Primary School Children.* Harmondsworth, Penguin.

Smith, F. (1982).   *Writing and the Writer. New York*, Holt Rinehart.

Tough, J. (1977).   *The Development of Meaning.* London, Unwin Educational books.

Wells, C.G. (1981).   'Some Antecedents of Early Educational Attainment', *British Journal of Education*, vol. 2, no.2, pp. 181–200.

Wells, C.G. (forthcoming).   *The Meaning Makers.* Exeter, NH, Heinemann Educational Books.

Wells, C.G., Barnes, S. and Wells, J. (1984).   *Linguistic Influences on Educational Attainment.* Toronto, Ontario Institute for Studies in Education.

Part Four

Writing Development

9 Early Writing

ANNE BAUERS and JOHN NICHOLLS

The need for enquiry into early writing

Theoretical background

Because writing is generally regarded as a derivative of spoken language and hence secondary to it, the attention of teachers of young children tends to be restricted to what are often called 'the mechanics' of writing — in particular to the correct formation of letter shapes and accurate spelling. The importance now generally accorded to creativity in work with young children has done little to alter such emphasis in early writing, which is scarcely surprising since, in later schooling, it seems to be widely assumed that successful writing demands little more than a stimulating environment and a basic understanding of 'the mechanics'. In the past few years, however, research into the processes involved in both writing and reading has drawn attention to features which suggest that the teaching of early writing may need to be carefully reappraised.

It is now clear that much more is involved in learning to write successfully than mere fluency in spoken language and competence with some of the more obvious surface features of the writing system. Indeed Kress (1982, Chapters 1–12 and in the present volume) argues that learning to write means learning an entirely new way of using language. Hence, also, the title 'Getting a Theory of Writing' which Clay (1983) chose for her contribution to a recent collection of papers on writing.

As regards the teaching of writing, a particularly important aspect of much of this research is its concern with the role of the reader in maintaining contact with the writer. The view that it is solely the writer's responsibility to sustain reciprocity of attention is no longer tenable as is made clear by Nystrand (1982, p. 70). A similar perspective is also explored by Gundlach (1981) and further explored by him with respect to young children in Gundlach (1982).

It would seem that the thrust of much recent research and theory concerned with children's problems in learning to write is to suggest that the teacher's traditional role is often unhelpful. Certainly a more appropriate role for the teacher of beginning writers would seem to be more like that of a supportive parent whose child is learning to communicate through speech. Such a parent, as Wells (1981, Chapters 2 and 7) shows very clearly, sees the achievement of communication as essentially a function of collaboration rather than a unilateral shaping of the child's language towards an adult model of correctness.

The beginning writing enquiry

Some awareness of these new perceptions of writing, coupled with the recognition that current teaching methods were still failing to produce consistently satisfactory results, led to the formation of a teacher enquiry group in 1980. The founding members were six class teachers working in infant or first schools in Norfolk. The purpose of the enquiry is to gather information about:

1. how children perceive the activity of writing; and
2. how children set about writing various texts, with examples of interaction, and some of the processes involved.

The method of enquiry

Perceptions of writing

Because it is felt that children's perceptions of writing might provide useful insights into how they interpret some of the things their teachers say and do when teaching writing, a number of questions were drawn up to explore their 'language awareness' through individual discussion. Our evidence here draws on each child's response to 'sentence-like' statements related to a picture. This acceptability testing of the concept 'sentence' is followed by an exploration of their understanding of 'word' and 'letter'. Such conversation foregrounds formal elements of language, so a further question 'What does a good writer need to know?' is pursued on a separate occasion. That question is proving to be extremely revealing and, as with understanding of formal elements, individual differences seems to be a more importance source of variation than chronological age or the effect of normal writing instruction.

Text construction

In order to collect information about individual writing behaviour each teacher in the original group chose four children — two boys and two girls — for detailed observation. To avoid too great a range in the data, no child of outstanding ability or with severe educational or emotional difficulties was included. Each child was observed for 20 minutes on two separate occasions in each term over a one-year period (where appropriate doing different kinds of writing, i.e. making up a story or reporting a personal experience). The resulting data is still being analysed but a number of interesting points have already emerged, some of which will be discussed later in this paper.

In order to organise the material obtained by observation we found it necessary to device a detailed schedule. This summarises the information recorded during the 20–minute periods of direct observation as well as some of the teacher's knowledge of the child and the task. Reference to the schedule makes it possible to see the particular strategies employed by a child in producing a specific text and to see how often those strategies were adopted.

It is not possible to give the complete schedule here (see Nicholls 1984). The information sought includes that on the source of the topic, its mode and possible audience; whether (and when) the writing was illustrated; the place of talk, and of vocalisation. Particularly important in the degree of dependence on the teacher during text construction. In some cases, for example, a text is *composed* by the child but *performed* (written down) by the teacher because the child cannot yet manage both the composing and performing aspects of writing at the same time. Subsequently such a text may be copied by the child and, as we shall show, observation of such copying can provide important evidence of developing understanding.

Towards a model of early writing

Levels of competence
Following a preliminary analysis and extensive discussion of the data assembled by these instruments of enquiry, the group has developed a tentative model of the writing process for young learners in their early years at school. The model identifies a number of levels of writing competence but we must stress that these levels are not intended to suggest an instructional sequence. Their purpose is to help one identify emerging skills and understanding in order to encourage further development.

We have adopted the term 'level' rather than 'stage' because the skills and understanding listed at level one, for example, continue to be developed alongside others listed at level two and the same is true for all other levels. It is also important to remember that children's apparent competence may be uneven and that they may be very much more successful in one kind of writing assignment than in another, a further reason for rejecting the notion of stages for beginning writers. A more important reason for using the term 'level', however, is that each level lists both skills and kinds of understanding that should be evident in a child's behaviour if a satisfactory balance is being maintained between the composing and performing demands of writing. It follows that observation, supported by reference to the model, can help to determine priorities for individual teaching.

Collaborative text-making
The model can also be used to inform discussion with individual children during collaborative text-making, which we see as an essential complement to individual work at each of the levels we identify. In this way it is possible, without loss of spontaneity, to provide feedback which is tailored to each child's own needs. Such collaboration is intended to reduce the need for corrections to complete text and, we think, is a means of promoting the kind of revision that Graves (1983) sees as a crucial outcome of 'conferencing'.

Pre-independent writing

Level one — orientation towards writing

The child is learning that 'writing codes meaning'.

Composing aspect	Performing aspect
Sign concept – that meaning can be conveyed visually as well as through speech.	To control writing implement. Directionality (i.e. left to right and top to bottom). To recognise some written words (e.g. own name).
Word concept — that writing makes use of written words, not pictures.	To recognise word spacing. To produce some letter shapes. To distinguish some initial sounds (though not necessarily to recognise the written symbol).

(towards level two)

Children's Perceptions
Most children do not attempt to learn to write until they come to school. Nevertheless, they bring with them a good understanding of the symbolic functions of gesture and of spoken language. Many will also be

able to represent objects and experience in drawing. Learning to write ought to be just one more step along the road and is one of the main tasks facing children on school entry. The teacher's role in enabling the learning to take place is vital. Certainly the purposes of writing are not always self-evident to children, as testified by one cheerful six-year-old who assured his teacher that to be a good writer you need to 'keep quiet, stay in your place and have a sharp pencil'. It may be that some teachers, by concentrating on one aspect of the writing process more than the other, unintentionally mislead children, thereby increasing their difficulties.

Children's text with examples of interaction
Scott produced the following piece of work soon after he entered school.

This 'text' shows a clear understanding of the purpose of *drawing*, but his writing resembles written text only in that it was produced in lines from left to right and that these lines succeeded each other from top to bottom down the page.

In many classes, as in the next example, there will be some children already able to demonstrate a knowledge of at least some letter shapes even before they have been given any formal instruction by the teacher. some will even attempt to write their own name, as in this example of early work by Krysha:

Some of these children are also able to ascribe meanings to their 'texts' so it is clear that they are ready to begin learning to write with their teacher.

In most classes, however, there will be a number of children who do not yet realise that text carries meaning and, if asked to write, they are merely 'drawing shapes'. These children still see writing in purely visual terms and may require considerable guidance through further work designed to increase their understanding of what writing is and does before they are ready to compose text with any real understanding. This does not mean that such children should be prevented from trying to write before they fully understand the purpose of written text. What is important is that the teacher, in her collaboration with these children, should continue to promote the kinds of understanding and skills listed at level one.

Level two — initial text-making

The child is learning that: 'my own meaning can be coded
in words which I can choose and order'.

Composing aspect   Performing aspect

Letter concept — the concept of   To form and orientate letters.
  alphabetic writing.   To begin to control letter size.
Sentence concept — writing is not   To recognise letter spacing.
  speech written down.   To analyse some words into pho-
                                          nic units.
Spelling awareness   To begin collecting a vocabulary
                                          of words that can be written
                                          unaided.
                                        To monitor letter formation in
                                          own text copy.

(towards level three)

Children's early preceptions

Those teachers in the Enquiry who are working with very young
children adopt the usual practice of collaborating with young learners to
produce some text. Typically teacher and child compose a caption to
accompany a picture drawn by the child. The teacher then writes the
words, probably uttering them as she proceeds, while the child watches
how it is done.

As we have already suggested, during these sessions children whose
understanding of the nature and functions of written text is still limited
may need considerble support in formulating their ideas. If the method
is working well, however, they will increasingly take the composing
initiative and choose their own words. They may soon become very
adept at this form of text-making and dictate passages of a length which
they themselves could never transcribe. Nor do they have any
consideration for the needs of their scribe who may find it difficult to
keep up.

Early text with examples of interaction

The following text was produced after the child had been in school
about two months: 'My daddy's got a pumpkin. He's made a face in it to
make a lantern.' Timothy has understood many of the features of writing
and obviously enjoys composing text with his teacher but, at this early
point of development he was not expected to copy the written text.

This transcript is taken from a tape recording made during the composing process (written text is in bold type):

Teacher:	What are you going to write for yours?
Timothy:	My daddy's got a pumpkin.
Teacher:	(*says and writes simultaneously*) **My daddy's got a pumpkin** And what's he going to do with it? Or what's he done with it?
Timothy:	He's made a face in it.
Teacher:	Really! has he really?
Timothy:	Yes.
Teacher:	(*says and writes*) **He's made a face in it.** Why did he do that?
Timothy:	To make a lantern.
Teacher:	(*says and writes*) **To make a lantern** Lovely. (*reads*) To make a lantern.

It is clear that Timothy had no difficulty in deciding what to say to begin with and the teacher transcribes his sentence repeating each word as she writes it. This demonstrates writing speed to the child and shows that spoken words are represented in writing as separated by a space. Then, in order to expand the text, she continues by asking Timothy for more information. His replies are transcribed in the same manner. This means that Timothy's text, although it reads like a narrative, was in fact composed through dialogue. The teacher, however, only writes down what the child says, omitting her own contributions. The idea is that Timothy will 'internalise' this process. This procedure resembles the facilitative strategies for extending children's text adopted by some experimenters, as in the attempts by Scardamalia, Bereiter and Goelman (1982) to extend children's written texts. 'From Conversation to Composition' is another paper by Bereiter and Scardamalia (1982) that looks in detail at children's composing strategies. The major difference is that the teacher does not necessarily restrict herself to what they call 'content-free inputs'.

In the early weeks at school, and sometimes much longer, it is the responsibility of the teacher as much as the child to make sure that any text they produce together adequately represents the child's intentions. Immediate feedback is a crucial element in the text-making process at this stage; that is to say child and teacher should engage in a relaxed conversation which contextualises both the meaning intended and the means whereby it is communicated.

Children's later perceptions

Collaborative text-making now begins to take on a rather different form as the description in this section will make clear. Children by this time are very familiar with the text-making process. They understand that meaning can be communicated in writing and that they can choose the words for their texts. They also realise that writing takes time and that spoken words are represented in writing by 'chunks' separated from each other by a space. They should also realise that these 'chunks' are words made up of a finite number of letters which are formed in a consistent manner. They will normally be able to spell a number of the more common words and will write these without referring to the teacher's model.

Because of their increased understanding, these children no longer need prompting in order to compose, but they are unlikely to compose more text than they can readily copy. They have come to realise that transcribing is a time-consuming business. Nevertheless, when copying, they now demonstrate considerable proficiency and reproduce letters with relative ease. Occasionally, when a word seems familiar, they will write it without looking back at the teacher's model after each individual letter.

Later text with examples of interaction

The following is part of a text composed by Peter after about two months in school:

The transcript of a recording of the collaborative text-making process shows clearly how Peter responds to the composing demands of written language:

Peter:	(*dictates*):	Roger

Teacher:	Roger

Peter:	(*dictates slowly as the teacher writes*):

went to the Village with Three corners.
He saw the old bus. He went in the old bus.
(*says in normal voice*): I'll watch you now, Miss Bauers.

Peter no longer needs prompting or encouraging. He has an idea for a text in his mind. He realises that writing takes longer to execute than speech and therefore dictates at writing speed a word at a time. His text is formulated in sentences which comply with the conventions of written language and the teacher now acts merely as audience and secretary for the child.

In copying the teacher's model Peter also showed himself very confident in the performing aspect as the following record of observation demonstrates:

says or does	*writes*
1. *where's my pencil*	—
2. —	*Roger we*
3. (*reads aloud from neighbour's book*) *my house*	—
4. *starts telling him how to spell 'open' — using letter names. Gets as far as 'ope'*	—
5. —	*nt*
6. *discusses 'ed' words with neighbour*	—
7. —	to the V
8. Teacher (*shows beautifully formed 'V'*)	—
9. I've nearly finished it	—
10. (*reads aloud*) Roger went to the	—
11. (*asks, of 'Village'*) what does that say? (*points*)	—
12. I've nearly finished it	—
13. —	illage with Three Corners

In this observation the only apparent teacher activity is to respond appreciatively to the proudly-presented 'V' and to read 'village'. In collaborative text-making the maintenance of reciprocity demands sensitivity to the individual learner and a readiness to respond according to observed needs at the time. It also requires a learning environment where children are free to make demands on their teacher, but also recognise that other members of the class may have problems too. This boy, with his knowledge of letter formation (a few reversals can be accepted), his reasonable formation of letters, his chunking of letters into words for copying purposes, his growing vocabulary of known words for spelling and his phonic knowledge is ready to move on towards independent writing.

Some problems with pre-independent writing
While many children manage to join in collaborative text-making with relatively little difficulty, there are some who find it rather more problematic. Kevin is a child who did not find reading or writing very easy.

On entering school he had no notion that it is possible to represent objects or events *even by drawing*. It could be argued that such a child is not ready to join in collaborative text-making with his teacher but, although level one presupposes an understanding of the symbolic function of written language, some children seem to need to be exposed to the text-making process at level two if they are ever to understand it.

An early observation made during an attempt to compose text with him gave the impression that Kevin was totally unaware of writing even as a visual medium. However, his question during this observation: 'What are you writing' came as a welcome indicator that he did recognise writing when he saw it being done and had an awakening interest in its purpose as well as some curiosity about its meaning. The observational procedure, which was designed to record and tabulate child strategies while writing, in this case provided two additional benefits. First, it demonstrated to Kevin how writing is done and, second, it reassured the teacher that, in spite of all the obvious difficulties, Kevin did have some understanding of what it was he was doing.

Independent writing

Level three — initial independence

> The child is learning that: 'I can make my own text by organising my message into sentences'.

Composing aspect   Performing aspect

Sentence *structure* concept (nam-   To recognise that letters have
ing part + verbal part — e.g.   names.

My mum is watering the flowers).

Awareness of syllabic structure of
words.

Awareness of textual cohesion (see
below).

To begin using upper/lower case
letters with some consistency.

To mark some sentence boundaries (capital and full stop).

To use classroom resources for
information on some spelling.

To invent other spelling.

To monitor spelling in completed
text.

(towards level four)

Children's perceptions

When children are familiar with the demands of the composing process
and are able to copy text with relative ease they are usually keen to begin
writing independently. By now they should know that written text can
extend beyond a single sentence and, having come to realise the rule-
governed nature of English orthography, they will usually have adopted a
number of strategies for discovering or inventing spellings. These
children normally write short coherent texts and speak as they write,
pausing frequently, often after each word. At first many may rely heavily
on the teacher for spellings but later, if encouraged to do so, they will
invent spellings freely as they come to realise the relationships between
symbol and sound.

Initial independent writing, however, greatly increases performing
demands for the child and this can lead to problems later on if the
transition is not carefully handled. Because of the vital importance of
this period it will be treated in some detail with examples from the work
of a number of children.

Texts with examples of interaction

Scott is a child who made the transition to independent writing with
relatively little difficulty. He was able to write the following at this
own request, after only two months in school:

We we r to the concert
we hadfun

Observation as Scott was writing shows that he behaved as follows:

says or does		*writes*
1.	—	We we
2.	—	went w
3.	(*deletes 'w'*)	—
4.	—	to the
5.	(*asks*) How do you spell 'concert' (*teacher provides*)	—
6.	—	conce
7.	(*says*) 'r' (*using letter name*)	—
8.	—	rt
9.	(*says*) 'w' 'e' (*using letter names*)	—
10.	—	we
11.	(*asks*) How do you write 'had'? (*teacher provides*)	—
12.	—	had
13.	(*asks*) How do you write 'fun'? (*teacher provides*)	—
14.	—	fun

Scott is a child who already knows how to write a number of the common words he needs — e.g. 'we'. 'went', 'to', 'the'. He also knows which words he cannot write and immediately asks the teacher to show him. At this point the teacher simply supplies the words without comment because holding the text in mind is burden enough without the addition of concern about orthography. Writing, for Scott, is largely a matter of spelling at present, but for the teacher there is more to be learned from other features of this independent text-making. There is evidence that he is monitoring his own writing — a point of fundamental importance for development. One can see that he spotted the intrusive 'w' after 'went" — though he did not notice the repeated 'we' at the start. In just eight weeks Scott had progressed from the graffiti of the earlier example (p. 138) to writing a cohesive two sentence report on a school visit. (His second sentence shows an example of cohesion by ellipsis — i.e. 'We had fun (at the concert)'?)

In the following term Scott wrote this text:

> wans they was a whes (witch) she was a verey bad whes and evey one how came to haR home she woold pot a sbel on and theat wood be the End of them

By now Scott has succeeded in extending his text beyond single statements. His second sentence is cohesive through pronominal reference ('she') and is extremely complex. While the inversion of object and subject it contains is unusual this certainly adds to the emphasis of his story-line and could be regarded as a deliberate stylistic device learned from stories. On the performing side there is evidence in the commentary that he knows the names of many letters as shown by the following comment: 'I sometimes forget how to do "one". I think it's "o", "e", "n"', where he uses the name of each letter. There is no evidence of punctuation or correct marking of sentence-initial position with an upper-case letter, but on the other hand there is plenty of evidence of invented spellings, as in 'wans' 'whes' 'evey' 'how' 'woold' 'sbel'. Furthermore, among these inventions, there is evidence that Scott is beginning to pay attention to visual detail as well as to word sounds before attempting spelling. He writes 'woold' with an 'l', and 'whes' with and 'h', which would be correct for 'which', and it is probably a memory of this word that prompted the inclusion of 'h'.

The teacher's response to this piece of writing was not recorded but, if the model is followed, it might have been appropriate at this point to discuss the use of full stops and capital letters and to encourage Scott to use these himself. However, as Kress (1982, Chapter 4) suggests, the adult notion of a sentence is acquired late and it is certainly unhelpful to insist on punctuation at this level. (See also Cazden *et al.* 1985.)

Some problems with initial independence

The obsessive speller
These are children who focus only on the performing aspect of writing and, within that aspect, only on correct spelling. Such children may come to the teacher to check every word before venturing to write it down. Kevin, whose early attempts at writing were referred to (p. 144) was later in danger of becoming one of these. In his case he was specifically encouraged to invent unfamiliar spellings during collaborative text-making — and thus helped to write more interesting as well as more extended texts.

The imaginative innovator
At the opposite extreme is Marie who let caution fly to the winds and innovated with abandon as in the following:

(I went to the fair. I had a go on the computer with my mummy and dad
and my brother. I put a money in the computer. Then we went home. We
had out tea. The End.)

There are obviously problems here, particularly for the teacher, as it is
her task to interpret the child's message and respond to it appropriately
without in any way inhibiting Marie's obvious desire to communicate in
writing. She saw writing almost entirely in terms of the composing
aspect and, here again, collaborative text-making was used to provide
the kind of instant feedback that helped Marie to take more account of
the conventions of the writing system.

The cryptic coder
Even more problematic is to decide how to respond to work like this
example from Tracey:

We was   goto Lowestot
and the bus alreagone
and at Lowestott we had
Some dinner

The teacher's initial reaction was to assume that she had merely lost the
thread of her story. The fact that Tracey's texts did not normally lack
coherence prompted the teacher to discuss the piece with her
afterwards. It emerged that her intended message was something like
this: 'On Saturday we had meant to go to Lowestoft but the bus had
already gone. We had hoped to have dinner in Lowestoft, as we had
done before when we did not miss the bus.' Tracey's ideas were far too
complicated for her to compose and write down without the support of a
conversational partner — another facet of collaborative text-making.

Level four — associative writing

The child is learning that 'whenever I have anything worth writing about I can do it quite easily'.

Composing aspect

Text *structure* concept (through 'story/not story' distinction as basis of genre planning).

Concept of spelling as 'rule governed' (see note below).

Performing aspect

To begin to regularise spelling towards conventions of the English writing system.
To begin using some punctuation other than full stop.
To monitor text for coherence of message.

(towards a personal style)

Children's perceptions

At this level of competence children are usually very confident writers and no longer too constrained by the performing aspect of writing. They usually enjoy exercising their newly learned ability to set down their ideas as they come to mind. These ideas are listed sequentially and the texts tend to end when the ideas run out. Indeed, that is why we use the word 'associative' to refer to this kind of writing. The term comes from a paper by Bereiter (1980). He is not responsible for the way we use the term, but we are glad of the opportunity to say how important his paper was in the development of our thinking about writing. Because many of their initial difficulties, especially with spelling, have been overcome children are now no longer obliged to stop painfully after nearly every word to think about the next one. When all goes well this means that they are able to devote more attention to expression and, with encouragement, to organisation.

Children's texts with examples of interaction.
Because of his own drive and enthusiasm Scott was already writing at
this level within a year of starting school, as in the following:

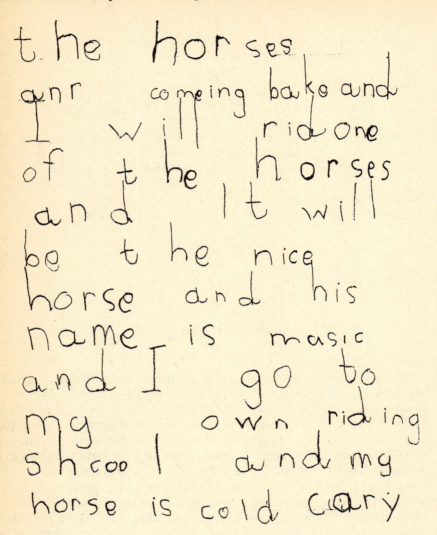

the horses
anr   comeing bake and
I   will   rid one
of   the   horses
and   It   will
be   t he   nice
horse   and   his
name   is   masic
and   I   go   to
my   own   riding
shcool   and   my
horse   is   cold   cary

Observation showed that he proceeded thus:

say or does	writes
1. —	The
2. (Checks word book for 'horses' — not there)	—
3. (Asks teacher for spelling. Teacher supplies)	—
4. —	hor + ses (syllables)
5. I get muddled up with 'are' I think it's 'a' 'n' 'r' (using letter names)	—
6. —	anr
7. (Reads) are coming back and	—
8. —	coming bake anr
9. I've made a mistake. I'll borrow Gavin's rubber	—
10. (Erases 'r')	d
11. —	—
12. (Asks teacher for spelling of 'one'. She finds it in his word book)	one ov
13. —	—
14. Have you got a rubber?	—
15. (Erases 'v')	f
16. —	—
17. (reads) 'of'	—
18. —	the
19. I don't write stories. I write news	—
20. —	horses and it will be
21. It's going to be long this one is	—

This text shows how Scott's awareness of sequence provides a framework for text construction. The follow-on or 'chain' text is familiar to teachers of writing at this level. The commentary made while Scott was writing this piece also shows that he is aware of the existence of different schemes for text-making, e.g. he says:

I don't write stories. I write news. (l.19)

Further evidence of development of composing is provided by his statement:

It's going to be long this one is. (l.21)

It shows that he has planned his piece in advance and knows what he is going to write about, but not how he is going to put it, of course.

On the performing side there is evidence that Scott is now monitoring his text for accuracy of spelling (l.9, l.15). His spelling of 'coming' and of 'school' later on, shows that he is paying attention to the visual aspect of written words and is no longer relying solely on his teacher or his knowledge of sound–symbol correspondence. Punctuation is not yet apparent, but it did appear a month later. Whether this was the result of deliverate intervention by the teacher or of the child's own observations from his reading was not discovered.

While many children achieve early fluency in the writing of stories and diary entries, other forms of writing can cause difficulty. This was very apparent in some of the texts written by older infants in response to the teacher's request that they produce instructions for the reception class on how to make an Aladdin-type hat. Most were quite unable to meet the demands of decontextualised writing of this order and found the absence of a conversational partner an insurmountable barrier. Karl, on the other hand, who had shown no particular talent for 'creative' writing, had a much clearer grasp of what was required. After the text was completed there was even a series of diagrams illustrating each stage in the construction process. It should be noted that Karl was an avid reader of non-fiction material and this may have helped him to internalise a framework for this kind of writing.

I wil tel you how to make a hat. you gt a hop you g t A bit of paper. you darw round the hop. you cut round the bit of paper. This is what we have. we have the Stapler. we have

the rulers. we have scissors.
you draw a line. you cut the line.
you have a pencil.

Finding a voice

Associative writing is often a pleasure to read, as is evident in Karl's account of the hat-making process. The following text is part of a four page story by Charles, a boy in his final year at infant school. The excerpt also demonstrates this charm but, in addition, it shows the beginning of a personal style or 'voice' as in the emerging modality of 'the horse seamed to be asking if he could stay'.

1

Once opun a time there
was a man his
name was Jim he lived
at the top of a
hill and he had a
farm. One day he
"Said want are you
doing here" he Said
this to a horse. the
horse had run away
from a man that lived
in a town it was
a lot of miles
away from the hill.
the horse Seamed to
be asking if he
could Stay the man
Said OK I have
got a Stable for
you Come on then
in here then

This extract from the teacher's record of observation shows how
Charles set about his story:

says or does	writes
1. —	Once upon a time it
2. What have I?	—
3. (*Erases 'it'*)	—
4. —	thr
5. (*Erases 'r'*)	—
6. —	ree
7. (*Erases 'ree'*)	—
8. —	ere was a man his m
9. (*Erases 'm'*)	—
10. —	name was Jim he lived at the top of a hill and he had a
11. How do you spell 'farm'? (*Teacher supplies*)	—
12. —	farm.
13. (*Long pause then reads aloud whole text so far*)	—
14. —	One day he "Said want are you
15. 'do' + 'ing' (*syllables*)	—
16. —	doing
17. —	here "he said this to a
18. Is 'horse' h,o,u,s,e? (*Teacher corrects*)	—
19. —	horse.
20. *Long pause, then*	the horse had ay
21. woops (*erases 'ay'*)	—
22. —	away from
23. (*Reads aloud from 'One day he said'*)	—
24. —	a man that lived in a town it was a lot of miles away from the hill.

The story was composed over a period of several days and must
therefore have been to some extent thought out in advance. The

commentary shows that there is evidence both of text monitoring and of subsequent correction. Most of this involved spelling changes but sometimes wording too was altered. There is also evidence that he was reviewing his text in large chunks. For example when he reached the word 'farm' he read aloud all that he had written up to that point (l.13) and later he read from 'one day' (l.23). Charles has very little difficulty with spelling. This does not mean that there are no spelling errors but that he feels sufficiently at ease to put down what he feels is correct and thus frees attention for the real business of writing, which is composing text.

The way Charles uses punctuation is interesting. When he stops to think what to write next he puts in a full stop (ll.12,19). Such 'errors' are to be welcomed as a sign of progress. He knows about the use of full stops and about sentences but his concept of sentence is still not that of an adult. For Charles, a full stop indicates an interruption in the flow of ideas rather than a grammatical boundary. He also has a very interesting system for the use of speech marks. His usage picks out the 'speech event' rather than marking the actual words used. Hence we get 'One day he "Said want are you doing here"'. Here too the error indicates growing understanding.

Directions for further research

Collaborative text-making
The text which has just been considered shows that Charles has reached a 'honeymoon' period of confident and increasingly competent associative writing. If he is to develop further it is necessary for him to learn how to diversify his writing with the same kind of sensitivity as he has, for several years, been able to modify his speech. Whenever possible he still needs to engage in collaborative text-making with his teacher but now such collaboration can also be done with other pupils working at the level of associative writing.

Although the exact nature and substance of appropriate dialogue during such collaboration with the teacher has yet to be researched it would seem likely that the kinds of sensitivity used by parents with their offspring and reception teachers with their new pupils could provide the key to effective learning for more advanced children.

Response to completed texts
How teachers can become more effective *readers* of children's work at this more advanced level has not yet been examined either. The model

we have presented is intended to discourage the still widespread practice of responding to young children's texts mainly in terms of 'proof reading' for performing errors. It directs attention towards both the composing and performing aspects of early writing — towards what a child has achieved and is attempting, rather than what he or she cannot yet do. It also emphasises the teacher's responsibility for helping each pupil to maintain an appropriate balance between these two aspects. It would seem that this to is an area in urgent need of investigation because, until appropriate interaction procedures are identified for facilitating children's learning, their progress will continue to be determined solely by their own motivation and the luck of their teacher's intuitions.

Biblography

Bereiter, C. (1980). 'Development in Writing' in Gregg and Steinberg (1980).

Bereiter, C. and Scardamalia, M. (1982). 'From Conversation to Composition' R. Glaser, (ed.) *Advances in Instructional Psychology*, Volume 2 in Glaser (1982).

Cazden, C.B., Cordeiro, P. and Giacobbe, M. (1985). 'Spontaneous and Scientific Concepts: Young Children's Learning of Punctuation' in Wells and Nicholls (1985).

Clay, M.M. (1983). 'Getting a Theory of Writing' in Kroll and Wells (1983), pp. 259–84.

Glaser, R. (ed.) (1982). *Advances in Instructional Psychology*, Volume 2. Hillsdale, NJ, Lawrence Erlbaum Associates.

Graves, D.H. (1983). *Writing: Teachers and Cildren at Work.* London, Heinemann Educational Books.

Gregg, L.W. and Steinberg, E.R. (eds) (1980). *Cognitive Processes in Writing.* Hillsdale, NG, Lawrence Erlbaum Associates.

Gundlach, R.A. (1981). 'The Nature and Development of Children's Writing' in C.H. Fredericksen, M.F. Whiteman and J.F. Dominic (eds.) *Writing (Volume 2): Process, Development and Communication.* Hillsdale, JN, Lawrence Erlbaum Associates.

Gundlach, R.A. (1982). 'Children as Writers: The Beginnings of Learning to Write, in Nystrand (1982).

Kress, G. (1982). *Learning to Write*. London, Routledge and Kegan Paul.

Kroll, B. and Wells, G. (eds) (1983). *Explorations in the Development of Writing*. Chichester, John Wiley.

Nicholls, J. (ed.) (1984). *Learning to Write and Teach Writing, 5 to 9 years*. Norwich, University of East Anglia School of Education.

Nystrand, M. (ed.) (1982). *What Writers Know. The Language, Process and Structure of Written Discourse*. New York, Academic Press.

Scardamalia, M., Bereiter, C. and Goelman, H. (1982). 'The Role of Production Factors in Writing Ability' in Nystrand (1982), pp. 173–210.

Wells, G. (1981). *Learning through Interaction*. Cambridge, Cambridge University Press.

Wells, G. and Nicholls, J. (eds) (1985). *Language and Learning: An Interactional Perspective*. London, Falmer Press.

10 Writing Counts

WILLIAM HARPIN

By the early 1960s, research in aspects of language development had reached a critical point. In the United Kingdom the test and measurment movement was under attack from those dissatisfied with the influence and effects of testing for secondary school selection. In primary schools a form of creative or personal writing was being strongly developed for which an analytical response was considered inappropriate. In both the United Kindgom and the United States traditional models for language analysis were in the process of being challenged: transformational-generative grammar', expounded by Chomsky (1957; 1965) elbowed aside the structural linguistics of Bloomfield, while a 'scale-and-category' (later 'systemic') model of language description was being developed by Halliday. Perhaps the most significant change was brought about by the assault on behaviourist psychology itself and particularly on its presumed inadequacy in purporting to explain the facts of language acquisition and development. Chomsky's revival of the rationalist position, postulating innate language-learning dispositions and turning crucially on the distinction between competence and performance moved attention away from actual language behaviour to the pursuit of a theoretical model to account for the ideal speaker-hearer's knowledge of language. Studies of performance became, if not trivial, at best of secondary importance.

The effect of this coming together of influences in changing the direction and emphases of studies in language development was by no means immediately apparent. Traditional approaches offered a secure base in design and methodology, particularly for projects embarking on fully longitudinal studies. They also provided the opportunity for comparative and contrastive analyses. Thus Loban (1963; 1976), in following his group of subjects for twelve years, broadly adopted the methods of analysis of his predecessors, though interestingly a linguists' panel was employed to draw up the detailed schedule and to cause it to be applied to a parallel project (Strickland 1962). Only in the material for the second report is there reference to an experiment in analysis with a transformational-generative grammar, and this for six subjects (out of 211). In the United Kingdom a longitudinal study of language development was begun at much the same time as Loban's, but the age-span was from 18 months to ten years (Sampson 1964). Analysis of the writing of these children at ten followed closely the methods of the major studies of the 1930s and 1940s.

Another development of the time contributed to the continuation of traditional approaches to language-development studies. The proposition that particular social groups were associated with distinct forms of language was not new, but its formulation in terms of formal and public languages (later elaborated and restricted codes) (Bernstein 1961) engendered a linguistic and socio-linguistic debate which still continues. One of the earliest effects was to promote studies of speech and writing on the established quantitative model with the variable of social class now the focus of attention.

After sixty years or so of endeavour in examining the development of writing, the curious position had been reached that, while the classic studies of the past were cited with appropriate gravity and frequency, they were treated largely as repositories of irrelevant information. This particular wheel had to be reinvented or, for some, forgotten. The case for a more informed understanding of how writing is learned, the purposes it is put to, and the language resources resources employed to realise those purposes, was plain, but serious doubts existed on whether such an understanding could be achieved by the established methods of enquiry. The sceptics could point to the history of research to assert the trivial or obvious character of many of the findings and their seeming irrelevance for the major issues of learning and teaching. Yet the case for such a study was a strong one: the challenge in formulating the enquiry was to link with past work while learning from its mistakes and to ensure that the purposes were clearly articulated and directed at practical outcomes.

The study

Origins and purposes
A group in the East Midlands of England of primary and secondary school teachers joined by tutors in teacher education had been formed in the late 1960s with the purpose of informing itself of new developments in linguistics and in the psychology and sociology of language, and considering their application to teaching and learning.

After considering a range of possibilities the choice was made to focus the study of writing in the junior school (age 7–11) and a series of reserach objectives identified. these were:

1. To study in detail evidence of the linguistic resources that children of differing abilities call on in writing and to examine the order and manner of development of those resources over a period of two years.
2. To relate this evidence to variables in the school situation which seem particularly relevant to the processes of language learning and use-teaching methods, class organisation, verbal interaction of teachers and pupils, teacher and school expectations, physical resources.
3. To set these results in the wider social context of the children examined, noting particularly socioeconomic status, parental aspirations, position in family and community influences.
4. To derive, from interpretation of and reflection on the data, suggestions for more effective educational practice in helping pupils to develop and refine their written language skills and in recognising and treating written language handicaps.

Design
Consideration of the evidence afforded by a survey of earlier research led to a swift decision to make the study longitudinal, to look for a large representative sample of writers from a variety of school settings and to take careful account of kind of writing and audience in specifying writing conditions. A two-year span for data collection, combined with the sampling procedure, ensured that evidence from all four years in the junior school would be available.

With nine contributory schools (one of which had a transfer age of eight years rather than seven), samples of 12 were drawn from each of the first three year groups, giving a notional sample size of 312. With the elimination of some children likely to move before the project's completion and others with birth dates falling outside the set limits, the final sample was 289: 95 aged 7.0–7.11; 96 aged 8.0–8.11; and 98 aged 9.0–9.11. Of these 146 were boys, 143 girls. At the conclusion of the second year of the study 276 pupils completed the final writing collection. Tests to establish the representativeness of the sample included the English Picture Vocabulary Test (Brimer and Dunn 1962), coloured and Standard Progressive Matrices (Raven 1960; 1963) and the Bristol Social Adjustment Guide (Stott 1966; 1970). In addition the distribution of social class membership in the sample was compared with that for the United Kingdom as a whole. On all these measures, when the effect of excluding non-writers was taken into account, the sample could confidently be described as representative of the population from which it was drawn.

Implementation

To provide the bulk of the non-linguistic information required, a questionnaire was compiled for completion by the class teacher and headteacher covering such matters as a physical description of each pupil, his interests and activities in and out of school, educational history, together with details of classroom setting, resources, organisation, and of the school and its community setting.

To supplement this and to gather information on characteristic classroom practices and the behaviour of individual children an observation schedule was devised, pilot-tested and, in a revised form, used on three occasions (in the third, fourth and sixth terms of the six-term duration of the project). Particular attention was given in the schedule to verbal components of the learning and teaching environment, notably pupil–teacher interaction, the range of reading, writing and speech activities engaged in by the pupil and language as a component in theaching style.

Arrangements for sampling the children's writing posed considerable difficulties. The original intention, to collect written output on any two days in one week of each term, proved after testing to be unsatisfactory. Wide variations of practice among the schools and the fragmentary nature of (and absence of context for) much of the writing led to the conclusion that a more carefully specified basis was necessary to produce writing amenable to analysis.

A distinction was drawn between writing that was essentially concerned with events and experiences 'out there' and writing springing from the imagination and feelings of the writer. These kinds were labelled 'recording' and 'personal' (following Clegg 1964), but amended to 'factual' and 'creative' as these were terms more readily understood from their own practice by the teachers involved. One other dimension was built in, to take account of a potentially significant variation in the preparation for writing. The introduction of forms of 'creative' writing in British schools in the 1960s had familiarised teachers with the technique of encouraging children to write directly from a stimulus, with little or no teacher (or class) intervention. The long-established practice of preparing for writing by extensive discussionof the topic co-existed with with the new style and suggested the usefulness of exploring the effects of these different settings for writing on the writer and his work.

The final writing sample consisted therefore of pieces in four modes each term.

Creative	Factual
(minimum verbal preparation)	(minimum verbal preparation)
Creative	Factual
(normal verbal preparation)	(normal verbal preparation)

Of these, only the factual writing with minimum verbal preparation was felt likely to cause some difficulties in implementation as a form likely to be comparatively rare in the repertoire of most teachers. In the event, the ingenuity and inventiveness of collaborating teachers were ample equal to the challenge. It should be stressed that writing requirements were imposed for kind of writing only: choice of content theme or focus was expected to derive from each teacher's existing programme of teaching and normal practice and no time limit for writing was stipulated. It was hoped that this division of responsibility would preserve the 'naturalism' of the setting for writing and identify the teacher in her normal role as audience for it.

With beginning writers there is, of course, no guarantee that the writing expected will be the writing delivered. Confirmation of this variability from the pilot sampling suggested the need for some assessment of writing outcomes on the creative–factual distinction. Accordingly a sample of typescripts from one term's collection (about 250 items) was scrutinised by an independent panel of judges who were asked to rate each piece on a four-point scale from 'certainly factual' to 'certainly creative'. The number of cases where there was a discrepancy between intended and actual outcome was encouragingly small, particularly when the immaturity of the writers was taken into account.

Excluding the material from the first term in which 'day's output' was employed, 20 pieces of writing were produced by each pupil over the five following terms; roughly 6000 texts in all containing just under 700,000 running words. In reporting the results, output or fluency measures are based on this corpus of data. Illness among the research workers unfortunately caused a curtailment in the scope of the linguistic analysis. The results presented are therefore derived from the collections for the second and sixth terms 2000 pieces of writing and 250,000 running words. The time-lapse between these two writing occasions was 17 months.

Analysis procedures and units of analysis
Since no single model could be predicted to fulfil all the project's needs in identifying and tracking indices of linguistic development, systemic

and transformational-generative analyses were employed alongside the work based on the traditional model.

After a promising beginning, the transformational-generative analysis had to be discontinued. The systemic analysis sampled processes from each of the three language functions: transitivity (ideational function); modality/modulation (interpersonal); thematisation (textual). In the event, it proved possible to complete this analysis for only one school of the nine (results reported Harpin *et al* 1973).

Analysis using the traditional model accordingly became the chief exploratory instrument and its concerns were extended to take account of the enforced reductions. Some elements — sentence and clause length, indices of subordination, kinds of sentence — were selected on the evidence from earlier enquiries that they provided relatively stable measures of progress towards syntactic maturity. Others were added in order to determine their value as indicators of growth and flexibility in the syntactic repertoire, for example the appearance of subordination other than noun clause as object and adverbial clause of time; the use made of non-finite constructions in the main clause. Interest in elements of cognitive functioning and particularly (following, among others, Moffett 1968) the development of point of view led to the inclusion of a study of the incidence of personal pronouns.

Though most research enquiries into language development have concerned themselves to some extent with the amount of speech and writing produced, this interest has usually been prompted by design and analysis considerations most notably in compensating for inter-subject variability of output. The absence of a comprehensive study in the literature of writing fluency and its relationship with other variables suggested its elevation in this study to a major theme worth investigating in its own right.

Findings

Measures of fluency

The amount of writing produced in responding to a need to write is controlled by a host of interacting influences, among them the writer's mechanical competence in getting the marks on paper, interest in writing in general and the topic in particular, time limitations, the nature of the task, presence or absence of external encouragement or inhibition, even physical circumstances. Yet, for all the variability introduced into performance by these influences, studies of writing output offer some insight into the growth of competence and confidence int the beginning writer. Individual variability is very great: among the 289 writers studied here, at one extreme is a child whose 20 pieces together total 500 words; at the other a writer who produces 7800. One part of the explanation of the difference is that the first is younger; 7–8 years against 9–10, but that still leaves much unaccounted for – a 7–8-year-old from the same class, writing on the same topics and in the same circumstances, produce more than 4000 words.

Ages Study	7+	8+	9+	10+	11+	12+
Harpin *et al.* (1973)	81	105	158	165		
Ford (1954)	68	95	133	168	175	195
Schonell (1942)	31	85	125	164	190	210
Harrell (1957)			202		224	
Heider and Heider (1940)		112	134	144	142	166

Table 10.1 Mean number of words per piece of writing, by age

Table 10.1 shows how, in various studies, the length of a piece of writing has been found to vary with the number of pieces of writing included (four each for Schonell and Ford, a single example for Harrell and Heider & Heider) and presence or absence of a time limit, the constancy of means across these studies is striking. The higher figures for Harrell's subjects may be explained by his practice of encouraging them to write more if he felt their compositions to be 'unusually short' (Harrell 1957, p. 28). No evidence seems to be afforded here for the contention that insistence on handwriting and the niceties of spelling and punctuation (supposedly a characteristic of practice in schools until the 1960s) inhibited writing production.

Creative, no preparation	145.8
Creative, with preparation	161.0
Factual, no preparation	97.1
Factual, with preparation	113.5

Table 10.2 Writing output and kind of writing (mean number of words per text)

When we consider the mean number of words in the various types of text (Table 10.2), the differences here are in accordance with the hypothesis that children are less confident in writing in descriptive or explanatory modes. Much, if not most, of the 'creative' writing adopted the narrative form. Though the means given here appear to suggest that verbal preparation encourages a more extensive response, the results, collection by collection, demonstrate that the difference diminishes steadily over time. By the time of the final collection, equivalance is established between the two preparation conditions.

	EPVT	Raven's Matrices
Writing production	0.401	0.456

Table 10.3 Intercorrelations : writing production and test scores

Intercorrelations were obtained of various measures with the Test Scores (Table 10.3). Measures of verbal and non-verbal ability are not unexpectedly shown to have a relationship with writing output, but the values are modest, supplying further support for the point made earlier that individual differences in writing are not explained by the operation of a single dominant variable. Of those others investigated in relation to writing output, social class membership and social adjustment (as determined by global score on the Bristol Social Adjustment Guide — see Stott 1966, 1970) made a significant contribution; size of family and position in family did not, the last despite frequent references in the literature to the advantages in language development and use enjoyed by first or only children.

In all, 12 language measures were selected for study: sentence length; clause length; subordination index; Loban index of subordination (Loban 1963); proportions of simple and complex sentences; incidence of non-finite verbal constructions in main clauses; 'uncommon' clauses (i.e. excluding noun clause object and adverbial of time — see Lawton 1963); use of personal pronouns; first and third person pronoun use; and non-subject uses of personal pronouns. Of these, five will be referred to in this discussion (full details of analysis procedures and conventions and results for all variables can be found in Harpin *et al.* 1973).

Age Study	7	8	9	10	11	12
Harpin *et al.* (1973)		9.0	9.8	10.2	10.6	
Schonell (1942)	7.5	9.0	10.9	13.0	14.0	14.9
Heider and Heider (1940)		10.2	10.9	11.1	11.1	12.8
Stormzand and O'Shea (1924)			11.1		12.0	13.5
Lawton (1963)						15.9

Table 10.4 Mean sentence length

Sentence length
Despite the lengthy arguments in the earlier literature on the unreliability of the measure (see particularly Hunt 1965, Chapter 3), it seemed too useful a construct to discard. It is the only grammatical unit

to be orthographically marked, apart from 'word', and embodies the syntactic and stylistic clause-combining operations. Using a set of working rules (Harpin *et al.* 1973, p. 73), the analysts achieved an inter-scorer reliability better than 0.90 in identifyng sentences in the writing (see Table 10.4).

Age Study	8	9	10	11	12
Harpin *et al.* (1973)	6.4	6.5	6.8	7.3	
Heider and Heider (1940)	5.2	5.3	5.4	5.4	6.2
Harrell (1957)		6.2		6.2	
La Brant (1933)		6.5	6.5	6.8	7.2

Table 10.5   Mean clause length

Clause length

A similar range of variation occurred with clause length (see Table 10.5) as with sentence length.

An explanation of the variability in the figures concerning both clause and sentence length may be related to the suggestions made earlier, particularly in respect of kinds of writing and number of pieces analysed. The 'working rules' for sentence definition, referred to earlier in the case of Harpin *et al.* (1973) were more tightly drawn than was the case for most other investigations and therefore likely to produce more conservative estimates. Here, as elsewhere in this section, reference to *rate* of development is of interest. The assumption of a steady change in language measures over time has to be rejected when a pattern of acceleration and slowing down, cyclically repeated, seems to fit the evidence more closely.

Age Study	8	9	10	11	12
Harpin *et al.* (1973)	15.5	18.1	18.6	19.5	
Heider and Heider (1940)	10.0	12.0	13.0	15.0	15.0
Harrell (1957)		11.6		15.6	
La Brant (1933)		17.8	19.0	21.2	
Sampson (1964)			21.3		
Hunt (1965)		22.2			

Table 10.6   *Subordination index*
(percentage of finite subordinate clauses to all finite clauses)

Clause subordination

We also calculated the proportion of finite subordinate clauses to all finite clauses (see Table 10.6).

By employing the device of subordination, speakers and writers can produce multiple clause structures of great complexity in the search for ways of realising intended meanings most fully. The speech and writing of young children is frequently marked by the absence of this construction, or its rarity. Instead, propositions are related in a linear fashion, commonly by co-ordination using 'and'. The discovery of this method of joining clauses and the exploration of its potential is charted in Table 10.6. Analyse of its use by mature writers indicate the extent of its employment. Boyd (1927), in looking for a measure of the maturity of his daughter's speech, analysed 'conversational' sentences from the work of 18 novelists and found a subordination index of 30 per cent. La Brant (1933) discovered in contributions to the volume *The Psychologists of 1930* an index of 46 per cent. In articles appearing in Harper's and Atlantic magazines, Kellogg Hunt (1965) noted an index of 42 per cent and observed that it was remarkably similar to that of the 18–year-olds in his sample.

The presentation of means inevitably conceals wide individual differences between children. Some ten-year-olds are confident users of the subordinating system; a few present no evidence in their writing over the two years of the study of an awareness of its existence. Variations in subordination related to kinds of writing are touched on below.

'Uncommon' subordinate clauses

Lawton (1963) attempted to test the hypothesis that there were social class differences in the range of types of subordinate clause employed in writing. For this purpose he identified the most commonly occurring as adverbial clauses of time and noun clauses as object; all others he expressed as a percentage of all finite clauses in the writing. For his 12–year-old group this yielded a figure of 13 per cent; for ten-year-olds in the study reported here the comparable figure was 8.3 per cent

A more illuminating measure, in developmental terms, is one that records changes in subordination over time, where the denominator is all subordinate clauses — not the total of all clauses (see Table 10.7)

	Group 1 aged 7½–9	Group 2 aged 8½–10	Group 3 aged 9½–11
Collection 2	10.5	20.0	26.0
Collection 6	19.5	36.0	36.2

Table 10.7   'Uncommon' subordinate clasues as a percentage of all subordinate clauses

Taken together with the figures in Table 10.6, those in Table 10.7 indicate that increased use of subordination is accompanied by a marked extension of the range of kinds experimented with. They also point to a phenomenon which is reflected in other measures, namely that the rate of development is variable. This seems markedly to accelerate as children move from the second into the third year of their junior school career and then to slow down again in the fourth year. One possible explanation links this variation with the growth of competence in meeting the mechanical demands of writing. With less attention necessary for handwriting, spelling, punctuation, fluency increases and with it the opportunity to test new ways of realising meanings, perhaps in part fed by increasing awareness of models from reading. A phase of consolidation could reasonably be suggested after this spurt as children become more conscious of themselves as writers and, influenced by teacher expectations, begin to concern themselves with economy and selection in shaping what is written.

Personal pronoun index
As Lawton (1968) noted, studies of language development tended to regard a diminution in the use of personal pronouns as an indicator of increasing maturity in writing. His findings recorded a fall from 7.4 pronouns per 100 words at age 12 to 5.5 at 15 (for his working-class group; the middle-class figures were respectively 5.4 and 4.9). Clearly the employment of personal pronouns will be strongly affected by kind of writing, but over a range of writing tasks this distortion will be to some extent minimised. If the move towards achieving the objective, impersonal stance in writing is accomplished by shedding elements of the personal, pronoun use might offer one perspective on this process in action.

	Group 1 aged 7½–9	Group 2 aged 8½–10	Group 3 aged 9½–11
Collection 2	13.1	11.9	11.1
Collection 6	13.1	11.6	10.3

Table 10.8   Personal pronouns per 100 words

If Lawton's figures (presented in Table 10.8) are representative of pupils eighteen months older than the oldest here, the pattern of results suggests a relatively late-developing and rapid change in this aspect of language use. the coincidence of the largest fall with the transition from the primary school to the secondary system at 11+ reflects other evidence that a radical change in writing tasks and expectations occurs at this point.

The influence of kinds of writing (see Table 10.9)

When the two preparation conditions are conflated, differences of means between creative and factual writing on these five variables are all significant (at the 5 per cent level or better). Such evidence lends considerable support to the view that factual and creative writing, as they were interpreted by participating teachers, are realised in linguistically distinct ways by these young writers. The nature of the analysis and the relative crudeness of the categorisation of kinds of writing must make any such conclusion provisional. A more delicate classification of discourse function (e.g. narration, explanation, argument) and an exploration of the effects of audience variation should be key features in further enquiries of this kind. A simple linear model of growth towards linguistic, and particularly syntactic, maturity is clearly inadequate.

Variable		Creative: no preparation	Creative: prepared	Factual: no preparation	Factual: prepared
1. Sentence length	Collection 2	9.58	8.74	10.09	9.56
	Collection 6	9.73	9.28	10.55	10.10
2. Clause length	Collection 2	6.64	6.24	6.78	6.96
	Collection 6	7.10	6.63	7.26	7.15
3. Subordination index	Collection 2	0.18	0.17	0.12	0.14
	Collection 6	0.20	0.18	0.15	0.18
4. Uncommon clauses	Collection 2	17%	20%	15%	27%
	Collection 6	29%	28%	26%	38%
5. Pronoun index	Collection 2	12.5	12.8	12.0	11.2
	Collection 6	12.0	12.4	11.9	9.8

Table 10.9 Kinds of writing — findings on five language variables

The influence of preparation on writing outcome is by no means obvious. The starting assumption was that, in general, the effect of intervention before writing would be to enhance the more mature linguisitc choices. The major contributor to pre-writing discussion is in most cases the teacher, not only selecting theme or topic and identifying its components, but also shaping the writing task and ways in which it might be tackled, including the provision of both lexical and syntactic resources. While the hypothesis holds, more or less, in the case of factual writing, the reverse seems to be true for the creative variety. The more mature choices are linked with the unprepared condition and the difference is maintained over time. Children may be more confident in the discourse mode, most frequently story-telling, that characterises creative writing themes and extensive preparation may inhibit experiment — beginning teachers (and others!) are often charged with talking a topic to death before writing ever begins. The less familiar discourse modes, including description and explanation, more likely to be required in factual writing, combined with a teacher's concern to be more in control of writing events for 'real life' experience, could make young writers more dependent on external sources of language models.

Though there is some warrant from the observation schedules for these general descriptions of writing circumstances, an enormous variety of practices may be concealed by aggregating them under the heading 'preparation'. The circumstances attending writing deserve careful scrutiny for their potential effects on the writing that emerges.

The impact of other variables on writing
School, setting, physical resources.
Though schools varied considerably among themselves in the writing performance of their pupils, these differences were more convincingly explained by reference to the measured ability of the children than on any other ground. Size, geographical location, ethos, existence of the implementation of policies for language development, and physical setting for writing offered no obvious clues to explaining differences in writing performance.

Teachers.
Just as the search for the school most effective in fostering writing development proved abortive, so, too, did the attempt to associate characteristics of teachers and their styles with writing performance. They differed widely in experience, training, special interests and methods and no common factor associated with success in promoting writing emerged, save one. Those teachers who strongly encouraged independent reading in class time when other learning tasks were completed appeared to have more than their predicted share of fluent, mature writers, but the link is at best a tenuous one.

Social class.
Of the association between social class membership and performance in written language reported by Lawton (1968) there was no sign. With intelligence test scores held constant, writing differences were insignificant. The age of the subjects may of course be crucial: Lawton noted that the differences between his social class groups widened with increasing age, from 12 to 15 years.

Handedness
The group of 33 left-handed writers in the sample had a marked advantage in test performance over their right-handed peers. The known difficulty experienced by such pupils in the physical act of writing

undoubtedly contributed to lower-than-predicted *output* figures; indistinguishable in fact from the outer group. Of more interest is that expectations of more mature performance on the language variables were also confounded, except for a slight advantage on sentence and clause length, and on the personal pronoun index. One possible explanation is that with relatively young and inexperienced writers, the very act of writing takes a disproportionate share of attention and a more restricted selection from the linguistic repertoire results.

Speech behaviour.
On each of the observation-schedule visits, project children were studied for a number of features of learning behaviour, among which was speech interaction with teacher and peers. On the basis of these observations four groups were formed: very vocal; moderately vocal; moderately silent; and very silent. The two extreme groups were similar in size, age distribution, test scores and balance of sexes but showed significant differences in writing. The 'silent' group produced more, tended towards more mature syntactic choices but the most marked contrast featured choice of personal pronouns. In a general movement for the whole sample over time of preference moving from third person to first, the 'vocal' group resist this change, while the silent set start with and hold on to a predominance of first person choices. If this in not a temporary phase in development, nor an arteface of either group definition or linguistic analysis, interesting questions arise. Which of the two groups will more readily adapt to impersonal writing? Will there be differences in sensitivity to audience? The groups are of course not homogeneous with respect to their distinguishing characteristics: one contains the inveterate chatterers together with the energetic, purposeful, curiosity driven; the other is composed of the absorbed, self-sufficient, well organised as well as the reserved, inactive day-dreamers. A more closely-controlled analysis could investigate the reality of these contrasts and explore their implications for more effective teacher interventions in promoting writing development.

Counters to counting

In the time since the enquiry reported here was completed, studies of the writing process, of writing performance and writing development, have identified new aspects of the activity for exploration, or, in some cases, have rediscovered old ones. Terms like 'development' and 'growth' abound in the literature on language acquisition, but only rarely are they carefully examined and defined. As Wilkinson *et al.* (1980, p. 14) point out, language development is heavily dependent on the social and situational demands made on the learner, not exclusively on an inner-driven, genetically-fixed process. He and his co-workers accordingly set out to chart the movement to maturity in writing on four dimensions — cognitive, affective, moral and stylistic — with some attempt to relate features in the writing to idenfifiable stages in the development process. Functional models (e.g.Britton *et al.*, 1975) have been suggested in which development, described in cognitive terms, is identified with increasing ability in tackling an ever-wider range of writing tasks. A more direct representation of the cognition–language relation in a developmental model rests on analysis of response structures: The Structure of Observed Learning Outcomes taxonomy (Biggs and Collis, 1981). Here the Piagetian stage of cognitive development of the learner is inferentially derived from writing by analysing it in respect of the kinds of relating operation employed, its degree of internal consistency and speed of closure.

Bereiter (1980) explicitly dissociates his provisional structural model from Piagetian stage organisation; for him stages are forms of organisation which may not be universal nor have a necessary order. The relationships among his six stages, from ideational fluency to epistemic writing, he describes (following Schaeffer 1975) as 'hierarchic skill integration' and their ordering as determined by the need to achieve automatic competence in the skill or knowledge system defining one level before progress is effectively possible to the next. Model-making of these kinds is not without its critics: some would argue for total rejection of the notion of stages of development (e.g. Collins 1984).

The disinterested observer of trends in the exploration of writing and writing development in children might judge that the age of quantitative analyses of writing samples is over: counting has been counted out. With Bereiter he might argue: 'However informative these analyses might be to the student of language development, they are disappointing from an educational point of view' (1980, p. 73). Some of the flaws have been instanced earlier in this discussion and the more extravagant claims for its usefulness discounted. To conclude from this that the method has nothing further to offfer is however to misinterpret the evidence. Ways of refining analysis and interpretation and of strengthening the design of enquiries are clearly discernible; some as yet modest advances have been been achieved (Watson 1983, Hunt 1983).

Of more significance is the realisation that no single approach is sufficient in itself to account for how writing is learned, how developed, how used. Andrew, a ten-year-old in a class of 32, had for two years been described as a 'reluctant writer'. When the class was taken to explore a large derelict house, once used as a school, and asked to write about the experience, his account was very different from the straight listing of observations and events the other 31 produced.

The Old School

Ivy hangs from the topmost windows like snakes hung upside down. It
lashes out at your arms and tries to hold you back. Where once feet
clattered and boys chattered moss grows. Where are the feet where have
the boys gone forever from the warm fires. The swimming pool rusts
every hour of the day. Everything everywhere is going to dust in that cold,
lonely place. Water no more comes forward from the taps no more do
boys play with the soap. Dormitories are dull, empty silent. A study stands
gloomy and bare. The wind streams in every crack and cranny.

Teachers are well used to the unpredictability of writing performance,
but have relatively little help in understanding how it comes about or in
assessing what part theirs is in the process. Is writing learned entirely by
writing or can it in some sense be taught? Which kinds of intervention
are beneficial, which obstructive? How should Andrew's teacher
construe his performance and how respond to it? Locating the piece
on some developmental model, establishing its syntactic maturity,
evaluating it with respect to judgement criteria, defining its rhetorical
purposes may help, but not if each act is seen as sufficient in itself.

All writers need a linguistic repertoire to call on in order to realise
their intended meanings effectively. More importantly the repertoire
needs to be fully accessible and the writer capable of judging selection
from the range of possibilities presented on the basis of fitness for
purpose. Syntactic analysis can offer insights into both the disposition of
language resources and their employment. Such studies should be seen
as a potent contribution to the knowledge base on which principled
policies or programmes for writing development in schools should be
founded.

Bibliography

APU (Assessment of Performance Unit (1981). *Language Performance in Schools. Primary Report No. 1*. London, HMSO.

APU (1982). *Language Performance in Schools. Secondary Report No. 1*. London, HMSO.

Bereiter, C. (1980). 'Development of Writing' in Gregg and Steinberg (1980).

Bernstein, B. (1961). 'Aspects of Language and Learning in the Genesis of the Social Process', *Journal of Child Psychology and Psychiatry*, vol. 1, pp. 313–24.

Biggs, J.B. and Collis, K.F. (1981). *Evaluation the Quality of Learning.* London, Academic Press.

Boyd, W. (1927). 'The Development of Sentence Structure in Childhood', *British Journal of Psychology*, vol. 17, no. 3, pp. 77–111.

Brimer, M.A., and Dunn, L.M. (1962). *Manual for the English Picture Vocabulary Tests.* Bristol, Educational Evaluation Enterprises.

Britton, J., Burgess, T., Martin, N., McLeod, A., Rosen, H. (1975). *The Development of Writing Abilities (11–18).* London, Macmillan Education.

Chomsky, N. (1957). *Syntactic Structures.* The Hague, Mouton.

Chomsky, N. (1965). *Aspects of the Theory of Syntax.* Cambridge, MA, MIT Press.

Clegg, A.B. (1964). *The Excitement of Writing.* London, Chatto & Windus.

Collins, J.L. (1984). 'The Development of Writing Abilities During the School Years' in Pellegrini and Yawkey (1984).

Copper, C.R. and Matsuhashi, A. (1983). 'A Theory of the Writing Process' in Martlew (1983).

Ford, C.T. (1954). 'Development in Written Composition During the Primary School Period', *British Journal of Education Psychology*, vol. 24, no. 1, pp. 38–45.

Gregg, L.W. and Steinberg, E.R. (1980). *Cognitive Processes in Writing.* Hillsdale, NJ. Lawrence Erlbaum Associates.

Harpin, W., Berry, H.M. and Williamson, J.G. (1973). *Social and Educational Influences on Children's Acquisition of Grammar. SSRC Research Report 757/1. London, Social Science Research Council.*

Harrell, L.E. (1957). 'A Comparison of the Development of Oral and Written Language in School Age Children. *Society for Research in Child Development*, vol. 23, no. 1.

Hayes, J.R. and Flower, L.S. (1980). 'Identifying the Organisation of Writing Processes' in Gregg and Steinberg (1980).

Heider, F.K. and Heider, G.M. (1940). 'A Comparison of Sentence Structure of Deaf and Hearing Children', *Psychological Monographs*, vol. 52, no. 1, pp. 42–103.

Hitchfield, E.M. (1973). *In Search of Promise*. London, Longman with the National Children's Bureau.

Hunt, K.W. (1965). *Grammatical Structures Written at Three Grade Levels*. Champaign, IL, National Council for the Teaching of English.

Hunt, K.W. (1983). 'Sentence Combining and the Teaching of Writing' in Martlew (1983).

La Brant, L. (1933). 'A Study of Certain Language Developments in Children. *Genetic Psychology Monographs*, vol. 14, pp. 387–491.

Lawton, D. (1963). 'Social Class Differences in Language Development', *Language and Speech*, vol. 6, no. 3, pp. 120–430.

Lawton, D. (1968). *Social Class, Language and Education*. London, Routledge and Kegan Paul.

Loban, W. (1963). *The Language of Elementary School Children*. Champaign, IL, National Council for the Teaching of English.

Loban, w. (1976). *Language Development: Kindergarten through Grade Twelve*. Champaign, IL, National Council for the Teaching of English.

McCarthy, D.A. (1954). 'Language Development in Children' in L. Carmichael (ed.), *A Manual of Child Psychology*. New York, Wiley.

Martlew, M. (ed) (1983). *The Psychology of Written language*. Chichester, Wiley.

Moffett, J. (1968). *Teaching the Universe of Discourse*. Boston, Houghton, Mifflin.

Myklebust, H.R. (1973). *Development and Disorders of Written Language*, vol. 2, New York, Grune and Stratton.

Pellegrini, A. and Yawkey, T. (eds.) (1984). *The Development of Oral and Written Language in Social Contexts*. Norwood, NJ, Ablex.

Raven, J.C. (1960). *Guide to the Standard Progressive Matrices*. London, H.K. Lewis.

Raven, J.C. (1963). *Guide to Using the Coloured Progressive Matrices*. London, H.K. Lewis.

Sampson, O. (1964). 'A Linguistic Study of Written Composition of Ten-year-old Children', *Language and Speech*, vol. 7, no. 3, pp. 176–82.

Schaeffer, B. (1975).   'Skill Integration During Cognitive Development' in A. Kennedy and A. Wilkes (eds), *Studies in Long Term Memory*. London, Wiley.

Schonnell, F.J. (1942).   *Backwardness in The Basic Subjects*. Edinburgh, Oliver and Boyd.

Stormzand, M. and O'Shea, M.V. (1924).   *How Much English Grammar?* Baltimore, Warwick and York.

Stott, D.M. (1966).   *The Social Adjustment of Children*. London, University of London Press.

Stott, D.M. (1970).   *Bristol Social Adjustment Guides: The Child in School*. London, University of London Press.

Strickland, R.G. (1962).   'The Language of Elementary School Children and its Relation to Reading Textbooks', *Bulletin of School of Education, Indiana University*, vol. 38, no. 4.

Watson, C. (1983).   Syntactic change: writing development and the rhetorical context. In Martlew, M. (ed.).

Wilkinson, A., Barnsley, G., Hanna, P., and Swan, M. (1980).   *Assessing Language Development*. Oxford, Oxford University Press.

11 Writing Development – Theory and Practice

ERIC CARLIN

Writing was long considered a simple clerical skill. Development of writing ability was a matter of making fewer mistakes and approximating more closely to models of complete adult writing. Fortunately consideration for the writing process has done much to change writing instruction methodology. Views of writing development, however, remain substantially theoretical and explanations and measurements of the sorts of change occurring in a child's writing are still being formulated. The study reported here considers some of the theories and measures of writing development and applies them to samples of writing from primary school children to attempt to show what development means in the writing of particular children. This, in turn, may justify some generalisations about writing which may help us enhance rather than inhibit its development. One contributory factor must obviously be the children's own concept of writing, and thus in addition the view of the writers are sought on what writing means to them.

The following piece was written by Laurel at the age of seven:

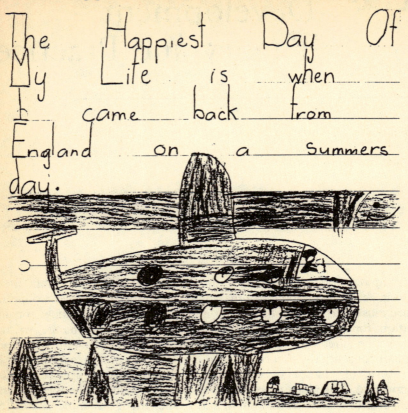

The Happiest Day Of My Life is when I came back from England on a Summers day.

When asked at twelve years of age what she could remember about the writing Laurel had this to say:

Laurel   I always remember coming back in the plane — having to get up and swapping planes in the middle of the night — I don't know — I can't remember much about England — just coming home on the plane — and getting ready to leave England.

Teacher   Was it important to draw a picture?

Laurel   Not too sure. What I remember of the plane was that it was really big — had two storeys —

Teacher   Was it difficult to write that much?

Laurel   Yes

Teacher	What was difficult about it?
Laurel	Forming the letters and things
Teacher	Were you saying things with the picture?
Laurel	Yes, I suppose — I think I was saying — because I went up in the pilot's cockpit and he was very nice — that's something I remembered and I remember him as the pilot.
Teacher	And that's why you put him in the picture?
Laurel	Yes
Teacher	And you remember it as two storeys high so you had two rows of portholes.
Laurel	Yes (*enthusiastically*). It was one of those double — two storey planes — and I can remember Dad saying we couldn't go on the top because it was too expensive or something. I remember when I was in England I was always drawing Koalas.

At age eleven when asked to write about a significantly happy or miserable day Laurel had returned to this same subject.

MY Best Day

My best day is when we where coming back from England
We were on a jumbo-jet and I was sitting in my seat rather boared (I was five years old) when one of the air-hostesses came around to me whith crayons and books. Then when starting to colour, the same hostess and asked if I would like to see the cockpit and where they prepare the dinners. From

the cockpit you see right out of
the big window then I went to
the kitchen where I got little tit -
bits and a drink. The loud speaker
broke in, Laurel could you please go
to your seats for we are landing
(the captain knew my name).

        We landed some where at
night to change planes. We went threw
this check out place and I was holding
my bear. The porter (who was saying no bears
allowed sorry. When to we arrived home
the first thing I did was ride my
bicycle.

The discussion with Laurel, now focusing on the second piece, continues. When asked why there were no pictures in this piece she replied:

> I think I explained it all in the story instead of saying it in the picture — when I write stories there are various pictures going through my mind and I think I wrote what was in my mind then and I didn't have to draw a picture and also I had to do everything quickly because I had only — I had to do everything like that. I don't know why I think it was important to draw pictures because all my former work has got pictures and I've got written expression from England and it's alway got a gigantic picture. I hardly ever draw pictures on my writing now it's mostly borders and fancy stuff like that.

I include these two pieces and Laurel's comments because they illustrate something of what is already known about writing development. There is the early dependence on pictorial representation as a stage in cognitive development; the young child's problems with motor coordination and the programming of written statements; the expressive–poetic nature of the seven-year-old's sentence; the later capacity to translate mental pictures into verbal symbols; the developing sense of audience indicated by the bracketed asides; the extended form of the second piece with the now more cognitively mature writer's capacity to included additional information, and so on. More importantly, perhaps, the two pieces give a graphic before/after contrast. How are the changes to be explained — how are they to be measured? What *is* writing development?

The project

In 1979 I began collecting samples of writing on five different topics from children aged seven in their second year of primary schooling. The children were in three suburban schools in Perth, Western Australia, with two class-size groups in one school (A — low socioeconomic area) and one in each of the other schools (B and C — both high socioeconomic areas).

As far as possible the writing samples were to be representative of the children's normal written work. The writing was promoted by the class teachers in their own individual ways having regard for the basic requirements of the topics which were:

- An account of a significantly happy or miserable day in the child's own experience.
- A description of something for which the child has strong feelings — a favourite or best thing.
- A story based on either one of two pictured scenes both of which featured children in open-ended situations.
- An account of an activity in which the child was involved such as an experiment, outing or excursion for someone who wasn't there and knows nothing about it.
- A story about an adventure in an unusual imaginary environment such as outer space, a haunted house or the like.

The topics were broadly defined in this way and the teachers were free to promote the writing in whatever way was usual for their classrooms.

Over the six-year period of the project the original 124 children were reduced to 48. Fortunately the proportion of children in each school remained fairly constant with 24 in School A (14 boys, 20 girls), 12 in School B (6 boys, 6 girls), and 12 in School C (7 boys, 5 girls). Whole class writing activities continued throughout in order to minimise any 'halo' effect on the children remaining in the project. In the final year (1984), after the collection of samples had been completed, the children were given a Language Abilities Test (Wilson 1980) and interviews with 18 of the children were audio-recorded.

Theories of writing development

Significantly helpful theories about writing development are advanced by Moffett (1968; 1981), Britton (1975), Britton *et al.* (1975), and Bereiter (1980). All these theories stress the close bond between writer and writing; that the development in the writer makes possible the development in the writing; that writing is the prism through which a writer's development is refracted and made observable. Writing development is directly linked with cognitive maturation.

Both Moffett and Britton suggest that development is marked by the child's capacity to process, in writing, increasingly abstract treatments of subject matter and to write for a more and more generalised audience remote from self. Similarly development is marked by a capacity to use increasingly complex forms for the expression of ideas. From a more analytical point of view Moffett (1981) sees the writing act as the integration of a number of constituent elements such as drawing and handwriting; transcribing and copying; paraphrasing, summarising, plagiarising; crafting conventional or given subject-matter; and revising inner speech. Moffett sees the need for children to draw on experience of all of these for any piece of writing but most importantly they should practise the expression of their own thoughts — their own inner speech — if they are to develop as writers. Too much time spent on activities that do not involve writers in expressing their own thoughts will detract from their developments as writers.

Although there may be evidence of all these elements of writing in Laurel's first piece, clearly the lower order elements predominate. She herself speaks of difficulty in, and therefore need for attention to, the formation of letters. There is the careful concentration on the crafting of the sentence and the reminder of borrowing in the final '... on a summers day'. Her capacity for revising inner speech is much more limited than it proves to be at eleven. By then her writing, with its greater information content, largely successful control of grammatical structures, control of spelling, punctuation and paragraphing, together with an obvious awareness of audience, suggests considerable growth in the mastery of Moffett's constituent elements. Such growth is, for Moffett, synonymous with writing development.

Bereiter (1980), who sees writing development in terms of cognitive maturation, would describe Laurel's development in terms of the successful integration of skill systems. In his terms her writing exhibits elements of associative, performative and communicative writing. He sees writing development in terms of the progressive integration of skill systems. With cognitive maturation the writer is able to focus in turn on: the process of getting ideas down (*associative* writing); shaping associative writing in terms of style and mechanics (*performative* writing); and shaping performative writing to have a calculated effect on a reader (*communicative* writing). Further skill systems are necessarily integrated by the exercise of critical judgement about, and reflective thinking on, the writing to produce respectively *unified* and *epistemic* writing. This model proved helpful in accounting for significant development in the project writing.

It is not necessary to view mastery of Bereiter's skill systems as discrete, finite accomplishments achieved in neat sequence — it is more likely that mastery of each is achieved at progressively more demanding levels during the period of writer maturation. Various mechanical skills can become sufficiently automatic without being completely mastered. What does seem to happen is that when new skills are being acquired, old ones may temporarily be lost. A writer's achievement can fluctuate widely under the pressure of acquiring new sikills even though the general trend of of development is maintained. New skills being integrated are as obvious as the stresses their integration causes. And it is not simply a matter of a writer learning new skills, for the writers who sees the need for new skills is, himself, changed. Cognitive and affective development demand new modes of expression — different language structures. Consequently, children writing need considerable support, particularly when they are making mistakes.

While some writers show earlier development, significant development is most marked in the project children's writing between their eleventh and twelfth years. At the time the majority seem to make their big leap forward. Here is a piece written by Arthur at eleven. It resembles closely the pieces he had written in previous years on this topic.

Pemberton

Pemberton is a very nice place it is very cold there. It is down South on the on the very tip of W.A. Pemberton have many forests including one of the only Karrie forests in the world. The trees are very tall there. There is a trout hatchery there there is the Rainbow Trout Trout and the Brown Trout. There are many Trout in the steams two to. At night time it very cold and rainy. I went to the Timber Mill there and saw all the different stages the wood goes through for cutting. In one of the forrests there is the Glouster Tree which was used for a look-out tower for fires. I enjoyed my self alot there.

This second piece, on the same topic, was written when he was twelve.

Adventure World

Adventure World is a place made just for fun. If you want to go to Adventure World you will have to take the 10.15 Adventure World Express. Adventure World is on the other side of the river at Bibra Lakes, it takes about three quarters of an hour to get there. On the way there, there is signs to tell you were to go. When I got there I saw a castle made of Limestone and wood. It is quite expensive but now there is a seven dollar all day pass it mean that you can go on all the rides for as many times as you want. As I walked through the entrance I first saw skull rock and swimming areas. The first ride I saw and went on was the racing cars, they were set up on a big tract. The cars were like go-carts with a motorised engine that went quite fast. Next I went to the shooting gallery there were targets which were actervated by a light flashed from the gun. After that a went to have lunch, there was a resturant which was up stairs. There was a balcony with the whole view of Adventure World. Frome the view you could see the paddle boats, the train, the tractor, the animal farm, the mono-rail and other things go there and enjoy it.

As in Laurel's case, but more subtly here, a more cognitively mature writer presents more information on each aspect of his subject. In the second piece the information is arranged in logically sequenced and extended segments. There is, however, some confusion at the margin between information on how to reach Adventure World and what is to be seen inside. There is also a lack of paragraphing and the punctuation he had inserted accurately a year earlier is missing from the longer and more complex sentences he is now attempting. Nevertheless the second piece by Arthur shows greater writer development and communicates more directly because he spreads his attention to cover the information, and how, and for whom it is presented. The new sense of a reader of his writing is one of Arthur's big advances at this time.

Similarly Jenny, who, like Arthur, had in earlier years produced very limited pieces, makes a sudden leap forward in writing development at twelve years of age. As with Arthur the leap is not entirely successful but the attempt is marked and obvious. Jenny had chosen to write in successive years about her cat, Sooty. At age 11, this is what she wrote:

My Cat

My cat is the most hamson cat in the whole wide world. He is black and he looks so cute and I like him. He has a girlfriend who lives down the road. And he is white, brown and black. My cat is greedy he eats half a tin of whistkas or snappy tom. He is quite large for a one and a half year old cat. When we had our guinea-pig he used to jump in his cage a play with him. My pussy cat is rather a bit of red on his stomach.
I
    Like
        Him!!

At age 12:

My Cat Sooty

I received my cat two days before Christmas because I had asked Mum and Dad so many times if I could have a black cat Mum wasn't really in favour of me having a cat, but she didn't mind if I had a black cat because she had one when she was young.

My cat's name is Sooty. Sooty is rather small and has very big eyes when he is in the sunlight his fur changes its colour into a light red. His paws are very soft when you touch them. At night he sometimes sits in the bean bag he purs very loudly just like dad snores in bed.

The description continues for two further paragraphs before concluding:

Sooty had a drastic disease on his back and some of his hair fell out. Mum quickly drove Sooty down to the vet one day when I was at school. The vet said it was lack of vatamin B and requested us to give him vatamin B tablets. After giving him tablets for a couple of week his back healed!
The End

Jenny's writing has developed in a number of areas at the same time. The differences between the pieces in amount of information, organisation and presentation, are both marked and revealing. There are also advances in social cognition and critical judgement — the latter signalled by a more personal style, a recognised view point. There are of course short-term costs to be paid for such developmental advances — they are paid here in terms of paragraph organisation, sentence structure and punctuation.

The majority of the project writers seem to show little advance before their obvious surge at age eleven but others show much earlier, if piecemeal, development.

The two pieces which follow were written by nine-year-old children — Robert in School A and Miranda in School C. The topic was the account of an activity for an uninvolved reader. (Only the beginnings and ends of the accounts are shown.) This is Robert's piece:

Walking in Fremantle

On the 3rd of November we went to the Fremantle Museum and when we got there we looked at the boats and we weren't aloud to climb on it. after that we went out side the entrentce and I waited for the lady to come. Then we went inside and got a rest board. then we went inside and went to the challenger room . . .

. . . and we got ont he bus and went to school and on the way back to school we saw a fair. It was an hours drive back to school.

Miranda's account goes like this:

A Day-At Teachers College

> Today we went to Teachers College. First we saw some books. There
> were drawings to match match. After that we imaginded we we were
> convicts I hated that it was disgusting. Soon after we had a drink. Then
> we listened to a dull story. We sung a song and played instruments. A few
> minutes later we had another icy cold drink. It got hotter every minute . . .
> . . . When we finnaly got back to school I thought what a boring disgusting
> day we all had yuck. Thats the worst excursion I have had.

While Robert's writing development may not have progressed very far
— not much more than associative in Bereiter's terms — there can be
no doubt that Miranda's shows aspects of communicative writing. She
has considerable reader awareness and is intent upon communicating
her feelings of persecution. A writer's intention and emotional involvement with subject matter appear to be prime factors in promoting
developed writing performance. Any model of writing development
needs to take these into account.

Britton's (1975;Britton *et al.* 1975) contribution to an understanding of
writing development is well known. Moffett's concept of cognitive
maturation and consequent mastery of hierarchies of abstraction
underpin Britton's well-known transactional–expressive–poetic model
of function categories. The expressive is synonymous with Moffett's
'inner speech' and is seen as being 'the seed bed from which more
specialised and differentiated kinds of writing can grow towards the
greater explicitness of the transactional or the most conscious shaping of
the poetic'. (Martin 1976, p. 26). Nevertheless, judging from the
samples collected, it is also true that the writing of even the youngest
writers is dominated by a strong sense of narrative. Whatever the task,
the time sequence which governs their own lives manifests itself quite
naturally in the chronological ordering of their own writing. Wilkinson
(Wilkinson *et al.* 1980b, pp. 10–11) makes a similar observation about
children's early writing in the Crediton Project.

Measuring writing development

How one measures writing developments depends very much on how
one views writing. The theories of development already examined in this
paper suggest that writing mirrors the cognitive, linguistic and effective
development of the writer. But measures have not necessarily been so
broadly based.

Historically, and predominatly, measurement has been in terms of count
measures based on a linguistic analysis of writing. The work on such

measures by Hunt (1965) and Loban)1976) is well known. Generally speaking, writing development is seen as syntactic maturity and measured in the length of T-units or communication units (a main clause and all its dependent phrases and clauses). Harpin (1976 and present volume) takes a basically similar approach but uses a number of measures which give more information about the degree and kinds of subordination used within each sentence. He also uses a personal pronoun index as a measure of decentration and elaboration.

More recent work on measurement by Wilkinson *et at.* (1980a) takes a more holistic and descriptive approach. Count measures are eschewed. Instead the child's writing development is analysed using cognitive, affective, moral and stylistic models of development. Wilkinson and his associates feel that 'writing is not just communicative; it is thinking and feeling, and learning to think and feel' so that any assessment of writing should address the question of 'what, in the communicating being, is the relationship between the communicating and the being' (Wilkinson *et al.* 1980a, p. 225). Wilkinson's measures thus relate closely to the theories of writing development already considered.

It was decided to analyse the children's writing using both Wilkinson and count measure systems and compare the information obtained. It is not possible of course to make precise comparisons but each system provides information about the project writing and thereby give some indication of its value as a measurement instrument.

For count measures Harpin's system was used. All the samples of writing were analysed using this system while a small representative set were analysed using the Wilkinson system.

The Harpin analysis of five samples from each of the 48 children in the six years of the project produced the mean scores as in Table 11.1.

Table 11.1   Count analysis by years.

Calendar year (school year)	Total word count	Average sentence length	Average clause length	Index of subordination	Weighted (Loban) index of subordination	Uncommon subordinate clauses as proportion of all subordinate clauses	Personal Pronoun Index
1979(2)	43.0	9.8	6.3	17.6	3.4	30.8	17.7
1980(3)	79.9	8.7	6.2	16.4	3.1	32.2	16.2
1981(4)	129.7	9.0	6.2	17.5	3.2	29.9	16.1
1982(5)	134.5	9.7	6.3	20.0	3.8	33.5	14.8
1983(6)	177.5	10.4	6.5	22.7	4.1	39.4	14.9
1984(7)	2323.0	10.9	6.8	24.3	4.2	42.1	13.6

Note: The disproportionately high figures in 1979 were likely due to the difficulty of analysing some of the very immature scripts.

These figures confirm what is generally known: that during the primary school years there is, in general, a steady increase in sentence and clause length, in the amount of clause embedding in sentence, and a growing diversification in the kinds of embedding used. There is a steady decrease in the number of personal pronouns used per 100 words of running text. Contrary to expectations there are no consistently significant differences, using these measures, in the scores of the boys and the girls.

Where significant differences do occur they are in the scores of individual school groups. (Table 11.2)

School A

Year	TWC	ASL	ACL	I/S	W I/S	USC/SC	PP1
1979	42.2	10.5	6.3	19.9	3.7	31.5	18.6
1980	79.2	8.4	6.2	14.5	2.8	35.0	16.0
1981	143.4	9.0	6.2	18.4	3.4	34.2	16.7
1982	115.8	9.6	6.2	19.2	3.8	34.9	15.1
1983	149.4	10.0	6.4	21.5	4.0	40.2	15.3
1984	187.3	10.2	6.6	22.3	3.8	40.3	14.6

School B

Year	TWC	ASL	ACL	I/S	W I/S	USC/SC	PPI
1979	53.4	10.0	6.2	21.6	4.4	37.7	18.2
1980	92.1	9.2	6.3	20.3	4.0	28.4	16.3
1981	170.4	9.9	6.5	22.4	4.2	34.0	14.5
1982	170.0	10.4	6.6	22.3	3.8	30.2	14.6
1983	236.8	12.0	7.0	25.1	4.3	36.5	13.4
1984	263.4	11.9	7.1	26.8	4.7	44.4	12.1

School C

Year	TWC	ASL	ACL	I/S	W I/S	USC/SC	PPI
1979	33.0	8.2	6.4	8.7	1.5	22.2	15.6
1980	68.7	8.7	6.0	16.2	2.9	30.5	16.6
1981	65.5	8.2	6.1	11.4	2.1	17.7	16.3
1982	128.8	8.9	6.0	18.9	3.8	34.8	14.4
1983	167.4	9.7	6.3	22.4	4.3	40.7	15.5
1984	299.1	11.3	6.9	26.2	4.5	43.4	12.8

Table 11.2 Scores of individual schools

Interestingly the differences in school performance shown here — differences which are quite marked and statistically significant — extend through the six years of the project. Of further interest is that the rank ordering of schools' performances on these measures reflects the rank order of their performance on the Language Abilities Test (Wilson 1980) given late 1984. Those mean score results were:

School A   106.9
School B   111.15
School C   123.5

(The Test mean score for 12-years-olds was 108.6). The differences are probably due to differences in ability or socioeconomic factors.

Count measures do seem to provide useful *general* information. For example, on the basis of the analysed project writing, sex does not seem to be a significant determiner of writing development using these measures. Age, home background, verbal ability do seem to be significant determiners. On the matter of school influence the verdict is probably not proven. At least six different teachers taught the children in this project with all teachers having had much the same sort of training and direction. Of some importance in this regard is that an examination of detailed results by schools shows that the results of school B retrogressed on all counts of all topics in 1981 and a similar slump occurred in school A in 1982. What is important, however, is that these events do not appear to have affected the trends of development using count measures in those schools. In other words the effect that a teacher may have in any one year does not seriously disturb the general trend of writing development of a particular group of children.

Count measures do, however, have their limitations when the nature of writing development is to be considered at the individual level. Patterns of development become less easy to distinguish where scores of individual writers on particular topics are concerned. In order to demonstrate this let us examine two writers, in terms both of count measures and of Wilkinson's developmental criteria. Michael and Andrew are the same age; they have identical scores on the Language Ability Test; they have attended the same school for the past six years and share similar socioeconomic backgrounds. The means of their 1981 count measure scores are similarly high (Table 11.3).

	TWC	ASL	ACL	I/S	W I/S	USC/SC	PPI
Andrew	201	12.9	7.7	23.8	4.4	39.2	11.3
Michael	202	10.9	6.7	30.3	5.9	40.3	12.4
Andrew	172	13.2	7.1	41.6	7.5	70.0	9.3
Michael	231	11.0	7.7	20	2.5	33.3	9.9

Table 11.3 Scores of two pupils writing on two different topics

These scores do not, however, reveal fully the differences in writing development displayed in these two pieces. Lets look first at Michael:

Teachers College

Early in the morning we walked tiredly to the Teachers College. It took us about 30 wasted minutes to reach there when we could have been sitting at school doing maths. That shows you how bad the excursion was to those who are listening to me.

First we saw a display. The display was filled with mainly books, science fiction, history and war. There were also a display of excellent pictures from books by Colin Thiele with some writing about the book, like a review.

Then we went to do some drama, prentending to be a convict in the 1800's, the old days. It seem a hard life as a convict. Mr XXX will know more about convicts. He's lived through the 1800;s. We also made a boat.

After that we learnt to concerntrate. The clown, Rainbow tired to make us laugh with funny noises.

When we had finished we listened to an aboriginal legend called "How The Sun Was Made." It was about two animals and they had a fight. One animal was full of rage so he threw a animals egg up into the sky. Unfortunately the egg hit a fire and the egg burst into flames. Then we had a relaxing drink.

We then came to school. It was very hot weather.

Andrew's version of the same events is as follows:

Teachers College

Today we walked in the scorching heat to the Teachers College, of course taking the long way. Thats because Miss XXX didnt know the way.

After the wasted ½ hour of walking we got there. Soon we went into a room which had little bits of writing about a certain story with a matching picture.

After that we went with a man so called Rainbow. We imagined that we were covicts. Some boys pushed a container away from the others while other boys pushed other people off.

Soon after that we went and heard a story called Cricket. It was about a farmer called Cricket who wanted to be famous and become more famous by accident.

We went to have an ice cold drink after the story which I think was the best thing there. Then XXX took us on one of his so called short cut which took us about 10 minutes longer.

Anyway wer'e back to school, even though I hate it, it was better than the ecursion.

By using Wilkinson's models (1980a, pp. 227–38) for the analysis of writing the differences in individual development become clearer — differences that are not obvious ont he basis of count measures alone.

Andrew offers evidence of rather limited affective development. His sense of affront is completely self-centred and concentrates on what for him are the negative aspects of the experience. He displays little sense of organisaton other than chronological. His vocabulary is limited and description vague. There is a monotony of style evidence by the repeated 'soon'. He does not consider, indeed seem aware of, the needs of a reader. He succeeds in conveying a sense of personal frustration.

Michael, by contrast, takes a more balanced approach; he is more aware of other people, of a reader and of the environment he is describing. The reader has a cleared sense of the place and what is happening. Michael's sense of task is clearer — he effectively marshalls information for his report. He has a clear sense of the reader's needs in matters of detail — as he sees them — which is not completely, as he fails to explain who 'we' are. His own feelings are under more control: the weather is perhaps more to be blamed than are people. Despite the occasional ellipsis his sentences communicate effectivley. Other than adverbs the vocabulary shows a developing range and capacity for exact description. Though there are few subordinate clauses — there is a commendable variety of sentence openings and use of cohesive devices.

Surprisingly on the basis of count measures alone Andrew's piece would be seen as indicating greater writing development. It seems obvious that count measures, useful as they are as indicators of *group trends*, provide an inadequate description of *individual* writer/writing development. An abbreviated version of the Wilkinson models for the analysis of writing would seem to offer more scope for assessing *individual* writer/writing development.

Children's concept of writing

The development of writing ability is an enterprise sponsored by adults but carried out by children. How do the latter view their task? We decided to ask them, and interviewed 18 of the children — ten from school A and four each from schools B and C. These children were representative of the full range of writing development is indicated by both count and Wilkinson measures and language ability scores. The same set of questions was used for all interviews though supplementaries were used to amplify particular responses. The interviews, made in 1984 when the children were 12 years old, were recorded and transcribed. The sample was small and though the analysis was unsophisticated the children's comments provide an interesting alternative view of writing development and factors which affect it and put our more abstract deliberations on development into a new and interesting perspective.

Writing, for these children, represents both training in a skill and a vehicle for vicarious experience but the two may not be seen by children as equally important in the same piece of writing. For many of the children the term writing is synonymous with 'story'. They prefer the term 'written expression' or a functional label like 'report' or 'project' for non-imaginative writing. Overwhelming their preferred writing activity is story-writing, especially stories based on science fiction or other forms of fantasy. These are preferred because they are easier to write and provide intrinsic rewards for the writer.

> Oh, just fun. When you write about things that you don't really know about. Just makes it up. (Russell)

> Er. When you write haunted-house — mystery stories you get very excited — and you've got all good words to use in them.
> *Where from?*
> Well, listening to the teacher's and reading out of mystery books. (Michelle).

> I hate doing realistic things. I prefer fantasy things. I hate having to do realistic and things that actually happen because then it is too difficult and you have to get all the facts right and I don't like it. (Catherine).

The appeal of stories as vicarious experience becomes even more obvious when the question of envisaged reader is adressed. There is no reader other than the writer. Imaginative composition is a closed circle.

> *Who do you like writing for the best?*
> Myself
> *So you put in there what you want to enjoy?*
> Yes (Courtney)

> *And are you the reader too?*
> Yeah, I read it. Well not actually, I am *in it*, kind of thing — most of the time.
> *So you're having an adventure in the writing?*
> Yes (Russell)

> *Who is the reader when you're writing?*
> I just write it
> *You don't think of a reader?*
> No
> *So you're not putting things that a particular reader is going to need — or like?*
> No. I put in what I like! (Robert)

Writers show a wide range of opinions on the importance of writing. Michael emphasises its functional aspect:

> Well it's one way of communicating with people and lots of people enjoy reading stuff, and it's a good way of speaking if you write it down first.

Robert's is a pragmatic view:

> Because when you get older you'll be coming across it a lot more — when you're older you'll have to write more — if you write when you're young you can get all the punctuation and that straight — when you get older you won't be embarrassed or anything.

Kylie values the therapeutic nature of writing:

> *Do you like writing about familiar — things that have happened to you — real thing?*
> Yeah. To get them out of my system I like writing about what's happened — the past.
> *How do you mean — 'getting them out of your system'?*
> So that you never — sort of — never said it out or written it out before and you just sort of want to give it once and put it in a story.
> *And what happens when you write it in a story?*
> I usually feel a lot better after I've written it out . . .

Courtney's view is monomanic:

> *Is writing important?*
> Science fiction is important.

David sees it as purely punitive:

> Writing is important at school. I don't write much at home.
> *So it's not important for you?*
> *Not unless I have to do it.*

In the matter of subject-matter for writing the more developed (though not necessarily the most mechanically correct) writers prefer to choose their own topics, while the less developed not only prefer to write on given topics, but also rely on teachers for ideas and relevant vocabulary. More-developed writers, who place a strong emphasis on mechanical correctness, are also inclined to rely more heavily on teacher-supplied topics, ideas, vocabulary, and so on. Outline plans for a piece of writing seem more likely to be prepared and adhere to by less-developed writers, constantly amended by mid-level writers and little used by the more developed writers.

In the matter of their concern, while writing, for words, sentences, punctuation, paragraphs, and so on, most more-developed writers claim that these aspects cause little problem as they are considered a natural part of writing ('probably since Grade 5', as Gerald said). Less-developed writers have difficulty handling these aspects, make many corrections while writing and usually need to rewrite the whole piece. This may not be due to maturational factors alone. It may well be the case in imaginative writing that an unconcern for these matters is due to the writer's total absorption in his or her own vicarious experience. All writers recognise the dual importance to a piece of writing of subject-matter and clarity of presentation but their theory may be at odds with their practice. ('You've got to think about both — you've got a sandwich when you write', said Arthur.)

All writers stress the importance of supportive response. Few writers say they experience teacher interest in the detailed content of what they write. Very few writers expect such interest.

Some implications

This paper has attempted a brief treatment of some theories and measures of writing development in the context of a small longitudinal study of a particular group of children. On the basis of their writing and interviews the implications for our classrooms seem to be as follows:

- While drawing may be a necessary precursor and accompaniment to writing for young children, the need to draw at any stage of the writing process declines with writing development.
- Children's concept of writing will be limited to their experience of it as a productive and receptive activity.
- Few primary school children — Kylie is a notable exception — reach a developmental level of being able to reflect on the significance of the content of their own writing.
- The wide range of writer/writing development, even in this small sample, underlines the negative reinforcement for most writers of numerical or alphabetic assessment. The complex nature of factors which contribute to writer/writing development makes assessment irrelevant unless it measures an individual within the context of his or her own general writing development.
- Considerable teacher support is necessary when children are showing enhanced development. It is then that they make most mistakes and need most understanding.
- Given the fact that emotional involvement of the writer often produces writing at a higher level of development this is not an argument for artificially involving the child's emotions by teacher motivation. If true authoring is revising inner speech such motivation is unlikely to promote inner speech adequate to sustain an even moderately extended piece of writing.
- Writer/writing development is more likely to be enhanced by stacking the shelves than by manning the check-outs. The shelves should provide writer security, plentiful opportunities for writing, self-chosen topics, positive vicarious experiences, a rich language environment, experience in a wide range of writing forms, writing experiences which provide positive feedback, activities which

sponsor affective, cognitive, moral and linguistic development. Writer/writing development is about having the goods, not about having them valued.

Bibliography

Bereiter, C. (1980). 'Development in Writing' in L.W. Gregg and E.R. Steinberg, (eds), *Cognitive Processes in Writing*. Hillsdale, NJ, Lawrence Erlbaun Associates.

Britton, J.N. (1975). 'What's the Use?' in A. Wilkinson, *Language and Education*. Oxford, Oxford University Press.

Britton, J.N., Burgess, T., Martin, N., McLeod, A., and Rosen, H. (1975). *The Development of Writing Abilities (11–18)*. London, Macmillan Educational.

Dierderich, P.B. (1974). *Measuring Growth in English*. Champaign, IL, National Council for the Teaching of English.

Emig, J. (1971). *The Composing Process of Twelfth Graders*. Champaign, IL, National Council for the Teaching of English.

Fredericksen, C.H. and Dominic, J.F. (eds.) (1981). *Writing: The Nature, Development, and Teaching Communication: vol. 2. Writing: Process, Development and Communication*. Hillsdale, Erlbaim.

Harpin, W. (1976). *The Second R. Writing Development in the Junor School*. London, George Allen & Unwin.

Hunt, K. (1965). *Grammatical Structures Written at Three Grade Levels*. Champaign, IL, National Council for the Teaching of English.

Loban, W. (1976). *Language Development: Kindergarten through Grade Twelve*. Champaign, IL, National Council for the Teaching of English.

Martin, N.C. (1976). *Writing and Leaning Across the Curriculum*. London, Ward Lock Educational.

Moffett, J. (1968). *Teaching the Universe of Discourse*. New York, Houghton Mifflin.

Moffett, J. (1981). *Coming on Centre: English Education in Evolution*. Montclair, NJ, Boynton/Cook.

Wilkinson, A., Barnsley, G., Hanna, P. and Swan, M. (1980*a*). *Assessing Language Development*. Oxford, Oxford University Press.

Wilkinson, A., Barnsley, G., Hanna, P. and Swan, M. (1980*b*). 'The Development of Writing', *English in Education*, vol. 14, no. 3, Autumn.

Wilson, C., (1980). *The Language Abilities Test*. Melbourne, Heinemann.

Part Five

Form and Style in Writing

12 Interrelations of Reading and Writing*

GUNTHER KRESS

Some Issues in Reading and Writing

Reading and writing are functionally differentiated aspects of one system, and of one set of processes. An exclusive concern with either overlooks essential characteristics shared by both. Most importantly, reading and writing are both activities the draw on the forms, structures and processes of language in its written mode. That makes reading and writing fundamentally different from listening and speaking (see Kress 1982, Chapter 3; Halliday 1985). Hence neither the process of reading nor that of writing can be understood in isolation from the other. Indeed I wish to argue that in order to understand the way in which children learn to write we have to understand how and what children read.

Yet reading and writing are also distinct activities. All of us read more than we write, and the proportions in which we engage in either vary hugely, in a manner which is largely determined by social factors — class, education, (social constructions of) gender, ethnicity. For some children, reading (including 'being read to') plays no part in their lives outside the sphere of the school; for others it plays a very large part. They do not all start at the same point. For all children language in its spoken mode is the major linguistic experience when they arrive at school; for some children it is the only linguistic experience. Already

---

* This paper differs somewhat in emphasis from that given by the author at the International Writing Convention.

then it is essential to understand what the difference between speech and writing is about, and how that difference can be and is negotiated by children in their years of schooling.

Reading and writing, like all language activity, always take place in a specific social context. The purposes, functions and organisation of the context shape the language that is part of that context. Two things at least follow from that. The relevant linguistic unit is defined by the social context of which the language is a part. That unit is the *text*. The text is therefore the point of departure in learning and in teaching, both for the child and for the teacher. Social contexts differ: a committee meeting is not structured like a fireside conversation; nor are the functions of either the same, or the purposes of the participants. These conventionalised differences of occasion lead to conventionalised differences of kinds of text. For these I have used the traditional term *genre*. In learning to write, children have to learn the genres — and their formal characteristics — which are characteristic of specific social occasions. The occasions in which speech and writing occur differ, along the lines of larger cultural and social structures. Hence written genres have to be learned as new forms, distinct from spoken genres. But that fact of social differentiation also points to the much larger issues of the social place and political power attaching to any one genre, and the positioning of readers and writers (and of speakers and hearers) within them. That matter has fundamental implications for the content of a writing curriculum.

In this chapter, I explore some of these interrelations: between spoken and written language; between the activites of reading and writing; between social structures and linguistic form. My aim is to put some issues in the learning of writing on the agenda and to suggest that the questions around the learning of writing need to be seen in a wide social context.

The interrelation of reading and writing

I wish to consider now certain aspects of the effect that reading may have on writing. The texts range from those written very early in the child's schooling to some written in year 10 (of the South Australian system), at the age of 15. I also consider some texts which form reading materials for learners of writing. The kind of reading and the notion of reading at issue changes in fundamental ways over that period.

In the case of the first text, written by a boy of seven, the experience is not from his own reading, but from being read to by adults.

The Two Poor People

1   Once upon a time there lived two poor people.
2   They longed to be rich
3   One day when they were in the woods looking for fire wood.
4   When they met a prince riding through the woods
5   The prince stopped and looked at them and said Are you poor.
6   At first they were to scared to answer.
7   But in the end they answer yes we are poor.

25   When they got her home the witch gave the king and queen a red apple.
26   The king and queen took the apples and went back home and eat the appler.
27   Nects day the prince found the king and queen dead
28   The prince knozu a wizard
29   That day the prince went to tel the wizard
30   The wizard came and made the king and queen aliv agen and ciled the witch and they live happyly evry efder

This text shows the evidence of much 'reading'. It is clearly not the result of the reading of one single text, but is the result of 'hearing read' many similar texts. The evidence lies in a number of features of the text. The child has brought together typical plots, and characteristic episodes from the genre 'fairy-tale' and produced a single text within that genre, even though the stitches between the various fragments show. However, it would be wrong to see this as a shortcoming or a fault. Rather it points to an attempt — and the ability — to draw together material from a diffuse reading and to integrate that into a coherent whole. The child is not merely retelling one story, or a series of stories, but rather he is drawing on a large number of texts, remembered largely in schematic terms, and reproducing that 'reading' as a new text. In other words, what we see here is one point in the process of the learning or writing at a general level, and of the process of the learning of a particular genre at a specific level.

Some of what has been learned from this reading can be described in summary form: the child has learned one type of larger narrative structure, as well as the structure of brief episodes within that; he has learned certain formulae, such as openings, transitions, endings. Other aspects of his learning are more complex. For instance, the child writer uses the *line* as a significant textual unit; at this stage the line equates for him with a narrative episode. Within the line there are a number of clauses which are here syntactically weakly integrated. However, the fact that these clauses are co-present in one textual unit is putting pressure on the writer to develop a different mode of syntactic integration. That is, he is moving towards learning about the internal organisation of sentences. Some of the words and phrases of the syntax of writing and of this genre are in evidence: for instance, 'There lived two poor people', 'They longed to be rich', 'they met a prince riding through the woods' (where the embedded relative clause '(who was) riding through the woods' is much more typical of the syntax of writing than of speech).

At a yet more general level, the child has learned about the 'staging' of narrative, and he has learned to give order to events. Here the order is that of (temporal) sequence, which copies and depends on the sequence of events in the imagined and narrated world. The conceptual order is sequential, through the conceptual effort goes beyond this: from a diffuse range of readings, held in his memory, to a competent implemenation of that genre. Conceptually, then, this text is about integration.

An important general point arises out of this discussion. What the child is doing seems clear enough. He has, from a diffuse reading experience absorbed story-grammars, narrative schemata, narrative episodes with their appropriate details, relevant syntax and words. He has generalised from these and has produced a plausible text in the genre of fairy-tale. How are we to assess this process and its result? Everything in this text is conventional, taken from other texts, we might even say plagiarised. Nothing in it is original or creative. Yet the cognitive processes in evidence here are of an enormously powerful, general and generalisable kind. I make this point for a number of reasons: it seems to me that the first and essential task which faces the writer is to learn and gain control of specific generic forms. In gaining control of these forms the writer at the same time gains control over the social and psychological structures, functions, goals and purposes which are encoded in the generic form. And it is only from this basis that any writer can attempt to move into areas which might be labelled 'creative' or 'original'. At any rate there is no sustainable case for an easy dismissal of the skills displayed here, and of the social and cognitive abilities that they imply.

In the case of the next text, 'Who was Goyder', the reading is of a different kind; it is a (nine-year-old) child's *own* reading, and the relation of her reading to the written text is more direct. Her reading materials consisted of two texts written by adult (amateur) local historians, part of whose texts are reproduced here, *The Story of Mylor* and *History of Mylor*.

Who was Goyder

(1) Most people think that Goyder was the founder of Mylor but he wasn't. (2) He was South Australia's Surveyor General. (3) The drainage of the South East and the planting of Pinus Radiata. (4) It was recommended by him. (5) Mr. Goyder lived at Warakilla an old coaching inn he got it in 1987. (6) He liked the country so much that he

didn't mind taking the trip daily.   (7) Goyders house is really two in one the original was built in 1842.   (8) In 1880 Goyder bought the house and named it Warrakilla.

History of Mylor

(1) Possibly the most outstanding citizen the Mylor had was the then South Australia Surveyor General, Mr. Goyder, after whom Goyder's Line was named; his interest in drainage in the South East and the planting of the *Pinus Radiata* were also recommended by him.

The Story of Mylor

In 1880 the property came into the possession of an outstanding public figure of the day. This man was George Goyder, the S.A.'s Surveryor-General. Goyder's name will always be associated with the delination of a boundary line for wheat-growing, based on an average 14 inch rainfall.

Apart from his name perpetuating this line of rainfall he also performed invaluable survey work throughout Central and Northern Australia.

In 1860, he was appointed Surveyor-General and it was after his return from a mission to England that he took over the Inn. Like William Warland he too was greatly impressed with the natural beauties of its setting. First he changed the name to Warrakilla, an aboriginal name which he acquired during wanderings in the Northern Territory. Then he set about enlarging the original premises.

While religiously preserving the character of the old inn, he added a substantial home built solidly of freestone with walls as thick as a fortress. Around the house he lavishly planted English Trees, shrubs and hedges, including the rare Oregon pine and English beech.

Some of the strategies employed by this writer can be seen by a closer analysis of her text, and by contrasting that with the model texts that she had read. First, take her third and fourth sentences. In the original *History of Mylor* the content of these two sentences is part of a subordinate clause in a larger sentence. There the two complex nominal constructions: 'His interest in drainage in the South East' and 'the planting of the *Pinus Radiata*' function as conjoined subjects of one clause. Complex nominals such as these are frequent in (adult) writing, indeed they are characteristic of and typify writing, due to the integrating and embedding strategies of writing. They are not characteristic of speech; speech characteristically proceeds by the aggregation of simple clauses. The child's strategy here is to resolve the complexity of the original text in part by treating the two nominal constructs as a separate 'sentence', and to do likewise with the remainder of the initial clause. In other words, the writer employs the strategies of the spoken mode — the adjoining and chaining of simple clasues — to resolve a difficulty and complexity posed by the model text. In effect, what she is doing is reading the structures of the written models back into her own knowledge of the syntax of writing, which at this stage is still shaped largely by the syntax of speech. In doing so she does have further justification in that both the nominal constructs are clause-like in their meaning — both describe processes: 'His interest in drainage in the South East' is related to 'He was interested in draining the South East'; '[His interest] in the planting of *Pinus Radiata*' is related to 'He was interested in planting *Pinus Radata*'.

The same process is at work in other parts of the text: for instance, the second sentence of the child's text is treated as part of a larger sentence in both of the two model texts. Similarly, the last clause of the child's fifth sentence, 'he got it in 1879', is adjoined in the typical manner of speech. In the model '. . . it was after his return from a mission to England that he took over the Inn' content is handled in the characteristic manner of written syntax. In this last example the child also changes the lexical form of the written 'took over' to 'got', which is both typically speech-like and more in tune with her own knowledge anduse of language.

The child's reading constitutes an active process, one in which she reworks and reconstitutes the written model texts in terms of her own linguistics knowledge. This is evidence which can be most useful to a teacher interested in the child's reading. It is evidence that the child's linguistic knowledge is not at the level of the model text; it is evidence of the degree to which the syntax of speech is still the dominant model and affects her writing and reading; it is also evidence of the fact that she has strategies for coping with this discrepancy; and lastly, it is evidence for the specific nature of the strategy that she is adopting to cope with the difference and discrepancy.

Clearly, too, it is not a question of the child's merely imitating or plagiarising the models. She does take over whole segments of the model text into her text, most notably 'The drainage of the South East and the planting of Pinus Radiata'. There are two things that need to be borne in mind here.

First, all texts, whether those of children or those of adults, whether of amateur or of accomplished writers, do precisely that. If I wrote, in some essay on Goyder, or said in conversation to someone who asked me about Goyder, 'The planting of Pinus Radiata was recommended by Goyder' or 'Goyder recommended the drainage of the South East' or even if I used a term such as 'the planting of . . . ' or 'the drainage of . . . ', would I be imitating or plagiarising? Yes, to the extent that all texts draw on other texts, and all language is a common resource for its users. No, to the extent that it is a harmful misconcepton not to acknowledge this crucial characteristic of language, and to talk vaguely of 'creativity' and 'originality'. Creativity and originality operate against a ground of the shared resources of language, against the fact that any one text draws on other texts, is constituted of elements of other texts, and is defined also in contrast to other texts, in the intertextuality of all language use. To ignore this in an educational context has the potential for damaging judgements made on child learners, judgements which are no less harmful and long-lasting for their being erroneous.

Second the two phrases, and the syntactic forms of writing which they represent, are 'there' in the child's text. And being there, they do pose a problem for the child. She needs to come to term with them, and ultimately to assimilate them into her own linguistic knowledge. As a linguistic strategy the device of 'borrowing' or 'lifting' parts of someone else's text is entirely common, and is general to all language users, child or adult, native speaker or learner of another language. The first time I used the word 'paradigmatic' it was no more and no less 'my word' than the phrases above are those of the child writer.

Other effects of reading which are noticeable here are the child writer's learning of a specific *genre*, which is, broadly speaking, that of scientific writing, and more specifically, (local) history writing. (Of course, the fact that the models are provided by amateur local historians has to be taken into account.) Some aspects of this are: impersonality (which signals objectivity): 'most people', 'It was recommended . . . '; the use of the passive: 'It was recommended by him', 'the original was built . . . '; the use of dates; and 'factual evidence'. Notice that both the originals show a very heavy use of these features. Whereas the text of 'The Two Poor People' followed an order of events arranged in a chronological sequence, the order of *Who was Goyder* is of a different kind: it is an order that pays attention to the demands of the material dealt with. Again, the focus on the subject-matter and its demands is typical of writing, and particularly of scientific genres. Of course, what seems like the 'internal logic' of the material is an order imposed by the child, in conformity with the demands of the genre.

My next example text was written by a 15-year-old boy, in year 10 of the South Australian education system. Reading here stands in a fairly direct interrelationship with writing. The subject is geology; the first text is part of a hand-out written by a teacher, the second text is a set of answers to a quiz set by the teacher. The numbers in the student's text are those of the answers.

Geology

Man's part in soil erosion
For centuries, man has mercilessly cleared as much of the native vegetation from the surface of the earth as he could, in order to grow his crops or pasture for his animals. He is only now beginning to realize that he has responsibilities towards the land if he wishes to keep it producing for him.

Soil creep
If soil particles lie on a sloping surface, they will tend to move downlhill. This effect is called 'soil creep' and is evident on sloping land by the presence of shallow, parallel 'steps'.
Normally, the trees and bushes growing on the slope would limit the amount of soil creep on a hillside, but if the land has been cleared, mass movement of topsoil can result. This can be aggravated by stock using the 'steps' continually as paths. Usually, the effects of soil creep take place very slowly, and cannot be seen, but sometime it is made obvious where fence-posts and trees are seen to lean downhill.
Prolonged wet weather will saturate the surface soil and 'lubricate' layers of clay which lie beneath the surface of some soils.
A section of the surface soil may then move rapidly downhill, causing a landslide.

Man's part in soil erosion
1. Soil creep is when soil particles on a slope move downhill.
2. Evidence of soil creep is the presence of shallow, parallel 'steps'. Also fence post trees tend to lean downhill.
3. The absence of trees and bushes and stock using the 'steps' as pathways aggravates soil creep. Also the same as in number 4.
4. Prolonged wet whether will saturate the surface soil and 'lubricate' layers of clay which lie beneath the surface of some soils. This makes a landslide.
5. We can excuse the early settlers because they weren't used to the climate of Australia and didn't realise the damage they were doing.

This text illustrates a further specialisation of genre which has taken place. The child can read directly on to a knowledge of the syntax of writing which is now well established, and on to a knowledge of many aspects of different generic forms — though the latter are still subject of some learning. In other words, the effect of reading is now in a significantly different area. While for the nine-year-old the syntax of writing was the major problem, the focus of learning has now shifted to detailed points of generic form. What are they, in this example? In the main they centre on three related features: on the full command of the specific technical/scientific language of a particular academic discipline – geology in this case; on the use of metaphor as a strategy of theoretical/scientific language (and thought and action); on the ability to sustain the features of a specific genre over an extended text.

The first of these lies most prominently in the knowledge of the special terms of a discipline: 'soil particles', 'sloping surface', 'soil creep', 'sloping land', 'shallow "steps"', etc. In fact, just about all the content-words are specific to this discipline; even where the words seem those of everyday use they appear here with a quite specific meaning. Note for instance 'shallow steps', or 'tend to move downhill'. This characteristic is overtly acknowledged by the teacher in some instances, where the discrepancy between the specialist meaning and the general meaning seems too large; in those cases the adult writer uses inverted commas to alert the reader and to signal the distance between the everyday and the specialist use.

The second feature concerns the use of metaphor. The most outstanding example is 'lubricate'. Here a process of one kind, perhaps not all that well understood, is explained in terms of another process which is familiar. Whether the teacher understands the geological process described here as 'lubrication' or not is not the issue. The point is that it is a common process in theoretical and scientific work and writing (as indeed it is in everyday life), and this is one kind of language learning for the child writer. Other examples are 'soil creep' (soil does not 'creep'), and 'steps'.

The third feature, the sustaining of genre, is perhaps not fully discernible in this brief text, though it is clearly evident in the last text considered, 'Telecommunication', below.

The interrelationship of reading and writing is clear. It interacts here with the child's assumptions about the teacher's aims in setting the quiz. At any rate, the structures, both linguistic and conceptual, of the model text have to be assimilated, integrated into the child's linguistic/conceptual knowledge, and reproduced in a text which attempts to interpret both the material and the teacher's aims. It might again be worth raising the question of imitation/plagiarism. In his fourth answer the child reproduces a part of the teacher's text nearly verbatim. Is this legitimate or not? The child has two tasks: to master the ostensive content, and the form in which this content appears. Not that these can be separated; I am using this formulation because the task is frequently framed in this way: 'State, in your *own words* . . .'. My point is that no one has 'their own words' in these matters, least of all a child who is on the path to learning specific genres.

The construction of readers in genres and discourses

I wish to turn now to a discussion of some texts which form reading materials in schools. We know that reading is an interactive process, in which a reader reconstructs a text in interaction with the forms, meanings and structures of the text. My particular interest is to see how a text structures or facilitates a certain kind of reading, and indeed how the text constructs a particular kind of reader. I will consider this mater from three points of view:

1. the generic form and discursive content of these texts;
2. how the texts construct the child as a reader; and
3. what models of writing and of the 'writer' these texts provide for the child learner.

I said earlier that genres are conventionalised textural forms which derive from (larger) social/institutional structures. They reflect, encode, and reproduce the meanings and functions of those social structures. The institution, in the case of these extracts, is the educational system, with its structures and meanings. Certain of these are reflected in the extract below, from a textbook (Harris and Stehbens 1981).

Regions

The area round a town in which its urban functions exert a strong influence can be described as a *functional region*. In highly urbanized countries this is probably the most useful way of division of large areas into smaller units for study. We need to remember, however, that the boundary of a region can be defined precisely only in terms of one factor, and then only if that factor can be expressed as a quantity. We can talk of part of northern New South Wales as within the region of 50 per cent or more commercial orientation to Brisbane; we can also talk of that part where 50 per cent or more of the people take in Brisbane daily newspapers; the boundaries are different, but they both mean something precise. To speak of the 'Brisbane region' without any indication of the way it is defined is vague indeed. In Chapter 2 the boundary of a population density region was defined from statistics in a precise way.

We have seen too that functional regions overlap and nest one within another. The fringe zones of the four New Zealand towns in Fig. 5.8 would overlap one another if plotted on one map. If the criteria used had been comparison rather than convenience goods, it is probable that all four towns would have have come within the functional region of Hamilton, a much larger town. Hamilton, in turn, in other fields could be considered part of the functional region of Auckland, the largest city in New Zealand.

Geographers have at different times thought of regions in different ways. Functional regions round towns as nodes are one kind, applicable in most places, but specially suited to industrial and commercial areas. French geographers early this century considered that a region was a part of the . . .

The institutional meanings reflected in this extract are those of the geography curriculum. It is important to bear in mind that the extract is not the complete text, and therefore does not display all (perhaps even the major) aspects of the genre, and of its forms and meanings (chapters, sets of questions, diagrams, instructions to teachers and students, etc.). Only some aspects of the generic form are evident. They include, at this level, a consistent set of modalities: 'can be described', 'probably', 'probably the most useful', 'however', 'can be defined', 'only if', 'without any indication', 'vague indeed', 'have seen too', 'would . . . if', 'If . . . [then] it is', 'if . . . then', 'could be considered'. These modalities express both care and careful distancing, as well as careful balance and nuance. They are matched by another set of forms, mainly adverbial, verbal and nominal, which indicate qualification and precision: 'in a precise way', 'defined precisely (only if)', '50 per cent or more', 'if plotted', 'defined from statistics', 'only if expressed as a quantity'. Passives, without agents, are common: 'can be described', 'can be defined', 'is defined', 'if plotted', 'the criteria used', 'could be considered', 'was defined'; as are indicators of impersonality: 'This is the most useful way of division', 'to speak of'; and of course all the agentless passives above serve to construct impersonality.

These features point to the meanings of the social institution of 'science' which here enters into and overlaps with the institution of 'education'. Certain generic elements point to the *didactic* function of such texts, and these are related to the institution of 'education': the use of 'we', which encompasses both the writer and the reader without the reader's permission being sought. A scientific text outside the genre of 'educational textbook' would not use 'we' in this fashion. Direct instructions are coded in the text: 'This term should not be confused with . . .'; and indeed in other sections of the text (not quoted) there are catechismic questions and instructions: 'find two towns . . . ', 'indicate a region . . . ', 'plot a set of lines . . .'. These occur as part of the text, not set off in any formal way. In all of these instances it is clear how generic features arise out of the meanings, processes, forms, and purposes of the social institution which gives rise to the texts.

Texts are structured by and constructed in generic form. Beyond genre, texts are also constructed in and by discourses. By discourse I mean a specific mode of talking, arising out of the meanings and organisation of given social institutions. That is, while genre codes the meanings of specific *social occasions* (say, a lesson, an assembly), discourses code the meanings of specific *social institutions*. The two are separate though related matters. Well-understood examples of discourses are sexism and racism, for instance. Through sexism the biological category of sex is constructed into the social category of gender, and that category is given valorisations which, in the case of Western technological society, reach into every aspect of our social lives, the family, work — or unemployment, leisure, social relations, the structures of knowledge, politics, and so on. Similarly with racism. As an example consider the next extract, again from a textbook (Marriott 1975).

Squandering our inheritance

We would have little respect for a young man who inherited great wealth but spent it so quickly that he died in poverty and left nothing to his heirs. But that is exactly the sort of thing the human race as a whole is doing today. We have inherited the earth and all it contains but we are using up its resources at a rate which, already alarming, is increasing rapidly. Unless drastic changes are made soon, our descendants will inherit a much poorer world.

How has this situation come about? First, the unprecendented rise in population (see Chaper 12) has meant greatly increased pressure on the world's resources. Second, the revolution in science and technology which has been mainly responsible for . . . The accelerated population growth has raised living standards to new levels in the developed nations. People in these countries not only expect high standards of living but hope for continued improvement. People in the underdeveloped nations are naturally anxious to reach similar standards. Governments and economists throughout the would have been obsessed with the idea of constant growth. The result has been an enormously increased demand for food, raw materials and energy. A contributing factor has been the extremely wasteful nature of large-scale commercial enterprises concerned only with increased sales (see Figure 14.4).

Part of the mischief has resulted from the belief that the resources of the world are inexhaustible or that even if we run out of some vital commodity, scientist will be able to find a satisfactory substitute. Such ideas are very dangerous, as they lull people into a sense of false security while irreparable damage is being done.

The world's resources can be divided . . .

Here you can see the operation of a number of discourses intersecting within the one text: a moral-conservationist discourse — which itself seems to be founded in a quasi-biblical-religious discourse — an economic discourse, a sexist discourse (the text was published in 1975 and would probably not be written in this form today), and an overarching common-sense discourse, — note the 'naturally'. These discourses, and the tensions created by their incompatabilities, contradictions, overlappings, and their contention with an absent technological/economic discourse constitute this text.

I wish to turn now to consider how child readers are constructed in these texts. First I wish to introduce the term *reading position*, to indicate that any text constructs a position for its ideal reader, a kind of vantage point, a preferred point of view from which to read a text, and in doing this indeed constructs an ideal reader. That is, texts make certain (unstated) assumptions about what their ideal readers should be, should think, should know, and should expect. The text, especially a successful text, coerces readers into that position, so that they read the text without resistance, 'naturally'. Of course, few readers are ideal readers, and indeed it ought to be the task of any reading programme to produce readers who are not ideal readers for any text; that is, readers who counter the text's attempts at coercion, to produce 'resistant readers'.

Generic forms — because of their total imbrication in social institutions — construct certain kinds of reading position. For instance, an interview — where the text is under the control of one participant, the interviewer — constructs a 'reading position' for the interviewee; so do conversations; so do the text extracts here. Discourses, because of *their* social institutional provenance, construct reading positions. Unless you are reading 'Squandering our Inheritance' from within certain discourses (sexism, certain moralistic-conservationist discourses), you will not be its ideal reader. It may be that you will permit the text to coerce you — even if only momentarily — or it may be that you will resist, in one or many ways.

I will look briefly at how reading positions are structured into a text in some details of grammar. Take agentless passives, such as 'The area . . . can be described . . . ': described by whom? Here the empty agent position provides a space for the reader — as agentive subject — to position herself or himself in the text. 'Ah', the reader is meant to say, 'can be described by *me*'. Similarly with 'To speak of the Brisbane region': who speaks? Again, in the non-finite verb form there is a space for the reader to become the subject of the utterance, and hence be part of the text. Or take 'this is probably the most useful way of division . . . ': who divides? Again, in the nominal form 'division', there is an implied verbal 'someone divides', and consequently there is a space for the reader to adopt that specific position within the text.

The abundant use of 'we' has exactly that function — it is an inclusive/coercive 'we', positioning the reader in an attitude of identification: 'We need to remember' — whose need is identified here? The point is probably clear enough. What I have said about the syntactic/grammatical level holds equally at the generic and discursive levels.

It seems, then, that texts do construct reading positions and, in so doing, attempt to construct readers of certain kinds. *All* texts are the same in this. Where texts in these educational genres differ from texts in other genres is in what I will call the politics of school-centred reading. Children, because of the power-relations in educational institutions and in the education process, are coerced into adopting the reading positions constructed in the texts, are forced into being ideal readers, are discouraged from being critical or resistant readers who can adopt distanced positions *vis-à-vis* the texts that they read. They are structured explicity and implicitly into the texts and into the larger contexts in which these texts occur, the purposes which they serve — as bases for assessments grading, ranking. These counteract the possibility of critical and distanced reading, of being a reader other than the determined by the text. It is an open question whether texts in the curriculum area of English are other and act differently than those I have discussed here, in their effect.

If the politics of children's school-based reading suggests that children are asked to be certain kinds of readers, this effect will translate itself into the kinds of writers children know that they can be. That process is further reinforced by the politics of children's writing, which is on the one hand an inversion of the usual situation of the powerful author/writer and producer of meaning *vis-à-vis* the relatively less powerful reader and consumer of meaning; and is, on the other hand a situation where children write for readers (i.e. teachers) who are not the appropriate audience for the texts that they constuct.

It is against this background that I wish to consider the last text, from a 17-year-old student's project on Telecommunication:

Telecommunication

THE ELECTRIC TELEGRAPH

Before the invention of the Electric Telegraph the fastest means of conveying a message had been shouting, the speed of sound, and signalling witt flags and the like. Both of these methods only good over very short distances and relied on good weather conditions. The Electric Telegraph seemed instantaneous in comparison to previous method. Telegraphy involves completing one or more electrical circuits being completed and broken to transmit a code . . .

THE TELEPHONE

Even though the electric telegraph was extremely fast at transmitting messages, all the messages had to be coded and sent along line one at a time with each word taking several seconds. So when the telephone came into operation it increased the speed of communication as well as making it more personal.

Chales Grafton Page (1812–1865) discovered, in 1837, that rapid changes in the magnetism of iron caused it to give out a musical note. Also that the pitch of the note depended on the frequence with which these changes occurred.

In 1860 Philipp Reis (1834–1874) was the first to transmit a musical melody electrically over a distance. He stretched an animal membrane over a small cone to which he attached a platinum wire with sealing wax. The wire was part of an electrical circuit and when the membrane vibrated the wire completed and broke the circuit at the same frequence as the sound. At the other end of the circuit was a knitting needle with a coil of wires rapped around it, and through the fact that Page had discovered the knitting needle reproduced the sound. Three years later he claimed 'that words can also be made out' . . .

THE RADIO OR WIRELESS

The telegraph and telephone had revolutionised communication but they had one big drawback in that they counldn't be used to communicate with moving vehicles such as trains or boats.

The story of radio perhaps begins with Joseph Henry (1979–1878) who, in 1842, show that electric discharges were oscillation. . . .

THE TELEVISION

The first developments of the television came at about the same time as the radio, but it took much long to develop than the radio. . . .

This sample text consists of a series of extracts from a much longer text. It differs markedly from the preceding texts in the relation between the writer's reading and the written text produced as a result of that reading. For instance, here the reading is documented in a bibliography, which marks a number of highly significant matters: the writer's awareness of the interrelationship of his reading and of his own text, which is an overt acknowledgement of intertextuality (that is, an acknowledgement of a special relationship between the texts cited, and his own text) a seriousness about the status of his text; and of course, an entering into another set of genres, that of serious, academic, research-based writing.

My main reason for including this text is to demonstrate both a new genre — the extended 'treatise' with formal chapters, and the achievement of sustained structuring of a text over an extended range. The whold text, a project on telecommunication, is about 3500 words in length. It consists of four 'chapters'; these are marked formally, each beginning on a new page, with a heading drawn in bold, capital letters. The project concludes with a bibliography, on a separate page. Within the chapters the paragraphs are clearly marked and function in formally developed manner. The text is interspersed with drawings of a technical kind, illustrating sections of the text. The syntax is fully that of writing, and is specifically that of a particular genre, the historical account of an area of technical progress.

The learning — and achievement — of writing which is at issue here lies in the ability to impose and maintain structure over an extensive text. The linguistic, conceptual and cognitive task is to devise, and to sustain, and order which is not in any significant way inherent in the material; which, while it is to a significant extent given by the formal features of the genre, yet still demands a sustained intellectual effort by the child. It is worthwhile to reflect again on the interrelation of reading and writing — for it is through reading, through assimilation and absorption of the formal aspects of these generic features and of their integration into the child's own schema, that a text of this kind can eventually be produced by a writer. Of course, knowledge and mastery of the generic features has at the same time certain cognitive consequences, a pay-off in terms of the ability to opearte complex linguisitic, conceptual schemata. And beyond these factors lies the whole area of social and cultural life, out of which the generic form arises, where the genre both encodes and performs certain specific functions, and where the ability to control the genre has high social valuation, and permits the writer to participate effectively in powerful areas of social and cultural life.

The major device used to sustain an integrated structure over the whole text is that of cohesion. The first paragraph of the second chapter establishes a cohesive link with the preceding chapter. It summarises and encapsulates the information contained in that chapter, and presents it in such a form that it becomes a useful stage-setting for the material following on. That is, it describes the achievement of the electric telegraph and at the same time it poses a problem left by that achievement. In fact, the very opening, the *theme* of the sentence, is the focusing on the problem — 'even though . . . ', suggesting both achievement and problematic via the modality. The rest of the chapter has the function of working towards a resolution of this problematic state. Notice that in its technique the text is not at all unlike the narrative structure of a text such as 'The Two Poor People' which is similarly, and characteristically, constituted around the dynamic of problem and resolution. Moreover that is also the characteristic structure of scientific papers, which follow a three-part structure of achievement/description of present state; introduction/description of problem; resolution of the problem. The second sentence of the opening paragraph of the second chapter picks up the problem, and suggests the nature of the resolution, as well as indicating an additional benefit. Of course, as this is the history of a technological area, the resolution lies in the detail of the technological achievement; and the second paragraph now moves to that detail. The beginning of the third chapter, 'The Radio or Wireless', again establishes a cohesive link, again by a summary of the material and by the positing of a problem, repeating the structure of achievement–problematic. this larger narrative structure is handled by a syntactic/textual variation: the problematic is introduced by the negating particle 'but'. The discussion of the larger topic of the third chapter begins in the second paragraph. In the fourth chapter, the cohesive link is established in the first sentence, as it is in the preceding chapters, though again with a syntactic/textual variation. The achievement/problematic structure is set up as before, though the problematic is of a different kind — not some weakness inherent in the prior achievements, but a problem inherent in the development of this technology.

These overarching cohesive spans give integration and order to this large text, and act at the same time as a motivating impetus for the development of the text. The text creates its own world, with its own logic and plausibility. The material gathered in the writer's reading is integrated in a text which makes a new, its own, sense of that material. As I said above, cognitive and formal properties of the genre are largely involved in that process but, of course, they can only be involved if child writers have internalised them, understood their function, and learned to control them for their own purposes. That is the basis, the essential, minimal foundation, on which achievements of an original and creative kind can be made. It is only when these achievements have been established that demands for creativity and originality can be made with any seriousness.

In a number of places, I have referred to the similarity between 'literary' narratives and 'non-literary' texts. I wish to draw one last analogy, namely the similarity of the opening of 'Telecommunication' with the opening of 'The Two Poor People'. Both seem to need a setting, a temporal placement and anchorage, which is both a setting off from previous time and from prior texts, and at the same time establishes a connection and a starting point. It is a general feature of many texts, and points to the need to keep thinking of the underlying unity of the linguistic and conceptual tasks of reading and writing in the different curriculum areas. The similarities between the earliest connections between reading and writing, and those which exist later on might also bear thinking about. Initially child's reading may be quite diffuse, and the interrelation of reading and writing indirect; the initial achievement by the child is to make his or her own sense of that reading, to integrate disparate elements into their own coherent texts. Certainly many features of that interrelation seem to be there in 'Telecommunication', over a time difference of eight years between it and 'The Two Poor People'. Certain factors have changed: the texts which the child now reads display an order which is derived from specific genres which are orientated towards the logic of the topic or the material; and learning of these genres and their meaning becomes the task for the child writer. Of course the genres that the child comes into contact with initially also display particular kinds of order, particular logics, derived from the world (re)produced in those genres. In the intervening stages there seem to be periods when the pressure from reading to writing is very direct, leading to quite direct lifting or quoting. The process, the interrelation, is that of a complex dynamic about which very little is known.

Bibliography

Halliday, M. (1985). *Spoken and Written Language*. Geelong, Deaking University Press.

Harris, D.D. and Stehbens, E.R. (1981). *Settlement Patterns and Processes*. Melbourne, Longman Cheshire.

Kress, G. (1982). *Learning to Write*. London, Routledge & Kegan Paul.

Marriott, K.L. (1975). *Man and His World, Book 4*. Melbourne, Macmillan.

13 The Development of Style in Children's Fictional Narrative

GORDON TAYLOR

Though concern with style has a long and distinguished history in literary critical studies and more recently in linguistic studies, the development of style in children's writing has received little systematic investigation. Not until recently with the work of the language team of the Assessment of Performance Unit (APU) in the United Kingdom, and more notably the work of Wilkinson *et al.* (1980) in the Crediton Project has any attempt been made to rectify this ommission. This paper outlines an attempt to develop the model of style put forward by Wilkinson with particular reference to the development of children's fictional narrative, and reports the progress made so far. It concludes with the preliminary results of an investigation of the writing of children aged between seven and 15.

The relevance of style

Style is by no means a simple or uncontroversial concept. In attempting to trace its development in children's writing the student of style is faced not merely with observing some clearly visible behaviour pattern but with having to define his ground before he begins. Style, as a glance at any of the numerous attempts at definition (Enkvist 1964; Grey 1969; Fish 1973) will illustrate, is an aspect of language that appears not to be clearly defined or even clearly understood. There is, therefore, a need to preface any observations on style in children's writing with some observations on the nature of style in general, how it may be measured and finally how it might be applied to the development of children's narrative fiction.

Given the controversial nature of style study it might at the outset be argued that it is likely to be a less than fruitful approach to children's writing. If the base on which the observations are made is insecure than the value of the observations will be undermined. To counter such arguments I would like to make two points. First, whatever that state of the theory of style, it is undoubtedly a reality in education. In the assessment of children's writing, stylistic criteria have traditionally been a commonplace and there is little doubt that they still are. The criteria used by the APU to assess writing in schools reflects this state of affairs by making style one of its four basic areas. Moreover, style is still an important aspect of assessment in O level examinations and questions relating to style are still frequent in literature examinations. In fact teachers are generally bemused that any difficulty might be encountered with the concept and its application. Style is also a reality in the wider social setting. In everyday speech the concept is accepted without question as is its definition. If style is so widely accepted, and if teachers, examiners and national monitoring units are using style for the assessment of children's writing, then there is a need to ensure that such judgements are made on a sound theoretical basis.

My second point is that, despite the difficulty of the enterprise, style study offers a perspective on the surface structure of language that is not covered by other approaches. For some decades past the study of surface structure has been dominated by purely linguistic approaches (e.g. Hunt 1970; Harpin 1976). Though valuable in their way, these I would suggest have been rather narrow and have somewhat limited our concept of maturity in writing. Style study can offer a broader view.

A definition of style

How can we begin to define style? Before beginning to do so it is salutary to bear in mind a comment made by Middleton Murry (1922, p. 3): 'A discussion of the word style, if it were pursued with only a fraction of the rigour of scientific investigation, would inevitably cover the whole of literary aesthetics and the theory of criticism. Six books would not suffice for the attempt: much less six lectures.' With this warning in mind I would identify four main characteristics of style. Style is:

1. a characteristic of the surface structure of writing;
2. a product of choice;

3. functional; and
4. related to contextual norms.

That style is a feature of the surface structure of language is hardly controversial. There is no theory of style that assumes otherwise. Aristotle writes of rhetorical devices, literary critics of verbal texture, and stylisticians of the expression plane.

Choice is central to most theories. It focuses our attention on the options available in language for constructing the surface structure of a text. Within choice, however, it is possible to distinguish two central areas. First the choice of appropriate language: lexical and syntactic choices that are appropriate to context, genre, purpose, subject matter or audience. This area of choice is widely acknowledged and forms the basis of the APU definition of style: 'the writer's choice and purposeful use of vocabulary and sentence structure with regard to the writer's subject matter, reader(s) and purpose, in so far as this can be determined' (APU 1981, p. 219).

The second area of choice is more problematic, though it is most often quoted as fundamental to style and is closest to the everyday understanding of the term, i.e. choice as different ways of expressing the same or similar meanings. This leads us into the difficult area of dividing content from expression, matter from manner, which would be strongly contested by many who would argue that a difference in the surface structure of language always involves a difference in meaning. Such arguments cannot be totally ignored but some distinction between underlying meaning and surface expression must be accepted if we are to retain a meaningful concept of style. Our everyday experience of saying the same or similar things in different ways would perhaps support the distinction but more objectively so would modern linguistics in the theory of transformational grammar. It argues that surface structure is produced by the operation of optional transformational rules on underlying syntactic or propositional structures. For instance, the two sentences 'The boy kicked the ball' and 'The ball was kicked by the boy' are said to derive from the same underlying deep structure or in case grammar from the same underlying propositional elements. There *are* differences but they are differences in perspective on meaning or emphasis rather than totally disimilar meanings. Apart from transformations, modern linguistics would identify language systems such as tense, aspect and mood as offering options for expressing perspective or attitude. Such theories not only support the concept of choice but provide some pointers to the origin and nature and possible function of stylistic differences.

This brings me to the third point — that style is functional. Again most theories recognise the importance of linking style with its function in the communication system of language if style is to be a genuinely

significant concept. The fact is that simply identifying a feature of the
text as stylistic is not in itself sufficient to explain its value. This can only
be done if stylistic choices are related to the function they serve in the
text as a whole and in the communication system of which the text is
part. What the function or functions might be depends largely on which
part of the communication process we focus on: the writer, the reader or
the text. These give rise to three main definitions of stylistic function:
expressive, affective and textual. What in detail these functions might be
and the way in which they arise can be explained as follows:

Expressive
Writing is clearly a matter of expressing meaning. However, a distinction
can be drawn between basic propositional meaning and the writer's
expression of that meaning: in the surface structure of the text. I have
given some indication of how this may work when discussing choice
above. Specifically, choice in this area may serve to express:

1. the writer's particular attitudes to the subject-matter;
2. emphasis, focus, or ranking of importance;
3. the writer's perspective on his subject-matter;
4. the writer's particular world view.

Affective
This function focuses attention on the way stylistic choice influences the
reader's response to the text. This involves affecting the way the reader
reads the text. Reading is a linear process involving a left-to-right
movement through the text during which the basic propositions of the
text are perceived. The nature of this movement can be affected by the
lexical and syntactic choices the writer makes. Specifically choice in this
area may serve to:

1. affect the pace of reading by choosing structures that are easy or
difficult to process or predict;
2. affect the reader's apprehension of the coherence of the text
through the manipulation of the range of cohesive links;
3. affect the reader's perception of meaning by choosing structures
that control emphasis or foreground particular aspects of meaning;
4. focus the reader's attention on the text itself above meaning. This
is sometimes referred to separately as the aesthetic function.

Textual
This function focuses on the stylistic choices that contribute directly to
the production of a well-formed text. As such it relates choice to the
overall organisation of the text as a complete unit, relating the parts to
each other and forming a unified whole. Specifically, choices in this area
serve to:

1. organise basic propositions into large textual units and delineate these larger units clearly. For example in narrative: orientation, episodic material, evaluation, resolution, coda. Other text types will have equivalent textual units.
2. link the parts of the narrative to each other clearly and cohesively. This includes the linking of basic propositions to each other as well as the linking of larger structural units.

Different theories of style usually emphasise one function at the expense of the others though there is clearly some overlap. Which one is chosen is perhaps a matter of the particular perspective taken. I would argue that each of these functions is suggestive of possible lines of approach to assessing the development of style in children's writing.

My fourth and final point is that style is related to contextual norms. This aspect of style deals with the expectations that are created by a given text and the way in which these expectations can be used to identify those features that are stylistically significant. There can be little doubt that we approach particular texts either as writers or readers with a set of expectations about the kind of features we will find predominating: for example, passivisation in science reports or strong action verbs in narrative. Such expectations are based on experience of reading such texts or listening to them and form a norm for the set of linguistic choices generally made by the writers in that genre (see Cullen, 1981). In addition there are those choices within a given text which frustrate those expectations for specific purposes or with specific results and which in turn form a characteristic of the text. These choices may be termed deviations from the norm. It would seem logical to accept that writers in composing texts either conform to or deviate from a contextual norm for specific purposes and that such conformity or deviation can be said to be stylistically significant. As regards the development of style in children's writing a contextually related norm would be a norm to which young children might conform while mastering the written system and its conventions but from which they might deviate as they develop as writers and individuals and realise the potential such deviations offer for fulfilling particular functions

A contextual norm for children's stories

On the basis of the above analysis of the major components of style in general we can now turn to consider the specific case of style in children's writing. If we examine the definition of style suggested by Wilkinson and Hanna (1980a, p. 177), we see that it has all the features outlined above: 'Style is the result of a series of choices made to diverge or not to diverge from the norm represented by the simple sentence.

The choices are made to the end of effective communication.' In this definition we have choice, function and norm. However, both the norm, the 'sentence', and the function, 'effective communication', are very general, which is not perhaps surprising given that it was devised to identify style in a range of different kinds of writing: fictional and personal narrative, argument and explanation. In working specifically on children's fictional narrative it seemed it would be more appropriate to identify a norm more directly related to narrative and more closely representing our expectations of its surface structure as well as a developing a more specific definition of function of stylistic choice in a narrative context.

The work of Labov and Waletsky (1967) and Labov (1972) on oral story-telling offers one such norm, and suggests some possible functions that conforming to or deviating from the norm might serve. In an analysis of the surface structure of the oral stories of children, adolescents and adults, Labov identified what he calls the 'narrative clause', a simple structure expressing a simple events. He argues that this it is the basic unit of narrative and defines narrative itself as a series of events in chronological order which are realised in the surface structure of the text by the basic narrative clause. Labov defines the characteristics of the narrative clause in some detail but essentially it consists of 'the simplest grammatical pattern in connected speech' (Labov 1972, p. 375): a simple sentence with simple subject, simple verb in the past tense without auxiliaries, and with additions restricted to conjunctions and a limited range of adverbials. As an example of a story composed entirely of narrative clauses he offers the following (Labov 1972, p. 376):

1. This boy punched me
2. and I punched him.
3. Then the teacher came
4. and stopped the fight.

In identifying the narrative clause as the basic unit of narrative and the minimum narrative structure as two temporally conjoined narrative clauses, Labov is identifying a contextual norm. The extent to which any given narrative conforms to or deviates from this norm can be measured and stylistic characteristics of the text identified. Although it is a norm derived from oral narratives this does not imply that it cannot be applied to written narratives. There is strong evidence to suggest that children in the early stages of writing conform to an oral model (Wilkinson *et al.* 1980; Stratta and Dixon 1981) and only gradually develop a more appropriate written model. The narrative clause as defined by Labov is likely, therefore, to be an early norm of children's narratives with modifications and deviations developing in later years.

The function of style in children's stories

On the basis of the theory outlined above and using Labov's narrative clause as the contextual norm, an analysis was undertaken of a selection of the stories of children aged seven, nine, 12 and 15. For the purposes of comparison the stories were all written under similar classroom conditions in response to the same photograph with a brief discussion beforehand on stories they might write in response to a sample photograph. The teacher's input was kept to a minimum in order not to influence the children's writing, the only instructions given being that the stories should relate to the photograph and should be of interest to the general reader.

The stories thus obtained were each analysed into clauses on the basis of their finite verbs. Comparing the clauses in the sample stories with the narrative clause revealed a number of different deviations at different ages. Certain regularities in these deviations were identified and these were grouped under three broad headings according to the function they served. Specific deviations in lexis or syntax were not attached exclusively to any one function. Assigning a function to any one deviation partly depends on where it occurs in the overall structure of the narrative as much as the form of the deviation itself. Thus a subordinate clause occuring in the opening of a narrative may serve a referential function but one that occurs in the episodic material may serve an evaluative function. Certain deviations are free of this situational restriction. Thus choices relating to certain transformations or transitivity relations seem to be evaluative wherever they occur.

Three broad functions of stylistic deviation were identified and these I have termed *comprehensibility*, *linearity*, and *evaluation*. These may be defined as follows:

Comprehensibility
Deviations under this heading serve a referential function. Choices are made for the purpose of providing information necessary for understanding the basic narrative situation. Their function includes;

1. the description of states, settings, people;
2. casual explanation;
3. summary or reference to events that occurred before the narrative proper began but knowledge of which is deemed necessary for full understanding of the events in the narrative.

The deviations which serve these functions include:

1. the choice of verb forms other than the simple past tense, particularly those forms relating to sentence aspect, e.g., progressives (expressing process or continuing rather then complete action) and perfectives (relating to actions that occurred prior to the time line of the story);
2. the choice of stative verbs e.g. 'have' and 'be';
3. subordination in finite and non-finite clauses;
4. complexity in the noun phrase, e.g. the addition of single or multiple adjectives and prepositional phrases.

Linearity

Deviations under this heading serve to control the forward progress of the reader through the text. In a narrative forward movement is normally undertaken by the narrative clause explicitly expressing action and carrying the story forward clause by clause in temporal sequence. Deviations break the steady forward progress of the action, halting it, speeding it up or slowing it down, leading to effects such as 'pace', 'suspense', 'anticipation' and the general intensifying of particular actions. More specifically these deviations function as

1. *reference*: adding detail or information through deviations similar to those outlined above serving comprehensibility but in this case acting outside the orientation section;
2. *focus*: through deviations that suspend the action and focus attention on specific acts at specific points such as repetition, parallelism, rhythm;
3. *disruption*: through deviations that are difficult to predict or that disrupt normally expected sequences as defined by the narrative clause, i.e. through elaboration of the noun phrase before and after the verb, the positioning of adverbs and adverbial clauses, the introduction of prepositional phrases simple and complex;
4. *facilitation*: through surface structures that permit prediction by conforming to the narrative clause.

Evaluation

Deviations under this heading serve to express the attitude of the writer to the narrative material or control the reader's attitude towards it. It is possible to see a distinction in this function depending on whether the deviations operate at a local level in the sense that they refer only to specific aspects of the narrative, an event or character, or whether they act globally in the sense that they express a more general world view. A further distinction exists between

1. *explicit evaluation*: through deviations similar to those serving referential functions, i.e. expressing states; and
2. *Implicit evaluation*: through lexical and syntactic deviations that imply evaluation, i.e. intensifiers (quantifiers, repetition); comparators (negatives, modals, futures); correlatives (participle phrases), explicatives (subordinate clauses); and transformations and transitivity relations.

These groupings represent a way of characterising the developments in stylistic choice at different ages. Specific examples of each category will illustrate the kinds of choice being made and the functions they serve.

Style in children's stories

The following examples of children's stories are offered as illustrations of the kinds of developments in style that take place using the model of stylistic development outlined above. For the purpose of illustration only the most salient points in each story are discussed.

Seven-year-olds
Two samples of the stories of seven-year-olds are discussed here to show the variation that can occur even at this early age. Christopher's story represents a very early stage.

> one day this boy was walking down the road and a stranger ran after him and the stranger had a knife and the stranger ran up to him and the boy got some of his marbles and threw on to the road and stranger tripped up and the knife fell in a drain and the boy went home.

Christopher's story is composed almost entirely of narrative clauses temporally conjoined describing a simple series of events. The subjects are simple, the verbs are in simple past tense without in most cases auxiliaries, and additions to the clauses are predominantly prepositional phrases expressing location: 'on to the road', 'in the drain'. The temporal conjoining is expressed solely through the conjunction 'and', giving a repetitious evenness to the movement through the text. Cohesion in the story is achieved largely through repetition of labels: 'the stranger', 'the boy'. The only deviation from the basic narrative clause occurs in the first and third clauses where we find a verb in the past progressive, 'was walking', and the verb 'have'. These verbs express state or continuing rather than completed action. The first clause functions as an orientation to the story offering information about the protagonist and the setting. This information is minimal, however, and represents only a nominal move in the direction of comprehensibility. This is emphasised by the use of 'this' from oral modes and indicates an assumption about his identity. A similar assumption of knowledge is indicated by the use of the definite article before 'road'. The third clause, 'the stranger had a knife', also serves a referential function, making the text comprehensible but it operates outside the opening orientation section. This may be a product of limitations in planning ability on the part of this seven-year-old but its effect is to halt the reader's forward movement through the text at this point. The narrative line, begun with the second clause, is halted until the fourth clause giving the stop-start linear movement that is characteristic of the style of this age group. There is no evidence in this story of any deviations serving evaluation.

The story written by Lisa has many features that are in marked contrast to Christopher's; they also have some points in commmon.

> One day there was a man he wanted to kill a girl but the boy got the knife out of his hand then they both started running. They saw a door in the wall so they made a hole in the door and then they climbed in. The girls name was Charlotte he had seen her once. When Monday came Charlotte and Michael went down the road. When they got to shcool Michael said to Charlotte look thats the same man that was trying to kill us so they rushed into shool their teachers name is Mrs illumination her proper name was Elisabeth When they went out to play they heard a bang so they whole school rushed in but Michael didn't he stayed outside the children were scared and thought he was going to get killed even Mrs illumination thought he was going to get killed, but he didn't but instead he got something he was allergic to. then he got a gun and fired the things that he was allergic to and then he was dead so they lived happily ever after.

Again the narrative clause expressing the sequence of events is a predominant feature of this story but there are some important variations beginning to appear. As with Christopher variations in the verb phrase occur in the opening two clauses where we find verbs in a form that expresses continuing state: 'was', 'wanted to kill'. Both these deviations contribute to increasing comprehensibility. However, comprehensibility is only minimally served here and in other choices made by Lisa. There are inadequacies in the introduction of new information in the continual use of the definite article in the early part of the narrative: 'the boy', 'the knife', 'the wall', 'the door'. There are ambiguities in the reference system in the early part of the narrative where it is not clear who 'they both' refers to and in the later part when 'he' is used ambiguously to refer to both the potential killer and the boy. This latter reference can only be clarified by assuming that the boy found something that the man was allergic to and which the boy used to kill the man. Other deviations from the narrative clause indicate additional attempts to make the text comprehensible but these, as with Christopher's, interfere with the linear flow of the text. On two occasions Lisa halts the flow of the narrative by introducing structures that act referentially: 'The girls name was Charlotte he had seen her once' and 'their teachers name is Mrs illumination her proper name was Elisabeth'. Here we have the verb to be in the past tense describing state and the perfect tense introducing information from before the narrative proper began. Both the structures carry the reader out of the narrative flow and produce the stop-start movement throught text that seems characteristic of writers at this age. The linear flow of the text seems to be further disrupted unintentionally by inadequacies in the reference system already referred to. The reader must at points accept these inadequacies and infer knowledge as far as possible though his progress through the final part of the story is difficult without confusion.

Most interestingly there is some evidence that Lisa is beginning deliberately to disrupt forward movement through the text by choosing structures that the halt progress and act evaluatively. There are two sections in particular where narrative clauses give way to other structures. The first involves the section describing the children's arrival at school. Subordination is an important feature of this section, particularly the use of the noun-clause object after the verb 'said'. Using this structure, Lisa can halt the narrative since what is being said does not itself forward the sequence of events. At the same time she introduces referential material by integrating it into the action clause rather than keeping it completely separate. Though this structure delays forward progress it does not completely stop it. The effect of this is to create a moment of suspense that focuses attention on the potential killer, emphasising his intentions and creating an expectation in the reader about future action. The return to the narrative clause at the end of this section, 'so they rushed into school', provides an effective contrast and picks up the narrative line again. The second section of interest is that dealing with the incident in the playground. There are a number of interesting features here relating to the control of forward progress and evaluation. The use of the negative in 'but Michael didn't' is and example of what Labov calls the 'comparator'. Through this device the writer describes what did not happen rather than what did and in so doing halts the forward movement, comparing Michael's non-action with other, unrealised possibilities, in this case the actions of the other children. This focuses attention on Michael, positively evaluating him by enhancing his character. The choice of the intensifier 'whole' in the phrase 'the whole school' also acts as an emphatic device contributing to the evaluation of Michael's character. Immediately following this there occurs a section in which the narrative clause once again gives way to structures that express state and duration, halting the narrative flow. These again involve subordination in the form of the noun-clause object, this time of the verb 'thought'. There is an explicit evaluation of the children at this point as well as an embedded evaluation in describing the thoughts of the characters. What is most interesting, however, is the use of repetition or parallelism of the structure, 'thought he was going to get killed'. This is an evaluative device that creates a climax in the story. The reader's attention is focused on the event or non-event at this point, waiting for the other foot to fall. Michael is further evaluated in the negative — 'but he didn't' — which itself parallels the previous negative and hence refers the reader back.

I have dwelt at some length on certain of the choices that significantly deviate from the narrative clause. There are others but the ones I have focussed on illustrate well the kinds of possibilities deviations offer the writer in terms of comprehensibility, linear progress and evaluation. They also indicate the lines along which stylistic development seems to occur. In comparison with Christopher, Lisa is a more mature writer. Her stories have more in common with nine-year-olds than seven-year-olds.

Nine-year-olds

Though there are similarities between Lisa's and Stephanie's stories, Stephanie's represents advances in some quarters.

> A man was walking down the street one day when he saw a super car. the window was left open and the keys were in the car. It was raining and nobody was about. So he put in his hand and opened the door and got inside. He turned the key and the engine started. It went much faster than he thought. Soon it was going about 60 miles per hour just then he saw a policeman in front of him. He stopped the car and got out. He ran away, the policeman came after him the man was a very fast runner. The policeman had got some other police men who were all looking for him. One policeman saw him but he got away. He came to a river across the river was a bridge. It was a long bridge began to run across. He got halfway when he saw a policeman at the other side of the bridge. He turned round and saw another policeman at the other side He didn't dare to dive because it was so far down He started to fight the policeman, but they put him in hand cuffs took him to the police station and put him in jail.

The tendency towards creating a more comprehensible text is quite marked here. Syntactic deviation of the type already referred to occurs in the opening section, marking the inclusion of referential material orienting the reader to place, protagonist and situation. This section is more extensive than in the work of either of the seven-year-olds, indicating a more adequate movement towards comprehensibility which is also reflected in more adequate choices in the referential and cohesive systems. As with the seven-year-olds, however, Stephanie halts the narrative line and narrative clauses give way to other structures that express referential material at several points in the main body of the story. For example: 'The man was a very fast runner. The policeman had got some other policemen who were all looking for him' and later, 'across the river a bridge. It was a long bridge'. In these cases, however, when compared to that provided by the seven-year-olds, the information here is clearly more relevant to the comprehensibility of the narrative at the point where the deviation occurs, though there is still a sense of the stop-start movement which is inevitable when structures, separate from the narrative clause, are chosen to express this information. The range of deviation from the narrative clause is increased in Stephanie's story and, as with Lisa's there is a move deliberately to affect linear progress and evaluate. In the early part of the narrative she uses a subordinate clauses expressing comparison, which focuses attention and evaluates the man's response: 'It went much faster than he thought'. As with Lisa there is a concentration of deviations towards the end of the story when the man reaches the bridge. The syntax chosen suspends the action and produces a sense of climax. There is repetition or parallelism of the phrase 'at the other side' which focuses attention and counters the effect of the narrrative verbs. In addition the section ends with a negative and a clause of reason expressing both an explicit and an embedded evaluation of the man. Interestingly, Stephanie avoids ending her story with a simple coda as Lisa does but returns to the narrative clause, facilitating the reader's processing of the text, and giving a sense of expectation fulfilled.

Twelve-year-olds

The increase in deviation from the basic narrative clause by the age of twelve is very marked. Very few of the basic units of Susan's story are simple narrative clauses. Most are modified in some way with a consequent increase in comprehensibility, manipulation of linear progress and evaluation. Most significantly there is a tendency to integrate these function in lexical choices and elaborate syntax.

> It was about 11 p.m. and everything was deathly still in the town, except for one place — at the jewellers shop. There was a young man there, expert at breaking in. Slowly he removed the pane of glass in the window. He cautiously put his gloved hand inside the shop and picked out a few priceless diamond necklaces. He reached for a few rings, but in his hastiness, succeeded in triggering off the burgular alarm.
>   Quickly he glanced round, pushed the jewellery in his pocket, and ran. The police were now coming. He could hear the sirens blaring away in the distance but they were getting closer, he was tirering now, but his face

was deturmind, and apprehenshious. There were now several police on
their feet and running after him, as well as some in 'panda' cars. The man
ran until he came to an alley way. He went down it, knowing that the cars
couldn't come down. He came to a turning, and ran down that. He could
hear the police getting closer all the time. In hid desparation, he jumped
over a airly small wall and hid in the coal shed.

After about ½ hour he thought the police would have passed but he
daren't move in case they were waiting for him. He stayed in the shed for
what seemed hours, until he could bear the suspence no longer — he
burst out of the shed, and to his relief, there was nobody there. He came
back over the wall and tried to decide whether it was worth going back to
the shop trying somewhere else, or playing it safe and leaving the shops
alone that night. He came to the the conclusion that the first two were too
dangerous the police would be on the look-out, so he abandoned those
ideas and went home.

In the opening of Susan's story we begin to see the way in which older
children add to the basic clause and elaborate the syntax to serve a
variety of stylistic functions. The first clauses are typically orientating
the reader, using the verb 'to be' to describe state. However, Susan's
ability to handle more elaborate syntax enables her to affect the reader's
progress through the text and evaluate even at this point. The structure
of the first sentence, for example, delays the focus of the story until the
final phrase 'at the jewellers shop'. The emphasis given to this phrase
through this final position is reinforced by the structure: 'everything-
. . . except'. This delaying of specific detail until the final phrase is also
the basis of the structure of the second sentence. Both of these
sentences involve structures that delay the reader's completion of the
sense of the sentence, creating a sense of expectancy. In addition, Susan
uses comparison to evaluate the setting. The addition of the word
'deathly' involves comparison, though clichéd, as does the implied
negative in 'except'. The kinds of lexical and syntactic choices made
here indicate Susan's knowledge of the textual structures of stories but
also the possibiliites for manipulating the reader's response through
particular stylistic choices.

Once the narrative is under way, Susan again disrupts the reader's
movement forward by simple means such as adverbs which delay
completion of meaning. The inclusion of 'cautiously' between 'He' and
'put' is one such example, dividing subject and verb, as is the elaboration
of noun phrases, for example 'gloved hand' and 'priceless diamond', and
the inclusion of prepositional phrases such as 'in his hastiness'. As in
stories previously analysed, there is a tendency to interrupt the narrative
flow by using syntax that expresses information and evaluates but an
interesting development is the way in which Susan manages to imply
continuing action, rather than completely halting it, by her use of
participle phrases. The action is not quite halted but continues in a state

of incompletion. Such choices also heighten and emphasise, creating a sense of building to a climax as well as explicitly and implicitly evaluating. The use of negatives, modals and participle phrases is particularly relevant here.

Susan is not able to maintain the narrative flow so effectively in the final part of her story, though the elaboration of syntax is still evident. On the whole, however, her story illustrates the tendency of this age group to want to write stories that deliberately excite the reader through the manipulation of the surface structure of the text.

Fifteen-years-old

By the age of 15 the stories written contain many complex structures as writers increase their linguistic resources and become more and more aware of the possibilities that stylistic choices offer. It is only possible here to give a flavour of the way these choices are realised. James for instance opens his story thus:

> As the sun rose over the grey dusty landscape of the excavation site, the electrostatic wakener woke convict no. 246537 from his deep slumber. The day had been a hard one, yesterday, and Alan Trudgoy was exhausted. As he dosed off again another bolt of electrostatic energy gave him a rude awakening.

Here we have considerable complexity and variety in the choices made, including subordination, embedding, complex noun phrases and multiple adjectives. Yet these opening sentences are largely based on the narrative clause which allow a focus on action that begins and maintains the narrative flow. What is produced is a pseudo-narrative clause foregrounding action but also functioning to introduce information to orientate the reader to character, setting and context. Complex syntax is used to integrate material necessary for comprehensibility. Information is implied rather than stated. The reader must infer rather than comprehend literally the fact that this story is set in the future, that it concerns a prison camp, and that the prisoners are treated harshly by robot guards.

Sarah's story, reproduced below, illustrates many of the possibilities open to writers of this age.

> The man's feet thud on the dry turf irregularly as he gets wearier and wearier. The painful beat of his heart vibrates through his body causing the whole of the body to ache. His stout shoes tied tightly on to his feet make them feel as if lobsters are pinching his toes and that tacks are sticking in his heel. His clothes now no longer feel rigid and cold as they did in side the prison but feel limp and sweaty. They cling to his tired body and become a handicap to him. A menacing horsefly explores the harmless man but he ignores it, he has not energy to flick it away.

They are gaining, the hounds are gaining. Hounds are determined eager to please their owners — the police.

The convict grits his teeth and his nostrils gasp for more air as his arms work like pistons at his side.

His state of mind declines steadily until it is worse than depressed. In one minute his brain summed up the whole of his live — nothing but unhappiness and emptyness. Crime like an evil woman had picked him up at an early age and had experimented and played with him and when she was bored with him put him in prison. Every day in the prison cell, the criminal felt that the four walls were drawing closer in, crushing the life out of him. He saw 'Death' painted in blood on every prison wall he saw and every long black corridor had no light at the end of it. Then his will power won a battle over his common sense and he found that he was determined to see the light at the end of the corridor and therefore, escape from the prison.

But now he was running in the wilderness, was he any better off? No. He was still nobody nowhere with nothing. And he had to ask himself why he was running. Surely he could never be free, free from the thoughts of his ruined life. As he realized that he had nothing to live for he collapsed. The triumphant hounds surrounded him and he died.

To illustrate fully the sophistication of the stylistic choices in this story is not possible here. I shall, therefore, simply indicate some of the major tendencies under function headings.

Comprehensibility

There is a confident integration of referential material into the basic narrative clause through subordination and elaboration of noun and verb phrases. Narrative flow is, therefore, maintained. The reader is impelled forward through the text, building a growing awareness of the situation, context, character, and so on.

linearity

Sarah indicates that she has a considerable awareness of the reader and of the stylistic choices that can be made to manipulate the reader's response. She uses structures that delay completion of meaning, creating suspense and surprise. The reader is focused on events through repetition. She uses rhythm on occasions to foreground the text over meaning, creating aesthetic effect. The overall structure of the piece involves beginning *in medias res* with a flashback half-way through so that the reader must infer and build meaning as he proceeds.

Evaluation

Evaluation seems to be the dominant function of this narrative. Sarah evaluates both implicitly and explicitly, and the range of evaluative deviations is very wide. She comments herself but also uses the character's thoughts and actions. In addition she uses negatives, comparisons, paticiple phrases, repetitions, extended metaphors, and many kinds of subordination. There is also a tendency to include both local global evaluation. Local evaluation involves evaluating characters, setting and events. Global evaluation is evident in the world view implied in the characteristic choice of role for the protagonist. He is consistently presented in the role of patient or object of action. This affects the reader's perception of the world in which the protagonist lives: a world of victims and persecutors.

Discussion

From the above analysis it is possible to suggest some tentative lines of development in style between the ages of seven and 15. The actual structures the children use are many and varied and to attempt to relate all of these to functions they serve is not possible at this stage of the research. However, a focus on the function that deviations from the norm of the narrative clause makes the following outline possible.

Comprehensibility
As writers mature they become more aware of the need to make their texts more comprehensible to a reader who does not share the writer's knowledge. At first texts are predominantly composed of narrative clauses which do not allow for the expression of referential information. As the child matures he incorporates structures that allow such information to be expressed but these structures are separate from the narrative, mere additions to the text, at first not clearly essential but later more relevant. The final phase is the development of structures that allow integration of referential material without disrupting narrative flow.

Linearity
In the early stages the narrative flow of a text is unintentionally disrupted by the addition of referential material. This gives rise to the characteristic stop-start movement of early stories. As the child matures he begins to develop an awareness of the control over the reader's response that variations in the surface structure offers. Thus there is an increase in the deliberate manipulation of the reader's movement through the text, creating effects such as suspence, surprise, climax and aesthetic pleasure.

Evaluation
Any kind of evaluation of the text is rare in very young children. Only those seven-year-olds who are exceptionally advanced seem capable of

it. As they develop, writers begin to incorporate varieties of evaluation into the text — at first in structures that express it explicitly but later in syntax and lexical choices that allow for its embeding in the text. The structures that allow such embedding are complex and only appear in older children as characteristic. In addition, older children show an ability to make choices the imply a global view and not just a local evaluation.

Conclusion

This study has put forward a means of defining and identifying the stylistic choices in children's fictional narratives and, furthermore, has indicated the functions such choices serve in terms of what the text communicates. On this basis it has been possible to characterise narrative style at different ages and to trace the development of children's linguistic resources and their ability to deploy them for particular purposes in a narrative context. What has been revealed is the children's growing understanding of the nature of narrative together with their growing mastery of the options available to them in language for expressing a range of meanings and, most importantly, for varying and manipulating the reader's response.

Style is not a simple concept, yet understanding it is an essential part of our knowledge of the nature of writing and the composing process. The better we understand it and the way it develops the more likely it is that our response to the writing that children produce will be informed and sensitive to their needs and the more likely it is that our attempts as teachers to help children become writers will be effective.

Bibliography

APU (Assessment of Performance Unit) (1981). *Language Performance in Schools: Primary Survey Report No. 1*. London, Department of Education and Science, HMSO.

Cullen, J. (1981). 'Literary Competence' in D.C. Freeman (ed.), *Essays in Modern Stylistics*. London, Methuen.

Dixon, J. and Stratta, L. (1981). *Achievements in Writing at 16 plus*. University of Birmingham, Faculty of Education.

Enkvist, N.E. (1964). *Linguistics and Style*. Oxford, Oxford University Press.

Fish, S. (1973). 'What Is Stylistics and Why Are They Saying Such Terrible Things About It' in S. Chapman (ed.), *Approaches to Poetics*. New York, Colombia University Press.

Gray, B. (1969). *Style: The Problem and its solution*. The Hague, Mouton and Co.

Harpin, W. (1976). *The Second R. Writing Development in the Junior School:* London, George Allen & Unwin.

Hunt, K. (1970). *Syntactic Maturity in School Children and Adults*. Chicago, University of Chicago Press.

Labov, W. (1972). *Language in the Inner City*. Philadelphia, University of Pennsylvania Press.

Labov, W. and Waletsky, J. (1967). 'Narrative Analysis: Oral Versions of Personal Experience' in J. Helm (ed.), *Essays in the Verbal Arts*. Seattle, University of Washington Press.

Murry, J. Middleton (1922). *The Problem of Style*. Oxford, Oxford University Press.

Wilkinson, A., Barnsley, G., Hanna, P. and Swan, M. (1980). *Assessing Language Development*. Oxford, Oxford University Press.

Wilkinson, A. and Hanna, P. (1980). 'The Development of Style in Children's Writing', *Educational Review*, vol. 32, no. 2.

14 The Mapping of Writing

DIANA DAVIS

The need for a map

The concept of mapping suggests the existence of uncharted or partially charted territory. With writing there are certainly some *terrae cognitae* but the main impression is of large *terrae incognitae*.

Early researched focused on central problems of assessing writing samples with reliability and validity, the concern being with accuracy of measurement at the moment in time rather than with age- or grade-related development. Yet such development is implicit in any attempt to sample and assess writing at a particular stage. Where research has taken place in this area it has concentrated on specific atomistic measures, that is, those constituents of a (written) language product which can be distinguished, quantified and manipulated numerically. Most have the advantage that they are readily quantifiable, that they are amenable to operational definition, and hence may be measured reliably. Such studies (e.g. Hunt's (1965) cross-sectional study and Loban's (1976) longitudinal study) have yielded useful information but as Wilkinson, *et al.* (1980, p. 32) compassionately acknowledge, that usefulness is fundamentally limited because '"count" measures . . . cannot account for meaning, and development lies essentially in the meanings that can be offered'.

Some attempts have been made to move away from the atomistic measures approach. By far the most influential of these attempts is that of Britton, *et al.* (1975). Britton (1978) himself acknowledges that the development aspect of the project was not carried as far or was as fully developed as he or the Writing Research Team would have wished. In essence, Britton *et al.* (1975) see the expressive as the matrix for the development of other forms of writing: transactional writing with its two major subdivisions; mature forms of the expressive; and the poetic which, like the expressive, is without subdivision. It remains a hypothesis about how writing develops rather than a developmental schema amenable to validation in the terms that the teams set up their research. While it is clearly an enticing hypothesis about the way individuals develop in their writing, it remains just that in the absence of substantive longitudinal evidence.

As a way of categorising writing products the Britton *et al.* (1975) schema has proved to be one of the best-signposted culs-de-sac of the decade. Not only has the model been seized upon in Australia as a blueprint (Thou shalt teach 'expressive' writing) in a way surely never intended by the authors, but also it has provided a false trail for research. Given the Britton *et al.* (1975) characterisation of the expressive as language close to the self, it is arguably presumptuous for a distant audience — teacher probably, researcher certainly — to make the judgement that example A is expressive, example B transactional, etc. Moreover the concept of expressive in the schema makes the fundamental assumption that the writing alone provides sufficient evidence for the reader to decide what function it was performing for that individual at that moment. The Pythagorean Theorem is purely transactional — 'language to get things done' — but for Pythagoras himself the dominant function might well have been expressive. There is little evidence in much of the mechanical research by followers of the Britton Schema that shortcomings like these are recognised.

Such limitations of the model became apparent when we considered it as a descriptive instrument in research we were carrying out at the Monash Education Faculty. The genesis of the project was the opportunity of access for the purposes of research to the scripts from a year 10 English Scholarship Examination together with the impression marks awarded. The English essay paper was 'experimental' in that it provided minimal structure and direction to candidates, who were required to write 'in any way you wish' in response to three separate selections of source material — set A consisted of a photograph; set B comprised two poems, one prose extract, one selection from the lyrics of a popular song, and one photograph; set C included one poem and one photograph. The resulting study by Davis *et al.* (1978) had two major but related thrusts. The first was to identify what was valued in marker assessments, and the second was to probe the extent to which the non-directive nature of the examination led to diversity in writing.

The achievement of both of these central aims led to the search for a way of categorising the writing. Existing function categories (e.g. those of Robinson 1972) were rejected on the following grounds (Davis *et al.* 1978, p. 17):

Function on its own . . . is not a satisfactory criterion for judging style or mode, as an apparently identical function may have linguistically different realizations. A candidate may appear to wish to persuade his audience, but though this is a single function, he may present his argument as a fable, as a very clear and logically argued essay or as a very emotional personal statement. To a reader, the modes, the styles are obviously different. These differing modes rather than differing functions were our concern.

This also was one of the reasons that the Britton schema was felt to be inappropriate. The decision was made to use the scripts as a basis for developing a more differentiated set of categories, based on mode.

The genesis of the categories may be traced to the traditional rhetorical classification referred to by Britton, Martin and Rosen (1966, p. 30) and exemplified by Edwards (1967, p. 24). These were extended and refined as a result of the experience of the four authors in reading and classifying the scripts. The resulting Taxonomy of Essay Modes represents the culmination of three consultative and tentative developmental stages.

In reverting to a traditional rhetorical base, the authors were sensitive to the need voiced by Britton, Martin and Rosen (1966, p. 30) 'to establish categories of writing which are both psychologically and linguistically meaningful'. Moreover, given the non-directive, non-prescriptive writing contexts of the examination which yielded the writing products, the Britton *et al.* (1975, p. 4) judgement that the traditional rhetorical categories show 'little inclination to observe the writing process', being concerned 'with how people should write, rather than how they do' did not have great relevance. The problem of a single piece of writing including, for example, both descriptive and narrative elements, was resolved to the extent of deciding that, on the basis of a corpus of independent judgements, it is possible to allocate to a dominant category — and finding that, in practice, this worked.

A Taxonomy of Essay Modes

The following reflections and definitions provide a focus for each of the categories.

1. NARRATIVE
1.1 *Personalised narrative (first person)*
1.1.1 *Sequential account of a real or imagined situation in which the writer is participating.*

This category is fairly straightforward. It focuses on actions and external reactions, e.g., on walking home at night, a meeting with a girl, a motor-bike race . . .

It is further defined by what is not, hence 1.1.2, 1.1.3 and 1.1.4.

1.1.2 *Sequential account of a real or imagined situation in which the writer is participating, plus introspection.*

This category was included because it was found necessary further to differentiate between the responses, since in a number of them there was comment on the actual feelings or thoughts of the character, while in others action predominated. The former were designated introspection and it was considered that the presence of this element might have influenced markers' valuations of the particular script. The team was also interested in determining which stimuli and which styles tended to produce this.

Introspection is the consideration of the nature of feelings or of the mental reaction to a situation. It is not merely the mention of a simple feeling or reaction. It is, as its name implies, a look forward, but it must do more than just look. It must consider what it sees.

1.1.3 *Introspection with a peripheral action basic.*

The previous subdivision, 1.1.2, had a strong story-line with some introspection. Quite a few scripts had less action and much more inward thought; their style was so obviously different to the mere sequential account that the team created this sub-category. While several scripts that fitted into it were obviously introspective, certain others with a similar style appeared just to be listing thoughts without any consideration of their nature. As in almost all sub-categories, it was difficult to draw an absolute dividing line.

This following extract, by Warwick, is one of the most obvious examples of 1.1.3 in that attention is focused throughout on the writer's thoughts in the situation, on his mental reactions to it.

I was excited by the darkness and the things that dwell around me, but, for some unknown reason, I felt lonely and frightened. I kept thinking of the deep water as though it was connected in some way with my thoughts. I felt as though I was near a place of evil. I could feel myself plunging down into the deep, dark water.

1.1.4 *Surrealistic writing in which the writer seeks, either consciously or not, to explore the subconscious* by representing the situations and phenomena of dreams.

This category was established to deal with personalised writing that was almost Kafkaesque or fantistic, writing that operated with the logic of dream rather than reality. It was often masked by its simple commentary and/or present tense recording of thoughts. Sue wrote:

This object still in my mind
coming closer and closer
I'm still cold
Object getting bigger
Too big
Bigger than 12 worlds
Dull colour
It's the same dull colour
Deeper and Deeper I get
Some object floating in my mind
Snow
Getting thicker and thicker.

1.2 *Interactive narrative*

This category deals with narrative, real or imagined, with the dialogue central to the narrative in the sense of expanding or modifying it. Much of the material in this category is obvious, being almost entirely interactive. However, some difficulty arises when there are only snatches of dialogue in the narrative. These are integral to the narrative in the sense of expanding of modifying it, but are not discernible as the dominant mode which was to be our criterion of judgement in cases of doubt. The omission of punctuation, it should be noted, does not change the category. Dialogue will be obvious from the style. Interaction may also exist in indirect speech.

1.3 *Externalised narrative (third person)*

1.3.1 *Sequential account of a real or imagined situation (single episode)*

This is fairly simple category to discern. It is always focused on an episode and on the actions and reactions in that episode. It almost always appears that the writer is a spectator. The action is immediately observable. It is always concrete and specific and generally, although not necessarily, encompasses a short period of time.

1.3.2 Sequential account of a real or imagined situation (chronicle)

Scripts in this category usually encompass a period of time. Although still closely related to concrete reality, they are marked by greater generality or vastness of subject. The theme or unity of the work usually lies in a subject such as life, a long journey, a relationship; in such cases the time factor is obvious.

1.3.3 *Sequential account of a real or imagined situation (single episode) plus introspection*

This category may be more easily understood by reference to the earlier section (1.1.2) which categorises personalised narrative plus introspection were introspection is both defined and exemplified. In this category we have episodic narrative with introspection in the third person. However, introspection is concerned with covert aspects of behaviour, with exploration rather than mere observation.

Steve's analytic comment 'Many a time he done wrong but never anything that troubled him so much . . .' is introspective in that the state of mind is compared to prior states of mind in order to explore its quality. Exploration of cause implies introspection where it is concerned with the cause of a mental state, or the mental cause of a physical state.

1.3.4 *Sequential account of a real or imagined situation (chronicle) plus introspection.*

The chronicle mode associated with some introspection.

1.3.5 *Didactive writing in which a moral is presented either explicitly or implicitly*

On occasions several narratives presented a situation but, though not stating a moral clearly, seemed to be using the story as a concrete example for the purpose of warning or advising. As in fables and parables, the meaning is inherent, not stated. The narrative is a vehicle for a message. Often the ending states the conclusion or moral explicitly.

One script by Alice is quite explicit, a warning against drug addiction, building up the picture of a girl going on to drugs and taking an overdose. The ending: 'What a way to go!! or is it best for her??' marks the emphasis on the moral aspect, the warning.

1.3.6 *Surrealistic writing in which the subconscious is explored* in terms of the situation and phenomena of dreams.

This category includes writing similar to that in 1.1.4 (surrealisic personalised narrative) except that the writing is in the third person.

1.3.7 *Introspection with a peripheral action basis*

This might well be considered an unlikely category and certainly there seemed to be very few scripts that fitted the description. Continuous introspection would appear to be more natural in the first person.

2. DESCRIPTIVE

Many of the responses in this category were primarily factually descriptive and the taxonomy was not developed to the same level of discrimination as for the narrative category.

2.1 *Literal descriptive*

Some writers simply described the stimulus or an object or event quite baldly and without observing any relationships of cause and effect. Such writing gave no evidence of thought about the scene or of an attempt to do more than state what cold be concretely observed. June wrote:

Out in the country you wake to the birds singing and the lambs baaing and the smell of flowers that may be out. Then just as dawn breaks the day begins, the farmer is out early as the day is . . .

2.2 *Embellished descriptive*

A second kind of descriptive response appeared stylistically different and showed what were felt to be different language functions. It was concerned with embellishment, with establishing and observing relationships in the scene being described, or embedding conclusions or thoughts, about them. Such writing tended to be syntactically more complex and made greater use of adjectives, adverbs and imagery than the writing in 2.1, as Bill's piece shows:

As the sun became higher in the sky, more light penetrated into the battle torn arena. Not only were there motionless machines, vehicles and weapons of destruction, but men also lay with their faces in the brown grey mud. Some poised as if they were ready to charge.

2.3 *Introspective perspective*

This category occurred most often in personalised description where, for example, a writer describes through sense perceptions a scene close to the self. On occasions, as in the following piece written by Paul, the writer's reaction to his observation is explored:

Only the dark coloured cars did not look this way as the lights showed true their sparkling variety of colours. The dismal looking scenery seemed to mock or betray my anxiety of reaching home . . .

In this case, the writer is observing the effect of the scenery on his thoughts.

2.4 *Speculative/philosophical descriptive*

The dominant mode is descriptive, but the description is accompanied by generalisations or abstractions such as the nature of man and the universe, as in this piece by James:

The sudden change of the traffic light
But brings no car to a stop
The moon peeps through to have a look
Man always looks for signs of light
All through the ages he has made night like day with light.

3. ARGUMENTATIVE

3.1 *Objective argument*

This category catered for scripts written in a classic debate style, characterised by an awareness of audience and an obvious attempt to persuade this audience by using clear and objective arguments. There were few scripts in this category.

3.2 *Personal persuasive argumentative*

This writing embodied an attempt to persuade but it tended to be non-objective and often emotive. It occasionally took the form of advice with little attempt to use evidence, as in this piece by Rodney:

Life is precious and should not be neglected and you will not benefit by war. Build your society, build your comfort, but also consider your natural environment. Now you must co-operate and consider these points as a guide to life and proper conduct towards society.

3.3 *Personal platform argumentative*

This category was added to cater for responses that make no attempt to persuade, being basically an avenue for an idiosyncratic expression of opinions or views without recourse to logic or system, as in this piece by Sarah:

ever since I was a child adults have been ordering me around . . . and I am gettng sick and tired of it.

4. EXPOSITORY

4.1 *Straightforward expository*

This classification is characterised by more generalised writing than in the narrative or descriptive categories. The organisation of the writing tends to require greater intellectual or mental organisation. It is only chronologically or spatially organised when it is dealing with subjects that, by their nature, are generalised.

Thus the following extract from Peter's script has almost the chronological form of narrative, but is expository, dealing with generalisations such as war, empires and the atmosphere. The incidents referred to in it are not visible to a single person. The incidents in a chronicle tend to be at a lower level of abstraction. Some writing was very general with no emphasis on chronological organisation.

Long ago, vast cities were built, with high buildings that reached for heaven. Great industries were formed to produce the necessary items for these cities.

4.2 *Speculative expository*

Speculative expository writing is characterised by very localised speculation relating to the stimulus material. Speculation on what an object is, what a picture portrays or what a poem means, is very different from speculation on the meaning of the universe. it is characterised by subjectives or questions and generally perseveres throughout a script. Luke speculates:

It might be that the picture was taken after a plague . . .
I think the most probable thing . . .

And Craig:

The man in the picture is being pointed out by someone, maybe it's meant to be us, or whoever looks at the picture . . .

4.3 *Interpretative expository*

This has a definiteness lacking in the speculative category 4.2. It is tied to the meaning of a picture or poem and goes beyond mere description of what is seen. It is not merely a story arising from a picture, it is a definite stylistic difference usually referring directly to the stimulus that gives rise to the interpretation. For Charles,

This picture tells its own story. There is a girl walking the street of one of many cities onone cold and wet night. I would estimate the time as being . . .

At times it may move near to philosophising, but is at a simpler level of generality and abstraction. Thus, in interpreting an abstract painting as an allegory, it is still fairly much bound to the concrete specific features of the painting.

4.4 *Introspective expository*

This category was added to cater for those responses where the general discussion of the attributes and characteristics of a topic included embedded personal comment and the examination of personal responses and reactions to the topic, introspection being defined in the same way as for earlier categories. Simon wrote:

This verse shows that the person concerned feels lost — put in exile — separated from society — rejected from the world. when at last this person sees someone he or she feels great relief or jumps to the conclusion that the other person might attack him or her or something of that nature.

Both interpretative and speculative material which moves to introspection is included in this category. In the extract above, the
presence of alternative feelings indicates an exploration of the mind.

5. PHILOSOPHICAL

5.1 *Embryonic nascent philosophical*

This category includes those pieces of writing in which the writer is
concerned with man and the nature of the universe, but is unable to
present thoughts cogently and infer relationships from a broad
perspective, and which consequently seem naive, idiosyncratic or
trite. Generally such writing deals with philosophical subjects, but is
undeveloped; it is more a collection of generalisations than an
organised and thoughtful development of a topic. The following
extract from Bevan's piece of 'Man nad Night' is full of thoughts of a
philosophical nature, but there is little exploration or development of
the thoughts.

Who are these creatures that lurk about the dark alleyways, are they
human, does man become a Jekyll and Hyde as soon as night falls, does
he change his appearance without anyone noticing, is there a difference
between day man and night man if so what, what makes him seem more
aggressive at night than in the day, do we possess two people inside our
bodies each with different ideas and morals and does night suddenly kill
one and create the other.

The writer is speculating on the nature of man (a generalised term).
Nature itself is abstract. His ideas are abstract, using analogy: 'Does a
man become a Jekyll and Hyde . . .' He is using Jekyll and Hyde as
representative of a certain concept, good and evil existing in the same
person, to speculate on man's nature. The idea conveyed is abstract.
However, the writer just keeps raising questions and does not attempt
to answer them.

5.2 *Speculative/didactic generalisation philosophical*

Writing categorised in this way is characterised by generalisations or
higher-level abstractions, but has greater organisation than the
embryonic category. Much of the writing is this class is metaphorical,
and deals with the nature of man. The metaphor is a generalisation
designed to carry considerable meaning about man's nature. This
extract from Frank's piece is a good example:

The man who travels his own road is a leader and not a sheep.

The concept 'The man who travels his own road' refers to a specific
subcategory drawn out of the class 'man' and embodies many of the
features abstracted to create it.

5.3 *Introspective generalisation philosophical*

This category contains writing in which the generalisations are often based on introspective data or on generalised comments about man's thoughts and feelings. Jack wrote:

We look to each other for warmth, security, well keeping and if necessary, help. We need to be wanted by someone. We like to feel important and most important all is to know that there is always someone to turn to in our times of distress. We humans are a frightened race always looking at shadows and looking corners . . .

6. POETIC

In all stages this category was simply called poetic, including a pot-pourri from blank verse to rhyming doggerel. These scripts were subsequently reclassified under the other categories.

7. PERSONAL EXPLORATION

Exploration of one's life and comments about it — this is different from expository in the specificity of reference, and in organisation. It is concerned with expression of one's own ideas and opinions rather than just one idea as in 3.3 (personal platform argumentative).

8. PERSONA

Writing of this type uses a persona to create the story, often an animal or a tramp. It is close in style to personal exploration since both may be givnig opinions and ideas about a kind of life, and the final product is likely to appear as a personalised chronicle.

9. STYLISTIC EXPERIMENTATION

This category was included to accommodate writing that is similar to that in category 8 but where students appear to be experimenting with more than language and content.

10. MISCELLANEOUS

Included in this category were those scripts were a student had simply copied the stimulus material or had submitted too brief a response.

Applying the Taxonomy

The application of the Taxonomy to the scripts enabled the answering of four major research questions as follows:

Which categories (modes) of response dominated the three tasks both individually and overall?

Associated questions were whether the stimuli resulted in different modes of response; and which modes dominated each task.

The incidence of each category of writing was calculated as a percentage of the total sample (see Table 14.1) and the percentage of scripts in each task which belonged to a specific subcategory was also calculated (see Table 14.2).

Table 14.1 Number and proportion of sample scripts in each category

Category title	Number of scripts	% $N = 1370$
1. Narrative	647	47.2
2. Descriptive	112	8.2
3. Argumentative	26	1.9
4. Expository	462	33.7
5. Philosophical	82	6.0
6. Poetic[*]	—	—
7. Personal exploration	18	1.3
8. Persona	14	1.0
9. Stylistic experimentation	8	0.6
10. Miscellaneous	1	0.1

[*] Scripts originally classified in category 6 were subsequently reclassified with other categories.

Table 14.2   Number and proportion of scripts in each task in each sub-category

Category title		Task 1		Task 2		Task 3	
		N	%	N	%	N	%
1.1	Personalised narrative	97	18.2	129	27.7	66	17.7
1.2	Interactive narrative	32	6.0	25	5.4	30	8.0
1.3	Externalised narrative	120	22.6	83	17.8	65	17.4
2.	Descriptive	45	8.5	56	12.0	11	2.9
3.	Argumentative	5	0.9	8	1.7	13	3.5
4.1	Straightforward expository	106	19.9	102	21.9	90	24.1
4.2	Speculative expository	36	6.8	6	1.3	18	4.8
4.3	Interpretative expository	43	8.1	18	3.9	22	5.9
4.4	Introspective expository	5	0.9	15	3.2	1	0.3
5.	Philosophical	27	5.1	17	3.7	38	10.2
6.	Poetic	–	–	–	–	–	–
7.	Personal exploration	6	1.1	4	0.9	8	2.1
8.	Persona	6	1.1	–	–	8	2.1
9.	Stylistic experimentation	4	0.8	1	0.2	3	0.8
10.	Miscellaneous	0	–	1	0.2	0	–
	Total	532	100.0	465	100.0	373	100.0

Note: As many categories were small, there seemed little point in comparing their incidence, unless there was an unusual loading in one category or one task, such as to suggest definite stimulus influence.

Clearly Table 14.1 suggests that the most preferred modes for writing are the expository and narrative modes. However, of the 462 scripts which were categorised as expository, 298 were subclassified as 4.1, that is as Straightforward expository. Of the 647 scripts written in the narrative mode, 292 were of the personalised narrative type and 268 of the externalised narrative type. The cross-task comparison (Table 14.2) yielded a similar pattern with the narrative and expository modes dominating all three tasks. Task 2 yielded more personalised narrative (1.1) than did either of Tasks 1 or 3. Task 1, however, gave rise to more externalised narrative. Task 3 produced the least descriptive writing but the most argumentative, philosophical, personal exploration and persona.

Which mode received the highest marks, and within each mode or category, which sub-category was most valued?
Table 14.3 presents within-category comparisions of marks given for scripts.

Table 14.3 Category and mode comparisons of marks given for scripts

Category	$\bar{X}$	σ	t	p
1.1.1 1.1.2	5.55 6.31	1.83 1.79	2.95	<0.01
1.1.1 1.1.3	5.55 7.04	1.83 1.65	4.00	<0.001
1.1.1 1.1.4	5.55 6.89	1.83 1.97	2.14	<0.05
1.1.1 1.2	5.55 5.81	1.83 2.14	1.04	—
1.1.2 1.3.1	6.31 7.04	1.79 1.65	1.83	—
1.1.2 1.2	6.31 5.81	1.79 2.14	1.55	—
1.1.1 1.3.1	5.55 6.12	1.83 2.15	2.46	<0.02
1.1.2 1.1.4	6.31 6.89	1.79 1.97	0.09	—
1.1.3 1.1.4	7.04 6.89	1.65 1.97	0.23	—
1.1.3 1.2	7.04 5.81	1.65 2.14	2.74	<0.01
1.1.4 1.2	6.89 5.81	1.97 2.14	1.45	—
1.3.1 1.3.2	6.12 5.67	2.15 1.85	1.61	—
1.3.1 1.3.3	6.12 6.05	2.15 1.84	0.15	—
1.3.4 1.3.5	5.57 5.59	0.90 1.77	0.44	—
1.3.2 1.3.5	5.67 5.90	1.85 1.77	0.52	—
4.1 4.2	6.08 5.40	1.82 2.02	2.59	<0.01
4.1 4.3	6.08 4.49	1.82 1.92	6.95	<0.001
4.2 4.3	5.40 4.49	2.02 1.92	2.74	<0.01
5.1 5.2	5.62 7.38	2.07 2.13	3.47	<0.002

Within personalised narrative marker valuations followed the hierachy of the Taxonomy with the basic category being significantly less valued than those differentiated by introspection, etc. This did not occur with externalised narrative where markers appeared not to differentially value writing in any of the sub-categories. Marker valuations reversed the taxonomy in the expository category with straightforward expository writing being more highly valued than either interpretative or speculative.

Did markers value certain kinds of writing more than other kinds both overall and within each task?
Markers did show a tendency to value particular kinds of writing both overall and within a task. Descriptive writing was valued significantly more highly ($p<0.01$) than either personalised or interactive narrative. More descriptive category scripts scored highly and fewer scored low marks in proportion to the total numbers in each category. Interpretative expository writing, on the other hand, was given a consistently low valuation.

Did individual markers differ in the kinds of writing they valued most highly?
Although more detailed work needs to be undertaken in this regard there did seem to exist for each examiner an idiosyncratic scale of values, different both in content and order from any other examiner. One examiner obviously valued very highly a clearly planned essay with accurate English. Another examiner appeared to value depth of thought most highly. Thus an inaccurate, jumbled exposition essay, that struggled to express complex ideas, was valued more highly by the second examiner than by the first. On this valuation scale there appeared to be an agglomeration of stylistic, holistic, grammatical, syntactical and calligraphical factors.

In reading the responses the team had rather loosely classified the mode of writing as narrative, descriptive, expository and poetic. This level of analysis confirmed the impression that the actual mode of response was a factor in the marker's valuation. Some markers seemed to value the traditional literary essay (or attempts thereat) highly, while often such markers attached relatively less value to free verse which, in turn, was highly regarded by other examiners. Rhyme seemed to be lowly rated by almost all examiners.

Reading the scripts left the team with the impression that there differential valuation between those stories that were concerned with a single episode and those that were essentially chronicles of events over a longer period of time. It appeared that the episodic writing was more highly valued. However, a closer examination of these somewhat tentative classifications and of the marks awarded to them showed that, in general, both styles tended to gain similar marks. It was noticeable that, whereas several episodes gained very high grades (A, A+) no chronicles achieved this.

On occasions the actual content of the scripts seemed to be a factor in assessment. Several scripts revealed discrepancies between examiners of three grades, with the only apparent factor of disagreement being that of content. One narrative was clearly planned and grammatically accurate, although rather pedestrian, showing little depth or syntactical variety. Our impressions of the markers' values would have led us to believe that it would at most have been given a grade C. Consistent with this impression, one marker gave it grade D. The fact that it was given a grade A by the other marker could only be explained by its unusual basic idea.

This judgement of content originality was paralleled by the negative reaction of examiners to responses which they seemed to regard as unoriginal or hackneyed. An apparently competent war story with insignificant spelling and grammatical mistakes, and with the virtues of varied and complex structures, appropriate vocabulary, clarity of development and force, received a grade C from one examiner whereas his colleague awarded it a grade A.

The study yielded a tentative model or taxonomy which could be applied to samples of writing with reliability. Despite a free writing context, certain writing modes were dominant and there was evidence that these were differentially valued by markers making impressionistic qualitative assessments.

Subsequent research studies have provided further validation of the extensions to the Davis *et al.* taxonomy.

Subsequent studies

Walsh (1983) sampled primary school children's writing within different modes of discourse to explore characteristics of this writing within and across grade levels, sex and modes of discourse. To this end she focused on two parallel tasks within narrative, argument, and description — autobiographical and concrete modes of discourse — and sampled 24 males and females at each of grades two, four and six. In addition to productivity and syntactic complexity measures, Walsh used the relevant categories of the Davis *et al.* taxonomy as a basis for modifying and extending the taxonomy to include more primitive forms of writing within these categories. Within each taxonomic category a more detailed analysis of specific elements was made. With the narrative category Walsh used 1.1.1, 1.2 and 1.3.1; in the cases of 1.1.1 and 1.3.1 she created three sub-categories (skeletal, skeletal plus detail, and expansive detail) to differentiate the narratives collected from her sample. With both kinds of descriptive writing, autobiographical and concrete, she found it necessary to distinguish between first the third person descriptions. Within each of these she distinguished between literal skeletal, literal embellished, and introspection, adding some sub-categories to the original four descriptive categories.

The most additions made by Walsh were in the argumentative mode, which in Davis *et al.* (1978) accounted for only 1.9 per cent of all scripts. In the Walsh study the argumentative mode was predicted by the nature of the task. Walsh thus found it necessary to sub-categorise within 3.1 and 3.2 on the basis of form — monologue, dialogue, and objective third person assertion with or without reasons (3.1 only). She added a further category to the argumentative which she termed 'didactic' to take account of arguments which took the form of moralistic narratives or dialogues, in either the first or third person, where the main thrust was to argue by pointing up a moral.

Walsh demonstrated that, with some modification and extension, the original Davis *et al.* taxonomy could be a vital tool for classifying the writing of younger children. She also made the point that rhetorical forms such as argument are within the repertoire even of very young children, albeit at a primitive level.

The taxonomy has also been applied usefully in other studies. Overend (1982) used it as a means of classifying writing derived from two free writing activities (one at the beginning and one at the end of an audience–awareness programme) from years 7–11 in order to explore and demonstrate the hypothesis that

> if the sense of audience can be inculcated, there would be in (the second free writing activity) a decrease in the frequency of selection of the narrative and descriptive modes, the less complex lower order modes, and a corresponding increase in the frequency of selection of the more complex higher order modes (Overend 1982, p. 154).

Ford and Hardcastle (1983) used the taxonomy as a means of establishing response-mode preference in the writing of a group of graduate students. It has proved to be a useful research tool and it has enabled these practising teacher-researchers to explore the writing of their students from a more detailed developmental perspective.

Both Walsh (1982) and Fraser (1984) have used the general categories of the taxonomy as a basis for analysing and describing the elements of narrative and/or expository writing as a means of further providing teachers with access to ways of helping students. Children in the Fraser study were asked to 'Describe your house including its good and bad points'. Her element analysis of the resultant descriptions focussed on the extent to which the children commented on the façade of the house; the interior; household furniture/appliances; property/ garden/personal details, other details and the good/bad points mentioned — and would provide a productive teaching and observation context.

Reflection

Writing research has progressed; previously unrecognised *terrae incognitae* have been identified and the charting has begun. For example, the process approach to the teaching of writing has quickly moved from the *terra incognita* of the late 1970s to the *terra cognita* of the 1980s. We need to consider the adequacy of the charting that exists in this regard. How appropriate is conferencing for all children? Earlier studies (Davis 1973; Davis and Taft 1976) of children's preference for speaking or writing suggests that there are some children whose preference for writing is predicated on their perception of its being a more private mode of communication. Certainly there are students in most classes whose silent profile in the classroom is belied by their capacity to express themselves in the written form. Travers (1981), Vestris (1983) and Farrell (1984) have found that some students find it extraordinarily difficult, even repellent, to verbalise about their writing process. It is important to explore whether process approaches have a similar effect on such children. There are *terrae congitae* in writing — but it is important to accept that this recognition does not mean we know all there is to know — the process of charting, evaluation and re-evaluation must continue. We must accept that we are still working with tools and not with high-precision instruments.

Bibliography

Britton, J. (1978).	'The Composing Process and the Functions of Writing' in Cooper and Odell (1978), pp. 13–28.
Britton, J.N., Burgess, T., Martin, N.C., McLeod, A., and Rosen, H. (1975).	*The Development of Writing Abilities (11–18)*. London, Macmillan.
Britton, J.N., Martin, N.C. and Rosen, H. (1966).	*Multiple Marking of English compositions*. Schools Council Examinations Bulletin no. 12. London, HMSO.

Cooper, C.R. and Odell, L. (eds) (1978).   *Research on Composing : Points of Departure.* Campaign, IL, National Council of Teachers of English.

Davis, D.F. (1973).   'Speaking and Writing: A Study of Some Socio-psychological Correlates of Skill in the Preference for the Use of Oral and Written Language'. Unpublished Doctor of Philosophy thesis, Faculty of Education, Monash University.

Davis, D.F., Ford, A.M. McBride, A.R. and Spicer, B.J. (1978).   *Towards a Taxonomy of Essay Functions.* Canberra, Curriculum Development Centre.

Davis, D.F. and Taft, R. (1976).   'A Measure of Preference for Speaking rather than Writing and its Relationship to Expressive Language Skills in Adolescents', *Language and Speech*, vol. 19, no. 3, pp. 224–35.

Edwards, H.J. (Chairman) (1967).   *The Certificate of Secondary Education Trial Examinations: Written English.* The Schools Council Examinations Bulletin no. 16. London, HMSO.

Farrell, L.E. (1984).   'What do we have to do this for? An Exploration of Writing Across the Curiculum: Process and Product'. Unpublished Master of Education thesis, Monash University.

Ford, A.M. and Hardcastle, L.A. (1983).   'Oracy and Literacy in a Professional Context: The Teaching of English'. Unpublished Master of Educational Studies project, Monash University.

Fraser, R. (1984).   'Writing in Context: An Examination of Current Practice inthe Primary School'. Unpublished Master of Education thesis, Monash University.

Hunt, K.W. (1965). *Grammatical Structures Written at Three Grade Levels*. Champaign, IL, National Council of Teachers of English.

Loban, W.D. (1976). *Language Development: Kindergarten through Grade 12*. Champaign, Il, National Council of Teachers of English.

Overend, H.M. (1982). 'The Perceptions of Audience in the Writing of 11–16-year-old Students'. Unpublished Master of Educational Studies project, Monash University.

Robinson, W.P. (1972). *Language and Social Behaviour*. Harmondsworth, Penguin.

Travers, D.M. (1981). 'Poetry in Context: Martyred in the Cause of Education. Unpublished Doctor of Philosophy thesis, Faculty of Education, Monash University.

Vestris, W.J. (1983). 'Writing: Process and Product'. Unpublished Master of Education thesis, Monash University.

Walsh, D.M. (1983). 'An Exploration of the Development of the Writing of Primary School Children within and across Modes of Discourse'. Unpublished Master of Educational Studies project, Monash University.

Wilkinson, A., Barnsley, G., Hanna, P. and Swan, M. (1980). *Assessing Language Development*. Oxford, Oxford University Press.

Index

Aborigines 81
Abstraction 32
Action knowledge/school knowledge 82
Affect 45, 66, 218
Affective stance 111
Affective model 14, 44
Agentless passive 210
Allen, D. 66, 72
Analysis of written text 111
APU (Assessment of Performance Unit) 6, 63, 64, 65, 72, 157, 215, 217, 232
Argument 5, Ch, 2, 241
Associative writing 149
Atkinson, D. 59
Auden, W.H. 47
Audience 2, 63
Australian Council for Educational Research 81
Awareness of reader 111

Backman, C.W. 58
Bacon, F. 2
Bain, A. 39
Barnes, D. 11, 21, 22, 43, 57, 82, 86, 129, 130
Barnsley, G. 19, 21, 176, 233, 253
Barthes, R. 34, 39, 72
Bauers, A. 3
Bell, R.Q. 58
Bennett, B. 79, 86
Bennett, N. 73
Bereiter, C. 130, 141, 149, 156, 157, 172, 173
Berger, P. 86
Berstein, B. 159, 173
Berry, M.M. 174
Biggs, J.B. 172, 174
Bowes, D. 86
Boyd, W. 167
Brimer, M.A. 174
Bristol Language Development Project 94

Bristol Social Adjustment Guide 165
British/Australian Ethos 84
Britton, J.N. 62, 71, 73, 87, 174, 195, 234, 235, 236, 257
Bruner, J.S. 2, 6, 57
Burgess, A. 73, 96, 174, 195, 235, 251
Burgess, C. 96, 108
Buxton Forman, M. 58

Camus, A. 61, 73
Carlin, E. 57
Cazden, C.B. 156
Chafe, W. 131
Chomsky, N. 158, 174
Churchill, C. 76
Clause length – narrative 220
  subordinate 166–8
Clay, M. 134, 156
Clegg, A.B. 161, 174
Cognition 2, 9, 212
Cognition and writing 2–3, 38, 67, 107
Cohesion 213–14
Collaborative textmaking 137
Collins, J.L. 172, 174
Collis, K.F. 172, 174
Communication 6, 66
Communication models 43–45
Communication skills 2
Comprehensibility 221–2
Competence, levels of 3, 136
Composing 136
Content 6, 38, 64
Context-free elaborations 2
Cooper, C. R. 252
Coping, 54
Cordeiro, P. 156
Count measures 3, Ch. 10
Creative writing 161
Creativity, 62, 206
Crediton Project 2, 215
Cullen, J. 219, 232
Curriculum, knowledge 38
  language 38

Dartmouth Seminar 1, 5
Darwin, C. 61
Davies, A. 6, 59
Davies, T. 9, 21
Davis, D. 5, 235, 249, 251, 252
Defending 54
DES (Department of Education &
    Science) 57
Description 4, 240–1
Desforges, C. 73
Development 172
Didactic writing 243
Dines, E. 92, 108
Directionality 137
Discussion 10–11
Dixon, J. 2, 6, 16, 17, 20, 21, 220, 232
Dominic, J.F. 156
Dunn, L.M. 174

Economics and Social Research Council
    22
Edwards, H.J. 252
Elaborated/restricted codes 159
Emotion 45–6
Emotional development 3, 46
Enkvist, N.W. 213, 233
Environment 48, 53–54, 75
Evaluation 221, 222–3
Exposition 16
Expressive 66, 235

Farrell, L.E. 251, 252
Faulkner 76
Fawcett, R. 90, 91, 108
Feeling 3
Fish, S. 213, 233
Fiction 23
Flower, L.S. 174
Fluency 162, 163–8
Ford, A.M. 250, 252
Ford, E.T. 164
Fowles, J. 76
Fox, G. 131
Frazer, R. 250, 252
Fredericksen, C.H. 156
Freedman, A. 86
Function 5, 221, 236

Garfield, L. 23
Genre 4–5, 17, 112, 199, 204, 206–14
Glaser, R. 130, 156
Giacobbe, M. 156
Gleason, J.B. 58

Glopper, K de 79, 87
Goelman, H. 141, 157
Goffman, E. 43, 58
Gordon, H. 67, 73
Gorman, T. 65
Grammar 111
Graves, R. 97, 108, 137, 156
Greenbaum, S. 108
Gregg, L.W. 156, 174
Grey, J. 213, 233
Growth 3
Gundlach, R.A. 156
Guntrip, H. 69, 73
Gusdorf, G. 73

Haaf, R.A. 58
Haffenden, M. 60, 63, 73
Halliday, M.H. 198, 214
Handedness 170–1
Handscombe, R.J. 96, 108
Handwriting 111
Hanna, P. 21, 59, 74, 176, 196, 219,
    233, 253
Hardcastle, I.A. 250–52
Hardy, T. 76
Harpin, W. 163, 165, 166, 174, 216, 233
Harrell, L.E. 165, 166, 174
Harrison, B. 2, 26, 67, 73
Hartog, P. 2
Hayes, J.R. 174
Heath, S.B. 79, 87
Heider, F.K. 164, 165, 166, 174
Heider, G.M. 164, 165, 166, 174
Henley, W.E. 48
Hirschbergm, L. 58
Hitchfield, E.M. 175
Hourd, M. 45, 46, 62, 73
Hunt, K.W. 163, 165, 167, 172, 175,
    216, 234, 253
Hurst, P. 45, 46, 58

Ideation 112
Inglis, F. 5, 6, 77, 87
Impression 63
International Educational Assessment
    (IEA) 79
International Writing Convention 1

Jefery, C. 86

Kadar–Fulop, J. 79, 87
Kahn, S.T. 86, 87
Keats, J. 56, 58

Kemp, G. 23
Kress, G. 4, 5, 134, 157, 198, 214
Kroll, B. 94, 121, 131, 157
Kulsdom, B. 54, 58

Labov, W. 220, 233
La Brant, 165, 166, 175
Language development 171–2
Lamm, Z. 130
Laurenson, D. 86, 87
Lawrence, D.H. 76
Lawton, D. 167, 168, 170, 175
Leech, G.N. 108
Lewin, K. 85, 87
Lewis, L. 58
Linearity 222
Literacy 81
Loban, W. 159, 165, 175, 234, 253
Luckman, T. 86

Macneice, L. 48
Marriott, K.L. 214
Marrou, H.I. 16, 21
Martin, J. 79, 87
Martin, N. 73, 79, 87, 174, 195, 235,
    236, 251
Martlew, M. 175
McBride, A.R. 252
McCarthy, D.A. 252
McLeod, A. 73, 174, 195, 235, 251
McPhail, C. 86
Medway, P. 3,6
Meek, M. 70, 71, 73, 131
Miller, J. 87
Mode of specification 30, 31, 32
Moffett, J. 71, 196
Moral model 3
    stance 111
Murray, J.M. 216, 233
Myklebust, H.R. 175

Narrative, development of 5, 9, 236–9
Newson, E. 58
Newson, J. 58
Nicholls, J. 3, 130, 187
Norm, deviation from 219
Norris, R.C. 108
Nystrand, M. 135, 157

Odell, L. 252
O'Donnell, 91, 108
Oracy, 109
Oral monologue 4, 129–30

Originality 206
O'Shea, M.V. 165, 176
Others 47
Overend, H.M. 250, 253

Paquette, J. 78, 87
Pellegrini, a. 175
Perera, K. 4, 108
Performing 136
Perkins, M. 90, 91, 108
Peters, R. S. 45, 46, 58
Philosophical writing 243–4
Place 5
    definition of 75
Polytechnic of Wales 90
Porch, B.E. 58
Pringle, I. 86
Process 62, 111
Product 62
Protherough, R. 62, 73
Proust, M. 64, 73
Purves, A. 79, 87
Pym, D. 62, 73

Quirk, R. 101, 108

Raine, C. 60, 61
Raven, J.C. 160, 175
Reading, 4
    and writer Ch. 12
    position 209–1
Reality effect 34
Reciprocity 44
Recording 161
Reflection 2, 44–5, 62–3
Rhetorical categories 5, 16, 236
Robinson, W.P. 235, 253
Rosen, C. 96
Rosen, H. 73, 96, 194, 195, 235, 236,
    251
Rosenblatt, L. 24, 38
Rushdie, S. 76, 77, 87

Sampson, O. 159, 165, 174
Scardamalia, M. 130, 141, 156, 157
Schonell, F.J. 164, 176
School knowledge/action knowledge 82
Schrofel, S. 15
Scott, C.M. 92, 108
Secord, P.B. 58
Self, 47
Self-definition 49–51
Sexism 208, 209, 210

Schaeffer, B. 172, 176
Sentence length 165
Shaughnessy, M.P. 96, 108
Social class and language 170
SOLO (Structure of Observed Learning Outcomes) 172
Sooby, a. 86
Source of validity 25–28
Speech and writing Ch. 7, Ch. 8
Spicer, B.J. 252
Steinberg, E.R. 156, 174
Sternglass, M. 58
Stromzand, M. 165, 176
Stott, D.M. 165, 176
Stow, R. 76
Stratta, L. 2, 16, 17, 20, 21, 220, 232
Strickland, R.G. 159, 176
Structuralism 61, 72
Style 5, 64, Ch. 13
Style – definition of 216–18
Subordination index 167
Sustained speech 129–30
Svartvik, J. 108
Swan, M. 21, 59, 74, 176, 196, 233, 253
Swingewood, A. 86, 87

Taft 251, 252
Tanner, D. 131
Taxonomy of Essay Modes 236–44
Taylor, G. 5
Ten Propositions of Writing 2–6
Todd, D. 11, 21
Tolstoy, L. 62, 73
Topic 28
Tough, J. 129, 131
Transactional writing 235
Transformational grammar 158, 163, 217
Transmission 2, 43–4
Travers, D.M. 251, 252
Twomey, A.M. 13, 21

Vaghan, P. 58
Vestris, W.J. 251, 252

Waletsky, J. 220, 233
Walker, A.B. 86
Walsh, D.M. 249, 250, 252
Watson, C. 172, 176
Wells, G. 2, 3, 4, 94, 109, 131, 135, 157
Welty, E. 75, 76, 87
Western Australian Writing Research Project 79

Whately, R. 6
Whitemore, M.F. 156
Wilkinson, A.M. 3, 5, 21, 42, 47, 54, 57, 59, 62, 73, 74, 176, 196, 219, 233, 235, 253
Williamson, J.G. 174
Wills, D.M. 59
Winnicott, D. 70, 74
Witkin, R. 66, 74
Wittstein, S. 58
Woolf, V. 61
Wordsworth, W. 5, 36
Worsley, G. 59

Yalden, J. 86
Yawkey, T. 175
Yeats, W.B. 47
'Your own words' 206